Professional Cod

Professional
CodeIgniter®

Thomas Myer

WILEY

Wiley Publishing, Inc.

Professional CodeIgniter®

Published by
Wiley Publishing, Inc.
10475 Crosspoint Boulevard
Indianapolis, IN 46256
www.wiley.com

Copyright © 2008 by Wiley Publishing, Inc., Indianapolis, Indiana

Published simultaneously in Canada

ISBN: 978-0-470-28245-8

Manufactured in the United States of America

10 9 8 7 6 5 4 3 2 1

Library of Congress Cataloging-in-Publication Data is available from the publisher.

No part of this publication may be reproduced, stored in a retrieval system or transmitted in any form or by any means, electronic, mechanical, photocopying, recording, scanning or otherwise, except as permitted under Sections 107 or 108 of the 1976 United States Copyright Act, without either the prior written permission of the Publisher, or authorization through payment of the appropriate per-copy fee to the Copyright Clearance Center, 222 Rosewood Drive, Danvers, MA 01923, (978) 750-8400, fax (978) 646-8600. Requests to the Publisher for permission should be addressed to the Legal Department, Wiley Publishing, Inc., 10475 Crosspoint Blvd., Indianapolis, IN 46256, (317) 572-3447, fax (317) 572-4355, or online at www.wiley.com/go/permissions.

Limit of Liability/Disclaimer of Warranty: The publisher and the author make no representations or warranties with respect to the accuracy or completeness of the contents of this work and specifically disclaim all warranties, including without limitation warranties of fitness for a particular purpose. No warranty may be created or extended by sales or promotional materials. The advice and strategies contained herein may not be suitable for every situation. This work is sold with the understanding that the publisher is not engaged in rendering legal, accounting, or other professional services. If professional assistance is required, the services of a competent professional person should be sought. Neither the publisher nor the author shall be liable for damages arising herefrom. The fact that an organization or Website is referred to in this work as a citation and/or a potential source of further information does not mean that the author or the publisher endorses the information the organization or Website may provide or recommendations it may make. Further, readers should be aware that Internet Websites listed in this work may have changed or disappeared between when this work was written and when it is read.

For general information on our other products and services, please contact our Customer Care Department within the United States at (800) 762-2974, outside the United States at (317) 572-3993 or fax (317) 572-4002.

Library of Congress Cataloging-in-Publication Data

Myer, Thomas.
    Professional CodeIgniter/Thomas Myer.
       p.   cm.
    Includes index.
    ISBN 978-0-470-28245-8 (pbk. : web)
      1. Web site development.   2. CodeIgniter (Computer file)   3. Application software—Development. 4. Internet programming.   I. Title.
    TK5105.888.M95   2008
    006.7'8—dc22

               2008024002

Trademarks: Wiley, the Wiley logo, Wrox, the Wrox logo, Wrox Programmer to Programmer, and related trade dress are trademarks or registered trademarks of John Wiley & Sons, Inc. and/or its affiliates, in the United States and other countries, and may not be used without written permission. CodeIgniter is a registered trademark of EllisLab, Inc. All other trademarks are the property of their respective owners. Wiley Publishing, Inc., is not associated with any product or vendor mentioned in this book.

Wiley also publishes its books in a variety of electronic formats. Some content that appears in print may not be available in electronic books.

About the Author

Thomas Myer currently resides in Austin, Texas, where he runs Triple Dog Dare Media, a consulting group that builds CodeIgniter applications, writes technical documentation and copy, and helps companies and business owners fashion successful strategies for the online world. He is the author of *Lead Generation on the Web* and *No Nonsense XML Web Development with PHP*, as well as dozens of articles on technology and business. If you have any feedback on this book or wish to discuss anything related to web development, writing, or marketing, contact him via his web site at www.tripledogs.com.

To Hope, for loving me anyway

Credits

Acquisitions Editor
Jenny Watson

Development Editor
Kelly Talbot

Technical Editor
Ed Finkler

Production Editor
Debra Banninger
Kathleen Wisor

Copy Editor
Cate Caffrey

Editorial Manager
Mary Beth Wakefield

Production Manager
Tim Tate

Vice President and Executive Group Publisher
Richard Swadley

Vice President and Executive Publisher
Joseph B. Wikert

Project Coordinator, Cover
Lynsey Stanford

Proofreader
Nancy Carrasco

Indexer
Melanie Belkin

Acknowledgments

My first tip o' the hat goes to my editor, Kelly Talbot of Wiley, who received all my raving, meandering prose and actually carved a book out of it. Although I kvetched a bit, he was a calm and steady hand navigating this project to a successful completion. (Yes, it's true, I did call him a slave driver in the heat of the moment. Yes, he is one of the most organized editors I've ever had the pleasure to work with. Other authors, take note. The editor is always right.)

The second acknowledgment goes to Ed Finkler, who pored over every line of code and made incredibly insightful remarks throughout. Despite the fact that he received the manuscript at quite an advanced stage, he bravely ordered a whole series of changes in order to bring my game up. He followed this up with a tenacious immunity to my whining and crying, and then nodded and patted my head when I finally came around to his point of view. Any technical difficulties you may have with the code are totally his fault. (Just kidding! Seriously, he's forgotten more than I'll ever know about software, and without him, this book would have been quite different.)

Neil Salkind, my agent, is a pearl beyond price. He's the kind of guy who will quietly listen to your half-baked ideas and help you shape them into a real pitch that will actually get a publisher's attention. Without him, I'd just be another guy with dreams of authorship and nothing to his credit.

With any book, there are dozens of folks who toil behind the scenes, and it's impossible to name them all, but I'd like to try. Jenny Watson, who acquired the idea for Wiley, thanks so much for listening to my pitch. Your guidance and feedback in the early stages were very appreciated.

Thanks, Debra and Cate, who took over during production edits — What can I say? Cate, I dub thee "World's Most Efficient Copyeditor" (although I'm sure you will make *Copyeditor* into two words, which will be funny as all get out — sorry, a little editor humor there). Debra — thanks for taking my calls out of the blue and for helping me put the last little touches on this puppy. Your solid Jersey wisdom on "data are" versus "data is" was much appreciated and a source of much mirth.

Thank you, good folks at EllisLab, for creating CodeIgniter — you don't know how much this framework has changed my relationship with web development and with my clients. In particular, thanks to Derek Allard for responding to my first tentative e-mails and giving me feedback. Thank you, thank you, thank you!

To my clients, who accommodated me as I pursued this book, even though you had pressing deadlines and requests of your own: You're simply the best, and I'm damn lucky to be working with you.

Lastly, I extend my thanks to my divine spouse, Hope, who endured many weekends of solitude while I wrote in my little study. And no, I can't forget the contributions made by Marlowe (our little Yorkie) and Kafka (our lovable mutt), who spent many a slow afternoon sleeping by my feet as I tapped away at the keyboard.

Contents

Contents

Contents

Introduction

When I first encountered CodeIgniter, I was pretty much at the end of my rope.

I'd spent seven years building up a thriving little web development group and had hitched my little wagon to various technologies (like SMARTY and PEAR), and things had run very well for a long time. And then it happened. What is "it"? Well, "it" wasn't exactly any one thing that you could point to and say, "There, that's the problem right there!" It was more like a combination of things. Regardless, "it" hit me with the force of a torpedo, and I felt my professional outlook implode.

I've shared my story with lots of developers over the past year, and they all seem to agree that in the life of every web geek comes a moment of clarity. This happens to us whether we're the worst decision maker in the world or some kind of digital *wunderkind*.

What am I talking about? I'm talking about some kind of tipping point where you look at everything you've done, and you don't want to deal with it any more. I'm talking about making one more really great choice (about architecture, performance handling, security, blah, blah, blah) and putting it in the box with all your other "great choices," and what you end up with is a box full of complexity, a kind of reverse Pandora's box of confusion and mischief.

The upshot is pretty simple. You end up with extremely complex code that you can't understand. Your mind can't stretch around all the hundreds (if not thousands) of little changes and one-off decisions you've made. You can't even follow all the includes, the third-party modules, and the classes embedded within each other like Russian Dolls. In point in fact, you end up with the Thing That Cannot Be Uttered: extremely complex code you don't even *want* to deal with.

And the customers that come with that code, who quite naturally want you to make things better, suffer from it. Big time.

So it was with me, as I contemplated the tens of thousands of lines of PHP I'd written with such good intentions. If you've ever had the pleasure of working with PEAR and SMARTY (and other similar technologies), you know that they solve a lot of problems … but they also bring a heinous level of complexity to even the simplest little web application. And all of it was hanging around my neck like an albatross, and boy, did I want to cut that sucker off and start over again!

But where could I go in my hour of need? Who could help me? Was there any way out of the complicated Rube Goldberg machine I'd built as my little fortress of certainty? At the time when I was feeling the most despair, there was a lot of media exposure for Rails. Hmmmm. Could this possibly be the answer to all my problems? I bought a few books and started playing around a bit. I liked Rails — it has a cleanness to it that makes you feel all giddy when you look at it, like buying a slick new sports car and driving around town with it so everyone can see how fabulous you are. It was easy to use, too, and you could get things done really fast.

But then, suddenly, the first-date warm fuzzies started wearing off. I realized that I was a PHP programmer and that I'd spent years developing solutions in that world. There were very few *gotchas* left, the learning curve was nice and pleasant, and it had been years since any of my customers had felt

Introduction

like I was learning on their dime. I realized, suddenly, that Rails wasn't going to do it for me and my situation. In other words, I realized that I didn't want a glamorous little sports car — I needed something a bit less showy and a lot more functional.

Yet there were lots of appealing things about Rails. The MVC framework brought simplicity and organization to the game. The convention-over-configuration approach made the code nice and lean. Where was something like that in the PHP world? I started my search, and I immediately found CodeIgniter.

In fact, I had CodeIgniter pointed out to me by one of my employees. CodeIgniter was still in the 1.0 phase at that point, and since I wasn't feeling too good about that, I started playing around with Symfony and Cake and some of the other PHP frameworks. None of them suited me, and so I came back to CodeIgniter around the time that it hit version 1.5.

Boy, am I glad I came back to it! It was like taking a really long trip around the world and coming back home to a good friend or loving family. It did what I wanted, right away, without all the complexity and baggage. I hardly even needed to spend time with the documentation, it was so intuitive.

I built my first customer application in CodeIgniter about six weeks after doing that first series of test runs. Over the next year, I built a dozen more, ranging from timesheet applications to scheduling apps to microsite managers and community boards for parents of children with special needs.

The results so far would give even the most hardened cynic food for thought. Instead of spending countless hours debugging needlessly complex code and dreading every call lest it be a request for yet another upgrade or change, I can now build entire applications in a weekend. Supporting them is a breeze, because the code is always organized in an easy, intuitive manner. Just about every time I receive a request, there is a CodeIgniter library or helper to ease my burden — or I'm able to write one for myself or reach out to the CodeIgniter community to find help.

In fact, I can now easily build something in a few hours that would have taken me days or weeks with just plain old PHP. It's getting to the point where I've had to rethink my entire billing process, because there isn't much sense in charging so little for a piece of software that helps to launch a significant part of a company's online presence.

From a non-financial standpoint, my relationship with clients has changed. Instead of being an adversary (saying, "We really shouldn't do that," when I really was thinking to myself, "Oh please, I don't want to do that!"), I became a collaborator, a helper, a guide. In other words, I'm able to fulfill my role as *consultant*. Not only that, but by spending less time with minutiae, I can spend more time with strategy and more meaningful conversations that help my customers move closer to their goals.

And then, in the Fall of 2007, I thought to myself, "We need a book on CodeIgniter!" Not just any book on CodeIgniter, and not just a repeat of the online documentation, but one that will walk a developer through all the phases of a project, from initial client meeting to launch.

That was the genesis of the book you're holding in your hands right now. At the end of the day, I wanted to craft a book that would take you from point A to point Z (and yes, we might be skipping a few of the less interesting points along the way) and give you a working knowledge of the relevant CodeIgniter pieces as we went.

With any luck, I've achieved that goal. I've had a lot of help and feedback along the way, of course, but ultimately, I wanted to show you how to navigate a typical project, complete with customer meetings, iterative cycles, and detours. I wanted to show you how to use CodeIgniter along with agile development processes to build a functional web site — hopefully, by the time you're done with the book, you'll have everything you need to create your own projects.

Here's to building great web applications, and here's to making customers deliriously happy! Most of all, here's to seizing the reins again and taking control of our professional lives!

Whom This Book Is For

My first assumption is very simple. You're a developer who knows his or her way around HTML, CSS, MySQL, and, of course, PHP. You have been doing all of this for a few years and have probably run up against the folly of ever more complex code and projects that always seem to tip over because they're so badly designed and managed. These projects rarely start out badly — in fact, one could say they start with the best of intentions — but they always end up in the same bad old place. I assume that you're sick of that and want to change things.

I also assume that you've probably looked at Rails (either a close-up look or just a cursory glance) and still, at the end of the day, you're committed to doing work in PHP, because that's what you know.

Furthermore, I strongly believe that this conviction to stay "with something you know" doesn't make you some kind of intellectual coward — far from it! You're a pragmatist, a person committed to doing good work for your clients, and you know deep down inside that having access to good tools and good processes can make for exponentially better outcomes than you've experienced in the past.

My final assumption about you is that you don't need a reference manual. You're smart enough to look up the more hairy details on your own. What you do need is some practical advice and know-how on the workings of CodeIgniter. Therefore, my aim in this book is to give you that know-how. With any luck, by the time you're done with this book, you'll be an "advanced intermediate" CodeIgniter user, well on your way to elite status.

What This Book Covers

I wrote this book about halfway between two version releases of CodeIgniter. In fact, I'd already written five chapters (and had them in technical review) when the new release introduced some fairly nontrivial upgrades that needed coverage. About 30 minutes after installing the new code from EllisLab, I'd upgraded the project the book is based on. It literally took me longer to update the chapters than it did to update the application. But I digress.

Throughout the book, you will meet a hypothetical small business owner named Claudia, who wants to build an online shopping site (Claudia's Kids). You, as the reader, will gather requirements from Claudia, draw diagrams, and build her application in record time. I tried very hard to make Claudia like a typical client (pleasant, but with a penchant for changing her mind), to show you how well CodeIgniter handles in this kind of environment.

You're going to encounter quite a lot of CodeIgniter. You're going to learn more than your fair share about Models, Views, and Controllers, naturally, but also about certain libraries and helpers. You're going to learn the differences between CodeIgniter sessions and PHP sessions. You're going to learn how to benchmark your application and cache your pages. You're going to learn something about security and the mindset you must bring with you when you're building iteratively.

Here's what this book is *not* about: It's not a book on visual design. You might openly guffaw at my creative sensibilities. That's fine, laugh away; just make sure you absorb the information presented in these pages and apply them to your own spectacular designs. This is also not a book on CSS, but it does contain some CSS in it. Furthermore, it is not a book on SQL design, but it does have SQL in it — you'll need it in order to create your tables.

At almost every turn in writing the book, as in my consulting practice, when it came down to a decision between discussing theory or getting things done, I opted for the latter. For me, getting something done is better than talking about all the possibilities. Some might fault me for it, but that's just the way I roll.

How This Book Is Structured

The first three chapters of this book introduce you to CodeIgniter, the Agile way, and to how you'll be working with Models, Views, and Controllers. Chapters 4 through 8 show you how to take the basic knowledge of CodeIgniter to build public-facing web sites, administrative screens, and much, much more. Chapters 9 and 10 cover security, performance, and some last-minute additions that lead to a successful launch of the site.

Throughout the book, you'll note that I keep coming back to certain themes in iterative cycles. For example, I keep returning to the theme of security — either because I'm putting in just enough security for the moment or because it really is time to slow down enough to do something substantial.

Iteration is at the heart of my working style, and I see a lot of my colleagues turning to this approach in their own work. I've learned over the years that it is impossible to predict every single nook and cranny of the customer's mental model of what the project should look like when it's all done. In fact, I've stopped trying. I ask my questions, I build my applications, and then I allow enough space for the client to play too.

I know from experience that most people are incapable of knowing what they want until they see it in front of them. This is doubly true for something as intangible as software. Does this mean that I throw all caution to the winds and just create things in a vacuum? Of course not — you always start with a client meeting and extract client requirements. There's almost always time to polish and iterate.

You'll also notice that I'm not afraid to say, "This is good enough for now," and move on to the next topic. Why? Because in real life, it's often pointless to harp on certain details until the customer has seen it and gives you a reaction. At other times, it is equally useless to let something go, when you know exactly what needs to be done and can't rely on the customer to make that call for you. True wisdom for the developer comes in knowing which way to go.

What You Need to Use This Book

First and foremost, you need a server that can run PHP 4 or 5 (CodeIgniter works with both) and MySQL 4+. You can set up your own development server with WAMP or MAMP, depending on your platform. You also need a good copy of CodeIgniter (available at `www.codeigniter.com`).

Furthermore, you need to have some familiarity with HTML, CSS, SQL, and JavaScript. I've kept the JavaScript down to a minimum, and most of it involves the Scriptaculous framework, and that's for a good reason: I consider myself to be primarily a back-end developer, and I focus more on those sorts of processes than JavaScript.

Two more notes: You really need to have a set of good editing tools (I use BBEdit or Dreamweaver, depending on the mood I'm in), and you really need PhpMyAdmin. If you install MAMP or WAMP, you'll have access to PhpMyAdmin. Without this extremely handy tool, you're limited to command-line interaction with MySQL, which can be a bit error-prone in the heat of battle.

Conventions

Several conventions are used throughout the book to help you get the most from the text and keep track of what's happening.

> *Tips, hints, tricks, and asides to the current discussion are offset and placed in italics like this.*

❑   Keyboard strokes look like this: Ctrl+A.

❑   Filenames, URLs, and code within the text look like this: `persistence.properties`.

❑   Code is presented in the following way:

```
Gray highlighting is used to draw attention to the blocks of code as
you work through the chapters.
```

Source Code

As you work through the examples in this book, you may choose either to type in all the code manually or to use the source code files that accompany the book. All of the source code used in this book is available for download at `www.wrox.com`. Once at the site, simply locate the book's title (either by using the Search box or by using one of the title lists) and click the Download Code link on the book's detail page to obtain all the source code for the book.

> *Because many books have similar titles, you may find it easiest to search by ISBN; this book's ISBN is 978-0-470-28245-8.*

Once you download the code, just decompress it with your favorite compression tool. Alternately, you can go to the main Wrox code download page at `www.wrox.com/dynamic/books/download.aspx` to see the code available for this book and all other Wrox books.

Errata

Every effort is made to ensure that there are no errors in the text or in the code. However, no one is perfect, and mistakes do occur. If you find an error in one of our books, like a spelling mistake or faulty piece of code, we would be very grateful for your feedback. By sending in errata, you may save another reader hours of frustration, and at the same time you will be helping us provide even higher quality information.

To find the errata page for this book, go to `www.wrox.com` and locate the title using the Search box or one of the title lists. Then, on the book details page, click the Book Errata link. On this page, you can view all errata that have been submitted for this book and posted by Wrox editors. A complete book list including links to each book's errata is also available at `www.wrox.com/misc-pages/booklist.shtml`.

If you don't spot "your" error on the Book Errata page, go to www.wrox.com/contact/techsupport .shtml and complete the form there to send us the error you have found. We'll check the information and, if appropriate, post a message to the book's errata page and fix the problem in subsequent editions of the book.

p2p.wrox.com

For author and peer discussion, join the P2P forums at p2p.wrox.com. The forums are a web-based system for you to post messages relating to Wrox books and related technologies and interact with other readers and technology users. The forums offer a subscription feature to e-mail you topics of interest of your choosing when new posts are made to the forums. Wrox authors, editors, other industry experts, and your fellow readers are present on these forums.

At http://p2p.wrox.com, you will find various forums that will help you not only as you read this book, but also as you develop your own applications. To join the forums, just follow these steps:

1. Go to p2p.wrox.com and click the Register link.

2. Read the terms of use and click Agree.

3. Complete the required information to join, as well as any optional information you wish to provide and click Submit.

4. You will receive an e-mail with information describing how to verify your account and complete the joining process.

    You can read messages in the forums without joining P2P, but in order to post your own messages, you must join.

Once you join, you can post new messages and respond to messages other users post. You can read messages at any time on the Web. If you would like to have new messages from a particular forum e-mailed to you, click the "Subscribe to this Forum" icon by the forum name in the forum listing.

For more information about how to use the Wrox P2P, be sure to read the P2P FAQs for answers to questions about how the forum software works, as well as many common questions specific to P2P and Wrox books. To read the FAQs, click the FAQ link on any P2P page.

Conclusion

You're now ready to get started. I start Chapter 1 by comparing CodeIgniter to something you're a bit more familiar with: regular old workaday PHP. I provide some fairly typical examples of non-MVC PHP code (some ripped right out of my own code archives, with enough changes in them to protect the innocent) and then show you how I would recast that code with CodeIgniter. Along the way, you'll learn a bit more about MVC, why it matters, and why you should care.

Let's get started!

Welcome to the MVC World

This book is about CodeIgniter and the world of Model-View-Controller (MVC) web development. Before venturing into the topic of CodeIgniter, it's helpful to put it into some kind of context. However, most programmers who are new to the world of MVC web development find some of the concepts hard to grasp at first — they've been so engrained in the old way of doing things that unlearning is difficult at first.

So even before you can learn anything about CodeIgniter or even MVC, it's probably helpful to start the discussion with something you already know and understand, and then move on from there. Therefore, that's where this book begins: with a description of a prototypical PHP project, most likely very similar to anyone's very first PHP project.

Many PHP programmers learn PHP either as their first language (having only been exposed to XHTML and CSS beforehand) or after learning another similar language (such as Perl). Most of the time, a PHP programmer's first few projects involve a pretty steep learning curve, but eventually the programmer finds a comfortable groove. He ends up with a project consisting of the following components:

❏   A series of PHP pages with intermingled PHP commands, SQL queries, and XHTML

❏   A series of JavaScript and CSS files that are linked from those PHP pages

❏   A series of universal includes — a footer file for all pages and a header file that contain the database connection and session initialization code

❏   A handful of database tables that store the application's data

In fact, a newbie programmer's first PHP page probably looks a lot like this one:

```php
<?php
include_once "db.php";

$sql = "select * from pages where status='live' and type='home' limit 1";
$result = mysql_query($sql);

while($data = mysql_fetch_object($result)){
  $title = $data->title;
  $css = $data->css;
  $bodycopy = $data->bodycopy;
  $kw = $data->keywords;
  $desc = $data->description;
}
?>
<html>
<head>
<title><?php echo $title; ?></title>
<link href="<?php echo $css; ?>" rel="stylesheet" type="text/css"/>
<meta name="keywords" value="<?php echo $kw;?>"/>
<meta name="description" value="<?php echo $desc?>"/>
</head>

<body>

<?php include_once "topnav.php";?>

<div id="wrapper">
<h1><?php echo $title;?></h1>
<p><?php echo nl2br($bodycopy);?></p>
</div>
<?php include_once "footer.php";?>
</body>
</html>
```

So far, so good, right? The pages render quickly; there's CSS for layout instead of tables, so it should be easy to re-skin; and life is good. The newbie programmer figures that keeping the project small enough means averting disaster. In fact, this first project does stay under a dozen PHP files in size and has one or two JavaScript and CSS files and three or four includes. Everything goes well during development, the project goes live, and the customer is happy.

Of course, the beginner programmer is usually blissfully unaware of some of the *gotchas* of this approach. For example, since the SQL code to retrieve the home page doesn't have any exception handling in it, what happens if the database is unavailable (or someone accidentally erases the home page content from the DB)? The code is tied to mySQL at the moment. What if the customer changes database servers at some point?

If these thoughts occur, they're usually put off. For now, everything works, and it's time to celebrate and move on to the next project. "Besides," the programmer thinks to himself, "you're using includes for the important stuff, like database connections, global navigation, and footer content. Doesn't that make the code more modular?"

Six months later, the programmer gets a call from the client, and the problems begin — not big problems at first, but they have a tendency to snowball. The client wants to add a few database fields, change the way the interface looks, and make the application more flexible in certain ways. Out loud, the programmer tells the client that everything is OK, but inside, a sense of low-level panic is brewing.

Why? Because the programmer barely remembers any details about the project in question six months later. Honestly, the programmer has worked on 10 other applications since that project ended, amounting to many thousands of lines of code written, rewritten, debugged, refactored, and rewritten again to meet the needs of changing requirements. This is not to mention that the programmer isn't exactly indifferent to learning about programming, so he's been reading books on the subject and applying what he's learned to current projects. The programmer knows that the approach he took with this particular project is off the mark. The approach wasn't *wrong*, in a strictly objective way (there are many ways to skin a cat, after all), but it sacrificed long-term support and flexibility in favor of ad hoc construction and initial speed.

Without a doubt, cleaning up the previous work will mean digging through the code to untangle PHP snippets, SQL queries, and XHTML markup; retesting everything to make sure it's working right; and making sure that the application code and interface match the database. It's also likely that the client will change her mind about many things along the way, requiring many course corrections (read: "rewriting code").

Even if the request from the client is relatively simple, involving a new skin or HTML layout, the programmer could find himself carefully picking through code to make sure no vital functionality is erased. The requests get more complex from there, and all of them are filed under "Let's hope they don't ask for that": supporting mobile devices, displaying content in foreign languages, rendering different views of the same data (such as pie chart versus spreadsheet), adding extensive Ajax controls, and so on.

So the programmer takes on the project, knowing full well that the relationship with the client is the most important thing — that, and a sense of pride that won't let him hand the project over to a completely new programmer, who will probably screw it up.

The first thing he decides to take on is that crazy SQL query right on the home page. The thing to do here is to create a functions.php file in which he stores all the functions. The function for that home page content (notice the minimal exception handling) ends up looking like this:

```php
<?php

function fetchHomePage(){
  $sql = "select * from pages where status='live' and type='home' limit 1";
  $result = mysql_query($sql);

  while($data = mysql_fetch_object($result)){
    $hp['title'] = $data->title;
    $hp['css'] = $data->css;
    $hp['bodycopy'] = $data->bodycopy;
    $hp['kw'] = $data->keywords;
    $hp['desc'] = $data->description;
  }

  if (count($hp)){
    return $hp;
```

```
    }else{
        $hp['title'] = "Welcome to our web site!";
        $hp['css'] = "default.css";
        $hp['bodycopy'] = "This is our web site!";
        $hp['kw'] = "welcome";
        $hp['desc'] = "our cool site";
        return $hp;
    }
}
?>
```

Now that the data-fetching code is in a separate file, the home page is a bit simplified. You could even say that things are a lot better now:

```
<?php
include_once "db.php";
include_once "functions.php";
$home = fetchHomePage();
?>
<html>
<head>
<title><?php echo $home['title']; ?></title>
<link href="<?php echo $home['css']; ?>" rel="stylesheet" type="text/css"/>
<meta name="keywords" value="<?php echo $home['kw'];?>"/>
<meta name="description" value="<?php echo $home['desc']?>"/>
</head>
<body>
<?php include_once "topnav.php";?>

<div id="wrapper">
<h1><?php echo $home['title'];?></h1>
<p><?php echo nl2br($home['bodycopy']);?></p>
</div>
<?php include_once "footer.php";?>
</body>
</html>
```

Soon, the programmer goes through all the PHP files and converts raw SQL into functions, depositing them into the same functions.php file. In no time at all, there exists a library of functions that extract pages, render calendar views, create RSS feeds, and do heaven knows what else. The programmer ponders this strange little file that's become so bloated and decides to tackle it later — there are more important things on the agenda.

So he gets to work on the rest of the client's requests. They want to add several fields to the pages database table, and they want to check for both browser language and client type (Mozilla, Safari, IE) to push custom content out to different users. They also want to incorporate analytics tracking packages from third-party vendors. Also — and they know it's last minute — but one of the founders of the company just got back from a conference and is really hot on using Ajax.

Through it all, the programmer's probably thinking, "There's got to be a better way!" Well, there is, and it involves learning about a way of thinking called *Model-View-Controller (MVC)*. With MVC, developers can separate their code into distinct parts, making the entire application easier to develop, maintain, and extend. Furthermore, MVC frameworks are usually pretty structured, allowing the developer to concentrate on what's important to the client and the project at hand and not worry about other issues that affect every project (such as security and caching).

The point here is not to chastise the programmer or call out deficiencies in his approach. Everyone has been there and done that. The point is to show you a better way, inspired by a belief in the transformative power of MVC, Agile methodologies, and CodeIgniter. Believe it: *All these things working together can radically change the way you work and interact with clients.*

You'll get to CodeIgniter and Agile methodologies very soon, but for now it's time to focus on MVC concepts. Once you have a strong foundation in the basics, the rest should progress naturally. As you'll soon see, MVC has been around for the past 30 years but has become increasingly popular of late, especially in the world of web development.

What's Model-View-Controller?

Model-View-Controller, as the name implies, is a design pattern that allows developers to cleanly separate their code into three categories:

- ❑ **Models** maintain data.
- ❑ **Views** display data and user interface elements.
- ❑ **Controllers** handle user events that affect models and views.

Figure 1-1 illustrates the relationship among the parts. The important thing to remember is that MVC takes the user into account — it begins with him or her. It's the *user* who clicks a link, moves the mouse, or submits a form. It's the *controller* that monitors this activity and takes the appropriate action (such as manipulating the *model* and updating the *view*).

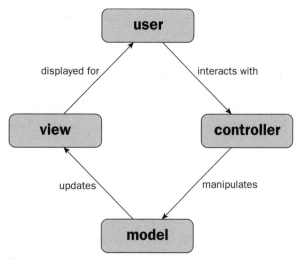

Figure 1-1

Because of MVC's three-part separation, developers can create multiple views and controllers for any given model without forcing changes in the model design. This separation allows for easily maintained, portable, and organized applications that are nothing like anything you've worked with before.

For example, imagine that most prototypical of early 21st century web applications, the blog. Blogs are everywhere these days, and they're not that hard to break into their constituent MVC parts:

❑ A model that keeps track of posts and comments

❑ Multiple views that display individual blog posts, a list of blog posts, or search results

❑ A controller that captures user interaction (such as clicking on an archive link) and then redirects requests to models and/or views

Drilling down further, an MVC blog application might involve the following flow of events:

1. The user visits the blog home page.

2. This simple event requires a controller action for the home page, which makes a quick call to the model to retrieve the last 10 blog posts in reverse chronological order.

3. The model's data are then transmitted to the view for the home page.

4. The view (including the data retrieved by the model) is what the user sees in his or her browser.

5. The user clicks on a link to see details on a particular blog post.

6. The underlying controller captures this user input (clicking the link), uses the model to retrieve the blog post in question from the database, and then loads the appropriate view.

7. The cycle begins anew when the user clicks a link to view comments or runs a search.

Another way of thinking about this breakdown of roles is to map it out this way:

❑ User Input and Traffic Control = Controller

❑ Processing = Model

❑ Output = View

This three-part analogy is a much simpler way of looking at things. Some might argue that the approach is much too simple. After all, it's possible, some might argue, to create an MVC application without a model, or to gang-press view code into the controller. It's not a good idea, but it can be done. For right now, this simple analogy holds. Different ways to approach problems in an MVC fashion are explored later in the book.

Why Bother with MVC?

Although at first glance the MVC approach seems like a lot of work, it really isn't. When developers of the hypothetical MVC blog application want to change something about the home page, they ask themselves about the nature of the change. Doing so allows them to zero in on the part of the application they need to work on.

❑ If they want to change the number of blog posts that get retrieved (or even the order in which they are displayed), they update the model.

❑ If they want to change the way the home page looks, they update the view.

❑ If they want to add a new page to their application, they first add a method to their controller and then build out any supporting views (to display content in the browser) and models (to gather data from a database).

The beauty of the entire system lies in the fact that none of those hypothetical actions on any given part of the MVC triumvirate affects the others. It's true that changing the model in some way (retrieving 15 blog posts instead of 10) will change the view, but the developers didn't have to dig through their view (or controller) to make that change, then later realize they had another SQL call embedded in other files that did the same thing. Theoretically, on large projects, you could have developers who focus only on views, controllers, or models, thus keeping clean lines of sight on deliverables and responsibilities. (Stop laughing. It is possible, you know!)

If you work as an in-house developer, you'll quickly learn to appreciate how MVC can help teams of developers create complex projects. Instead of lashing together ad hoc coding projects, you'll be creating systems of value to your organization and its clients.

If you're a freelancer or own a small technical consulting group or development shop, you'll love the power that MVC (and in particular, CodeIgniter) brings to your arsenal of tools. In this book, you'll learn how to combine CodeIgniter and MVC with Agile development processes to quickly build flexible and powerful applications in half the time with half the hassle.

Before you get too deeply into all that, it's time for a quick history lesson on MVC. The lesson is brief and provides some context for CodeIgniter. After this chapter, the focus is solely on CodeIgniter and how the processes and tools associated with it can help you build better applications.

A Brief History of MVC

Model-View-Controller was first described by Xerox PARC researchers working on the Smalltalk programming language in the late 1970s and early 1980s. Smalltalk was an object-oriented, dynamically typed, reflective programming language. Its first use was in the realm of educational learning, and it differed from mainframe data and control structures in that Smalltalk programs involved:

❑ Windowed user interfaces

❑ Object-oriented programming concepts

❑ Passing of messages between object components

❑ The ability to monitor and modify their own structure and behavior

In the Smalltalk world, the model knew nothing about the controllers or the views that worked with it. The model could be observed by the view and manipulated by the controller, but other than that, the model simply represented the problem domain. Whenever the model changed, it fired off messages to the views, so they could update themselves. Views themselves were subclasses of an existing View class that knew how to render what you wanted to render. For example, if you wanted to draw a rectangle or a circle, you'd subclass an existing class for the appropriate rendering. Controllers, in the Smalltalk world, were originally conceived as being very thin, providing a means of sending messages to the model.

This is not a book on Smalltalk, but Smalltalk's impact on modern computing in general and programming in particular can't be overstated. The Macintosh, Windows, and X Windows development efforts have borrowed heavily from the Smalltalk windowed interface. In fact, the early Apple GUIs were indistinguishable from Smalltalk-80 v2 (as illustrated in Figure 1-2). Many of the text-based user interfaces in DOS used Smalltalk offshoots like DigiTalk (Figure 1-3).

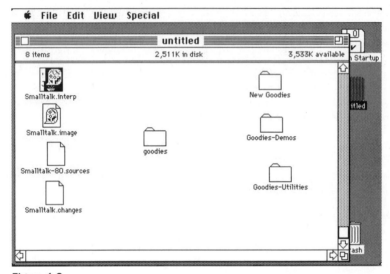

Figure 1-2

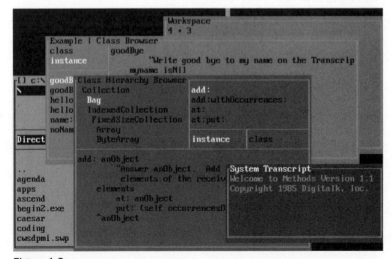

Figure 1-3

The next step in MVC (no pun intended) occurred with the arrival of the NeXT operating system and its software. NeXT was a company founded by Steve Jobs in the late 1980s that remained on the market until the early 1990s, when it was purchased by Apple. The NeXT MVC developers found a way to create ever more powerful views and ever more fine-grained Controllers (i.e., one could now track mouse movements and click events). This meant evolving the notion of the "thin" controller to a "fat" controller, as the controller took a more central role in the architecture. What's the difference? A *thin controller* is one that does just the basics and relies on models and views to do most of the work. A *fat controller* is the exact opposite, a software design choice that puts most if not all the processing responsibility in the controller.

On the desktop front, languages like Cocoa (on Mac OS X) provided developers with an MVC framework. The Cocoa MVC framework simplified the pattern by routing all messages through the controller. The controller updated the model, received a notification from the model, and then updated the view, thus mediating the flow of data.

With Sun's Model2 approach to MVC, controllers evolved again, mapping user requests to actions. Model2 featured reusable (but stateless) views, fat controllers, and independent models. However, it became quickly apparent that some of MVC's historically relevant functionality (such as views that updated themselves after receiving a message from the model) didn't really map to the stateless request/response world of HTTP.

But that didn't stop the emergence of MVC frameworks and languages for the Web. So far, there have been Django, Struts, and most famously, Ruby on Rails. In fact, if you're a PHP developer, you've probably been watching the Ruby on Rails phenomenon with a mixture of curiosity and dread. It appears from a distance that tools like Ruby on Rails allow small teams of developers to create web applications in a tenth the time, with less debugging and fewer headaches. Ruby on Rails web sites have slick interfaces, have easy to understand URLs (no more query strings!), and are generally more compact and secure than the sites you've been creating with your own custom PHP.

One overt design strategy for Ruby on Rails is the idea of "convention over configuration" — in other words, is there a way to create a set of defaults that works 80 to 90 percent of the time, thereby reducing the amount of configuration you have to keep track of? This pervasive idea has been incorporated into every single PHP framework, CodeIgniter included. The result has been an enormous amount of time saving and effort reduction in development.

From the perspective of the PHP community, several difficulties remain with Ruby on Rails — many PHP programmers don't have the time or desire to switch to it, hosting is not as ubiquitous as with PHP, and the strict database design conventions make porting legacy applications harder. All of these create an understandable reluctance on the part of the PHP programmer to switch. After all, you create and support PHP applications, and you don't feel ready to take on a brand-new programming language and the learning curve associated with it. Even if the language is easy to learn, there are still many things about it that you haven't mastered, and doing so on the client's dime seems wasteful and unethical.

Luckily for you, several PHP MVC frameworks have emerged in the past few years, among them CakePHP, Symfony, and CodeIgniter. The next section provides a brief comparison of these three PHP MVC frameworks.

Comparing PHP MVC Frameworks

When you look at CodeIgniter, Symfony, and CakePHP, you'll notice quite a few similarities. For example, all three:

❑   Allow you to create models that bind to a data source, views that display content, and controllers that monitor user action and allow updates of models and views.

❑   Use structured folders to separate your application's components from a central core.

❑   Use configuration files to help you maintain vital metadata, such as the location of the database, base URLs, and the like.

❑   Use controller callback functions that are surfaced to the GUI. If the user clicks on a link that opens /post/view/3, then the view() callback function in the post controller is called, with the ID of 3 passed to the model for data retrieval.

❑   Allow you to extend the core code and build your own libraries and helper functions.

The next few sections provide an extremely concise summary of the differences between CodeIgniter, CakePHP, and Symfony. The intent here is not to list every single difference among them, nor to proclaim that any one MVC framework is better than the others. The intent is to discuss the differences briefly, thereby giving you a more realistic appraisal of where CodeIgniter fits into the scheme of MVC thinking.

Making Life Easier for the Developer

CakePHP's automatic approach allows the developer to create web applications quickly. For example, the automation allows a model to map easily to a database table. If you don't really care how things work underneath, this approach can be strangely liberating. However, if you really want to understand what is happening, you sometimes have to dig around in the core code.

Symfony took a page from Ruby on Rails, providing developers with a series of command-line tools to help build admin panels, object-relational mapping schemes, views, and other niceties. Run a few scripts and suddenly you have a surprising amount of work done for you.

CodeIgniter has a different approach. Just about all your work will be in the controller. That's where you load libraries, extract data from the model, and pull in views. Everything's in plain sight, so it's easy to keep things organized and troubleshoot problems if and when they occur. The drawback, of course, is that beginners tend to create very general (and hence very fat) controllers that can become more difficult to maintain as time goes on.

Models

CakePHP automatically loads a model that matches the current controller. Yes, you can turn this off, but many CakePHP development efforts leave in this admittedly useful feature. CakePHP also establishes all the model associations for you, allowing developers to quickly pull in, for example, all comments associated with a blog post after only minimal association on the developer's part. This approach requires strict naming conventions for models, views, controllers, and database tables (not to mention primary key and foreign key fields). It can get a bit frustrating to remember to use the singular form of the database table for your model (your model is person, and the database table is people), but it can all be overridden. And yes, you can use raw SQL queries if you need to.

Figure 1-4 illustrates a typical CakePHP model.

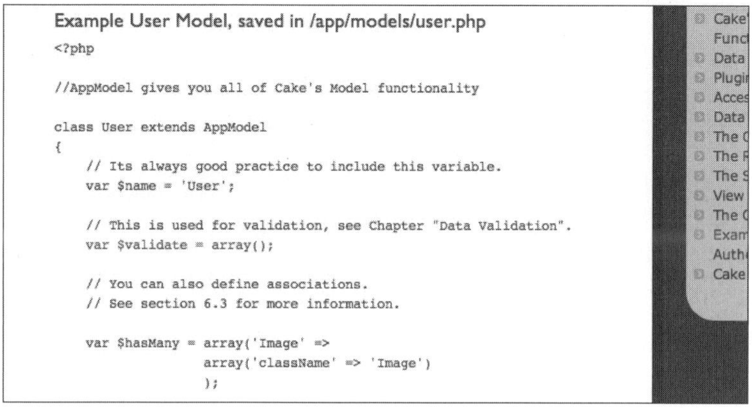

```
Example User Model, saved in /app/models/user.php
<?php

//AppModel gives you all of Cake's Model functionality

class User extends AppModel
{
    // Its always good practice to include this variable.
    var $name = 'User';

    // This is used for validation, see Chapter "Data Validation".
    var $validate = array();

    // You can also define associations.
    // See section 6.3 for more information.

    var $hasMany = array('Image' =>
                    array('className' => 'Image')
                    );
```

Figure 1-4

Symfony's approach allows you to use either built-in methods or raw queries to access the database abstraction layer. Symfony has several built-in methods to create, retrieve, update, and delete database records. Sometimes, though, it makes more sense to use raw SQL (e.g., you want to return a count on a number column). Using raw SQL (or synthetic SQL) involves the following steps: getting connection, building a query string, preparing and executing a statement, and iterating on the result set returned by the executed statement.

CodeIgniter's approach is a bit more manual, but a lot more flexible. There is no standard naming convention for models and controllers. Developers can manually load models or autoload them in the main configuration, and the models don't have to be named a certain way to match up to tables. What this means is that legacy applications are extremely easy to port over to CodeIgniter, and integration with outside database systems is generally very easy.

CodeIgniter also allows a great deal of flexibility when querying tables. For example, given a database table called *users*, the following approaches will all work if you want to extract all records:

```
//place raw SQL in the query() method
$q = $this->db->query("select * from users");

//or pass in a variable
$sql = "select * from users";
$q = $this->db->query($sql);

//or use the built-in get() method
$q = $this->db->get('users');
```

Throughout the book, you'll see how easy it is to create, delete, and update database records. (In fact, some of you may think that the repetition of the key database queries might be too much, but getting the basics down is the right foundation for your development success.) You can use SQL or CodeIgniter's built-in methods to do this.

Strictly speaking, CodeIgniter doesn't require models at all. Although this may seem a bit confusing at first (after all, how is it an MVC framework without the M part?), dropping this requirement gives you a lot of flexibility. For example, it could prove useful if you're developing applications without a database or XML backend or if you need to prototype something quickly using placeholder data in your controller.

Views

CakePHP uses layouts with placeholders (`title_for_layout` and `content_for_layout`) for other views. This automatic approach is pretty handy, but again, it requires a certain level of discipline in your file naming. Of course, it's easy enough to override this feature and use any kind of naming convention you want.

Symfony uses templates that support XHTML and PHP snippets, along with a variety of helper functions [such as `input_tag()` and `link_to()` to help you create text inputs and links, respectively]. Symfony also supports the use of separate layout files that can be assigned to templates.

CodeIgniter's approach is, predictably, more straightforward and flexible. You can almost think of view files as includes. You can load them one at a time with your controller and then render the pieces into a final view, or you can just use a master view with placeholders. Layout is typically controlled with CSS, or you can use a lightweight templating class that uses pseudo-variables in much the same way that SMARTY does. There are also many helper functions available to help you create forms, links, and other HTML elements. The preferred template format is pure PHP, which means that it's easy for PHP programmers to build views and then optimize them.

Helpers and Libraries

CakePHP is pretty light on built-in helpers and libraries, but it makes up for it with the Bakery, an online resource full of tutorials, snippets, add-ons, and third-party classes. However, as previously mentioned, it comes with a nice set of query methods, such as `find()`, `findAll()`, `query()`, `findBy<fieldname>()` (where `fieldname` is your database field name), and more.

Symfony's suite of tools for unit testing, scaffolding, and admin generation is probably the best of all three. These tools may not be used every day, but they offer plenty of shortcuts for the developer.

CodeIgniter comes with an amazing range of libraries and helper files that cover a lot of what you will encounter in just about every project: caching, security, file uploads, link building, form building, text parsing, regular expressions, database queries, FTP, e-mail, calendaring, sessions, pagination, image manipulation, validation, XML-RPC, dates, cookies, XML, and more. You can also extend built-in libraries and helpers and create your own.

Revisiting the Opening Example

Now that you've got the basics of MVC down and understand how CodeIgniter differs from other PHP-based MVC frameworks, it's time to revisit the opening example. Instead of struggling with the original code, imagine that you had access to CodeIgniter and you were recoding it from scratch.

In the following sections, you see how you'd go about doing that. The examples provided in the next few pages don't stop long enough to explain how to install and configure CodeIgniter (that's Chapter 3) or talk about all the advanced features like caching, routing, and the extensive libraries. The assumption is that all that's been done for you, and that you have a properly working CodeIgniter environment. The goal is to show you, at high speed, how a CodeIgniter application might look and behave.

First Things First: The Model

Depending on your work style, you may be inclined to tackle the views or controller first, but a good place to start is the model. Why? Because the model serves as the data foundation for your entire web application. Many of the controller's functions will rely on the model, so it's a good idea to have those tools all ready to go.

All CodeIgniter models have the same initial structure:

```php
<?php
class Page_model extends Model{

  function Page_model(){
    parent::Model();
  }
}
?>
```

Notice that the name of the model (in this case, Page_model) is both the name of the class and the name of the initializing function. This file is stored in the /system/application/models/ folder of your project, more than likely with a name like *page_model.php*. If this were the user model, you'd likely call your model User_model and store it in the file user_model.php.

Later in the book, you learn the ins and outs of placing and naming files. But here, you need to add a few functions to your model. The first function is the code that retrieves the home page:

```php
<?php
class Page_model extends Model{

  function Page_model(){
    parent::Model();
  }

  function fetchHomePage(){
    $data = array();
    $options = array('status' => 'live', 'type'=> 'home');
    $q = $this->db->getwhere('pages', $options, 1);

    if ($q->num_rows() > 0){
      $data = $q->row_array();
    }
    return $data;
    $q->free_result();
  }
}
?>
```

The `fetchHomePage()` function is very simple, but it pays huge dividends to understand what is going on. Here's what's going on in the `fetchHomePage()` function, step by step:

1. The first line initializes the `$data` array. You're not required to do this, but doing so is good practice and is an effective way to avoid unnecessary carping by PHP if you end up returning a null set at the end of the function.

2. The second line establishes a list of options that will be passed to the `getwhere()` method. In this case, the options set are any status fields marked as "live" and any type fields marked as "home." The `getwhere()` method is built in to CodeIgniter and allows you to extract data from a table while passing in an array that serves as the `where` clause in the SQL statement.

3. The `$this->db->getwhere()` line is where the model extracts the data from the database table. You need to pass in three arguments to this method:

   a. The first argument is the name of the table.

   b. The second argument is the list of options previously discussed.

   c. The third argument is how many records you want to extract (in this case, the limit is set to 1).

4. After the query runs, use the `num_rows()` method to make sure you're getting back the number of rows you want (in this case, anything more than zero) and then dump the fields from the result set into an array with `row_array()`. In other chapters, you see how to loop through multiple rows in a result set using `result()`. In this particular example, each field from the database gets placed into the `$data` array that was initialized at the top of the function.

5. Finally, the function returns `$data` and then frees the memory being used by the result set. It's not necessary to do this, because PHP will clear out all result set objects when page execution ends, but having numerous result set objects might slow down your application. It's a good habit to get into.

Now that you understand what's going on in the model, it's time to turn your attention to the controller. Basically, everything you've done in the model will become reusable data-fetching functions for the controller's use.

Creating the Controller

Now that a working model is in place, it's time to create a controller. Controllers in CodeIgniter function as the brawn of your application. Anything that a user can do on your site, including going to destinations, should be represented in your controller.

First, here's what a standard controller would look like. Notice that in the following example the controller is for the Page application you built the model for above:

```php
<?php
class Page extends Controller {
  function Page(){
    parent::Controller();
  }
}
?>
```

As before, this controller is bare-bones, consisting of just an initialization function that ties this particular controller to the master class Controller. Once again, notice that with this simple notation, CodeIgniter allows you to extend the basic core classes and create something specific and powerful with very little work.

When you're working with a controller, every function or method maps to an address in your application. If you want users to view a page with the address of /page/foo, there had better be a Page controller and a foo() method inside that controller.

For now, all that's needed is an index() function to represent the site's home page.

```
function index(){
    //code goes here
}
```

Right now, if a user were to go to your home page, they'd see a blank page. That's because nothing particularly interesting is happening inside the index() method. To change that, just simply load the Page_model so you can access the fetchHomePage() method you created previously.

```
<?php
    class Page extends Controller {
        function Page(){
            parent::Controller();
        }
    }

    function index(){
        $this->load->model('Page_model','',TRUE);
        $data['content']  = $this->Page_model->fetchHomePage();
    }
}
?>
```

Notice that once you load the model you want, you can access the methods inside that model by simply invoking the name of the model: $this->Page_model->fetchHomePage(). Storing the information from the database into the $data array makes it easy to display the information in a view.

You've loaded the model and invoked the method to retrieve the data; now all you need to do is print out the data to the screen. In extremely simple applications, you could get away with simply printing out what you need right there in the controller, but that isn't smart to do unless you need a quick and easy debugging method.

The best way is to load a view. You haven't created one yet, but for now, use the name home. Later you can create a home.php file in the Views directory. When you load a view, the name of the file (sans *.php*) is the first argument, and any data you want to pass in are the second argument. Here's what the entire controller looks like:

```
<?php
    class Page extends Controller {
        function Page(){
            parent::Controller();
        }
```

```
  }

  function index(){
    $this->load->model('Page_model','',TRUE);
    $data['content'] = $this->Page_model->fetchHomePage();
    $this->load->view('home',$data);
  }
}
?>
```

When you look at this controller, notice how organized it is, and how easy it is to figure out what is going on. Any visitor to the site's index or home page will kick off a discrete process: Invoke the model, retrieve the data, and display the view with data. There's nothing hidden about any of it; there are no other configurations to look up. Simple, clean, tidy.

Creating the View

The final step, creating the view, is quite possibly the easiest. Simply create the appropriate file in the / system/application/views/ folder (in this case, a file called home.php):

```
<html>
  <head>
    <title><?php echo $content['title']; ?></title>
    <link href="<?php echo $content['css']; ?>" rel="stylesheet" type="text/css"/>
    <meta http-equiv="Content-Type" content="text/html; charset=UTF-8"/>
    <meta name="keywords" value="<?php echo $content['keywords'];?>"/>
    <meta name="description" value="<?php echo $content['description'];?>"/>
  </head>
  <body>
    <h1><?php echo $content['title'];?></h1>
    <p><?php echo nl2br($content['bodycopy']);?></p>
  </body>
</html>
```

Please note that the $content['css'] in this code example is just a file name! You're not storing the entire CSS file in the database. You could if you wanted to, but it makes more sense to keep this information in a separate file.

Notice that the view is mostly HTML markup with PHP commands interspersed. The view contains a title tag (with dynamic content pulled in from the database), a dynamically inserted CSS filename (again, from the database), and other information, such as the UTF-8 charset declaration. You may be wondering what the point of all this is if you're eventually going to have PHP mixed in with your HTML. It's important to understand that:

❑   You have a lot less PHP in your HTML at this point.

❑   All the important business logic and data extraction have occurred in the controller and model.

❑   Because the view is PHP, it can be cached by CodeIgniter or by another server-side optimization process.

Notice the use of the $content array whenever you access what you need. You may be wondering about that. Take a look at the model again:

```
if ($q->num_rows() > 0){
    $data = $q->row_array();
}
```

When the fetchHomePage() function retrieves the home page content from the pages table, notice the use of row_array(), which converts the results into an array. The keys of that array are the field names, with field values populating the array values. In other words, the row_array() method is a simple way of keeping parity between your database tables and result set objects.

If you were to inspect the $data array within the model with print_r(), you'd probably see something like this:

```
Array
(
    [id] => 4
    [title] => test
    [keywords] => test
    [description] => test
    [status] => live
    [bodycopy] => test
    [css] => default.css
)
```

Once called from the Page controller, however, this array is dropped inside $data['content'], which, when passed to the view, is accessible via the $content array. Why? Because you told the template to accept the $data array when you loaded the view:

```
function index(){
    $this->load->model('Page_model','',TRUE);
    $data['content'] = $this->Page_model->fetchHomePage();
    $this->load->view('home',$data);
}
```

Once the view is loaded, it unwraps whatever is in $data (itself an array), and the first thing it encounters is the $content array embedded inside it. You see this kind of approach taken throughout the book, so it becomes second nature to you.

Figure 1-5 illustrates the application flow.

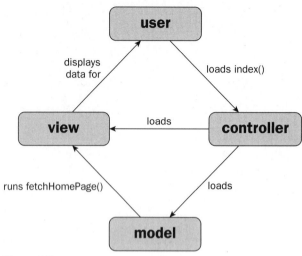

Figure 1-5

A Slightly Different Approach: Templates

Along with standard PHP templates, CodeIgniter offers a lightweight template parser. To use the parser, all you have to do is load it into your controller and pass in the data from the model. The view would then use pseudo-variables instead of actual PHP variables, thus making your views free of PHP altogether. If you are familiar with SMARTY templates, you will see that these pseudo-variables and pseudo-structures align with your expectation of how the SMARTY world works. If you are new to this type of template parsing, you won't have any direct experience with it, but it's pretty easy to pick up. For example, instead of calling $title as you did before, you'd use {title}. Semantically, the structures and naming conventions are similar enough to the PHP variables and structures that you won't have much trouble following along.

One final note before continuing the discussion: There's normally no need to modify the model if you're going to work with the template parser. Why not? Well, it just so happens that the template parser will accept the data structures you give it. The only thing that changes is how you call out and use the data structure from the parsed template.

Using Third-Party Templating Systems

Most of the time, you'll want to use PHP templates with CodeIgniter, as it offers the fastest way to both develop and generate views. However, there might be some cases in which you'll want to use a third-party templating system, such as SMARTY.

Why use a templating system? Some developers swear by them, as they allow a clean separation between PHP code and the pseudo-variables that designers and front-end developers can be trained to use without harming the rest of the application.

In most cases, these third-party templating systems work like CodeIgniter's template parser. They almost always use pseudo-code and pseudo-variables in place of "real" PHP code. If you've never worked with pseudo-code, it looks a bit like this:

```
<title>{title}</title>
<h1>{header}</h1>
```

You would normally pass variable structures into the template via your controller (establishing values for $title and $header above) so they can be replaced by their corresponding pseudo-variables.

The biggest template engine out there is SMARTY (available at http://smarty.php .net). Others include TinyButStrong (www.tinybutstrong.com) and SimpleTemplate (http://sourceforge.net/projects/simpletpl).

One of the common pitfalls of using third-party templating solutions is that they can provide too much complexity and overhead (both from maintenance and performance standpoints) with minimal return on convenience.

Modifying the Controller

Here's what the controller would look like:

```php
<?php
class Page extends Controller {
  function Page(){
    parent::Controller();
  }
}

function index(){
  $data = array();
  $this->load->library('parser');
  $this->load->model('Page_model','',TRUE);
  $data = $this->Page_model->fetchHomePage();
  $this->parser->parse('home',$data);
}
}
?>
```

Note the two additions to the `index()` method: loading the parser library and then calling the parser, passing in as arguments the name of the view and the data retrieved from the model. Also note that the data from the model can be safely stored in the `$data` array (which has also helpfully been initialized). In the view, you'll name your pseudo-variables from the keys of this array, which helpfully map to the names of the database table fields. For example, `$data['css']` can be accessed with `{css}`.

Modifying the View

Here's the view, with pseudo-variables in place instead of real PHP variables.

```
<html>
  <head>
   <title{title}</title>
   <link href="{css}" rel="stylesheet" type="text/css"/>
   <meta name="keywords" value="{keywords}"/>
   <meta name="description" value="{description}"/>
  </head>
  <body>
   <h1>{title}</h1>
   <p>{bodycopy}</p>
  </body>
</html>
```

This approach certainly involves a lot less typing, and the overall aesthetics can be very familiar and pleasing to anyone who's worked with a template system in the past. Also, some HTML specialists who are unfamiliar with PHP find this format a bit easier to work with.

What about `{bodycopy}` ?

However, notice that the `{bodycopy}` pseudo-variable in the example has lost some of its functionality. In the previous PHP incarnation of this template, the bodycopy data were processed via `nl2br()`, a PHP function that converts line breaks into HTML `<br/>` tags.

One way to fix the problem is to add two lines of processing to your controller, like so:

```
function index(){
    $data = array();
    $this->load->library('parser');
    $this->load->model('Page_model','',TRUE);
    $data = $this->Page_model->fetchHomePage();

    //fix the body copy
    $fixcopy = nl2br($data['bodycopy']);
    $data['bodycopy'] = $fixcopy;

    $this->parser->parse('home',$data);
}
```

Of course, you could also rewrite the model, replacing `row_array()` with `row()` and then processing each field as it comes off the database query. That way you can process every element as it is extracted from the database.

```php
<?php
class Page_model extends Model{

  function Page_model(){
    parent::Model();
  }

  function fetchHomePage(){
    $data = array();
    $options = array('status' => 'live', 'type'=> 'home');
    $q = $this->db->getwhere('pages', $options, 1);

    if ($q->num_rows() > 0){
      $row = $q->row();
      $data['title'] = $row->title;
      $data['css'] = $row->css;
      $data['keywords'] = $row->keywords;
      $data['description'] = $row->description;
      $data['bodycopy'] = nl2br($row->bodycopy);

    }
    return $data;
    $q->free_result();
  }
}
?>
```

In a lot of ways, this is a more palatable solution, because now the model does all the work of preparing the data for display. However, others might argue that there may be a need in the future to have access to the raw `bodycopy` field unprocessed by `nl2br()`. In that case, you'd want to keep the processing in the controller or create a second method in the model to address this issue.

There is a much better way to do all this, of course, and it involves using a built-in CodeIgniter helper called *Typography*. This helper has an `auto_typography` function that does all the hard work of converting line breaks to `<br/>` tags and converting quotes and dashes to the appropriate entities.

First, load the helper in the controller function:

```php
function index(){
  $data = array();
  $this->load->library('parser');
  $this->load->model('Page_model','',TRUE);
  $data = $this->Page_model->fetchHomePage();

  $this->load->helper('typography');

  $this->parser->parse('home',$data);
}
```

Next, use the `auto_typography()` function in the view:

```html
<html>
  <head>
    <title{title}</title>
    <link href="{css}" rel="stylesheet" type="text/css"/>
    <meta name="keywords" value="{keywords}"/>
    <meta name="description" value="{description}"/>
  </head>
  <body>
    <h1>{title}</h1>
    <p><?php echo auto_typography("{bodycopy}");?></p>
  </body>
</html>
```

If you put five MVC experts in the same room and asked them to tackle this particular problem, you'd probably get at least three different answers, if not more. But you get the idea: CodeIgniter is fairly easy to work with, very flexible, and leaves you, the developer, with easily maintained, well-organized code artifacts.

Conclusion

This chapter serves as a basic introduction to MVC and CodeIgniter's place in that world. You've learned about the concepts behind MVC and why you should use it, and been given a brief history lesson. Specifically, you've learned how to transform a non-MVC application into a working CodeIgniter application, with a simple model, controller, and view.

As you continue with the rest of the book, remember these key facts about Model-View-Controller frameworks and applications:

- ❑ Models maintain and update an application's data.
- ❑ Views display data and user interface elements.
- ❑ Controllers handle user events that manipulate models and render or update views.
- ❑ In CodeIgniter:
    - ❑ Most of your work will be done in the controller.
    - ❑ Views can be regular PHP files or parsed templates with pseudo-variables.
    - ❑ Models aren't required, but most of your applications will have them.

The next two chapters cover Agile development practices and provide a high-level overview of CodeIgniter's structure and installation process. By the time you finish with Chapters 1–3, you'll have the necessary background for creating the projects outlined in this book.

2

Agile Methodologies and Approaches

With our preliminary overview of MVC and CodeIgniter complete, let's take a slight detour. Don't worry, you're not being taken on a joyride; this detour lays some pretty important foundational blocks. In other words, the goal of this chapter is for you to be able to marry what you've learned about MVC with Agile methodologies. Knowing about MVC and Agile and combining that knowledge with CodeIgniter allow you to build applications very quickly.

What Is Agile?

A lot of different definitions for Agile exist, ranging from the superficial to the authoritative and pedantic. Not every definition is useful, nor is every definition really applicable to your job as a software developer. Things only get more confusing once you realize that various Agile methodologies exist, all of them competing for your attention.

At the end of the day, the most important thing to remember is this: Agile software development is a conceptual framework that seeks to minimize risk by developing software in short amounts of time. A typical iteration can last 1 to 4 weeks, during which time a software team performs tasks from a complete project life cycle (planning, design, coding, testing, documentation). Each iteration usually starts with stories (what Agile calls *requirements*) and culminates in potentially shippable software. Another important aspect of Agile is the team's ability to self-organize as they communicate face-to-face with stakeholders and other team members.

If you're not familiar with Agile, you probably have one of two reactions:

❏ "How is this different from cowboy coding? Agile sounds just like every chaotic code-and-fix project I've ever been part of."

❏ "How does anyone get anything done in so short a time? Agile sounds like a perpetual hamster wheel where everyone burns out."

First of all, if you have doubts when you first encounter Agile, welcome to the club. Rest assured that everyone who takes a closer look and sees Agile in action usually crosses over.

Second, many people out there made the initial mistake of distinguishing Agile methodologies as somehow "lightweight" (as opposed to the heavyweight models like waterfall) or "unplanned" (which inspires the mistaken belief that Agile developers are undisciplined).

A better way to look at Agile is to say that the entire process is *adaptive* instead of predictive. For example, if you were to start a project using waterfall methods, you would spend a lot of time trying to nail down schedules, resources, requirements, deadlines, milestones, and the like. If anything changes, you have to go back and reevaluate your initial inputs. It's very much like planning a road trip to Las Vegas down to the last detail (including where you would make rest stops, how much gas you would buy at each gas station, what sandwiches to pack) but then encountering a sandstorm right at the edge of the city and having to turn back home to try again later.

An Agile road trip to Vegas would be different. The process would start with a focus on gambling in Vegas, and then a minimal amount of work would be done to get the car ready and rolling. Everyone would bring his or her own snacks and gas money. Once on the road, travelers are free to take advantage of opportunities. Perhaps someone sees a casino just outside the town they left from, and the group decides to gamble there. After all, the goal is to gamble, right? It's this kind of adaptive thinking that gives Agile its power and flexibility.

Third, many outsiders have a bone to pick over the short iterations in Agile. They can't conceive that quality software can be developed in a week or two. Normally, this assertion would be true, but with the right tools (i.e., CodeIgniter and other MVC frameworks, especially those that focus on delivering convention-over-configuration benefits), you can achieve in hours what normally would take days or weeks. Most people don't stop to consider that an enormous amount of overhead time is devoted to non-programming tasks. Developers tend to forget the painful hours spent in meetings, all the hours devoted to planning and analysis, and all the time spent debugging. On a typical project, a developer might spend 2 to 3 hours a day programming and the rest in meetings, debugging, documenting, or researching a tough problem. If she's lucky! On the other hand, it is possible, with the right tools and the right methodologies, to create shippable software in very short iterations. The result is working software, happy customers, and developers with a sense of job satisfaction. What could be better?

Are there places where Agile is not a good idea? Of course: Agile works best when you have smaller teams in one location, more experienced developers, quickly changing environments, and a culture that is not exclusively driven by top-down command and control structures. In other words, trying to build a giant weapons software platform for the Army that involves 1,000 developers in three geographically separate locations would probably not make a good case study for any Agile methodology.

That being said, your average web application can easily be built following Agile. It doesn't matter what kind of application: blog, newsletter tool, content management, shopping cart, or content portal. If you can keep the team under 20 developers (or better yet, a dozen) and keep them communicating well, you can pull it off.

Post-Agilism

Any successful movement will have some members who eventually move on to something else. In the case of Agile methodologies, there is Post-Agilism. What is Post-Agilism? It's a loose group of developers and other IT professionals who have experience with Agile but have now moved on to other approaches.

The most thoughtful Post-Agilists (if they would allow themselves to be labeled as such, and even that is up for grabs) make a fine distinction between being "agile" (defined as being adaptive in a social or commercial circumstance) and being "Agile" (living by the rules, dogma, or inherited wisdom of a particular Agile methodology, like Scrum or XP). It's therefore possible to be "agile" without necessarily having to take on all the trappings of any particular Agile approach.

> *Of course, the way I am using "agile" and "Agile" here is merely to differentiate the concepts. Within the Agile community and throughout this book, "Agile" is the way you see the word presented. There is no formal distinction between "Agile" and "agile."*

Another extremely valid concern brought up by Post-Agilists (again, please forgive the use of broad labels) is that the Agile movement was once about shaking the industry out of the waterfall methodology, the predictive mess to which everyone was so well accustomed. Now they feel that everyone is trying to follow the *Agile Manifesto* (and other touchstone documents) as some kind of canonical bible, replacing the earlier problem with a newer adherence-to-dogma problem.

To be clear, any time that "Agile" is mentioned in this book, it is in the spirit of little-"a" "agile." It is more important for you, the developer, to be adaptive and successfully complete a project than to adhere strictly to the rules of a certain methodology.

Resources/Further Reading

Robert Wysocki has two books that include information on and examples of Agile methodologies:
Effective Project Management: Traditional, Adaptive, Extreme *deals with the Adaptive Project Framework and Extreme Project Management (in addition to traditional project management methods). His other book,* Effective Software Project Management, *covers a lot of information. Part IV covers the evolutionary development waterfall method, Scrum, Rational Unified Process, and Dynamic Systems Development as iterative software development project management strategies. Part V covers the Adaptive Project Framework and other adaptive software development strategies. Part VI covers INSPIRE and flexible model extreme strategies. If you want more information on Agile methodologies, Wysocki's books offer a wealth of information. Other good places to find information are at* www.agilealliance.com *and* www.agilemanifesto.org.

Notable Agile Methodologies

Because so many Agile methodologies are out there, and because each of them has different parts that take a bit of time to absorb, this chapter briefly touches on just two of them: Scrum and XP. Once you take the brief tour of these methodologies, you can incorporate the ideas you want from each to make things work.

Some people feel a little anxious about mixing methodologies. However, that is actually at the heart of being *agile*. Where *Agile* with a capital "A" focuses on the purity of the model, *agile* with a small "a" focuses on freeing you up to do whatever will help you quickly and easily achieve your goals. Being "agile" is about being adaptive and fast on your feet.

In the real world when you are working with clients, any time you have to decide between getting things done on schedule and strictly adhering to theoretical rules, always err on the side of getting things done. It may get under your skin a bit, but it's really the only way to keep the customer happy.

Scrum

Scrum is an Agile project management methodology that offers small teams a great deal of flexibility (even by Agile standards). Here are the typical attributes of a Scrum undertaking:

- ❑   You need a **product backlog** — a prioritized list of work items that need completion.

- ❑   The self-organizing team uses the product backlog to create **sprint backlogs**.

- ❑   Each **sprint** is a short period of duration (usually 1 to 4 weeks) in which highly focused activity takes place.

- ❑   Each sprint begins with a **sprint planning session**, in which backlog items for the sprint are defined.

- ❑   Each sprint ends with a **retrospective**, in which a postmortem is performed.

Each team has a ScrumMaster, who acts as coach, facilitator, and buffer against the outside world. The ScrumMaster is not the leader of the team! Many outsiders view the ScrumMaster as the chief project manager, but it's not so.

Scrum recognizes that customers are wont to change their minds about what they want. Sometimes the changes in direction are subjective and capricious, and other times they come about because of market pressures. Regardless of the reason, change happens, and normal predictive methodologies have zero chance of predicting these changes (ironically). Instead, Scrum accepts that change is inevitable, unpredictable, and indefinable, and focuses instead on maximizing the team's ability to adapt to change and still deliver a great product.

The team works closely with stakeholders (such as business owners, marketing managers, the CEO, CFO, etc.) to develop a backlog of requirements that need to be addressed. Normally, this backlog of requirements is maintained by a certain stakeholder called the "product owner." In most cases, the product owner is the CEO, but it can also be a marketing manager or project manager.

The *backlog* is essentially a list of prioritized requirements that emanate from the end-customer. At the start of each sprint, the team takes the top remaining items from the product backlog and turns them into tasks on the sprint backlog. It's important for the team to only take on as many tasks as can be completed in any given iteration.

The goal of any iteration is to create potentially shippable software — in other words, by the time you're at the end of the time box (1 week, 2 weeks, whatever), what you have could be considered ready to ship. It is functionally complete, reasonably bug-free, and reasonably documented.

For example, a product backlog might have several prioritized items on it, like so:

- ❑ The customer wants to be able to securely check page views and other stats about their web site.
- ❑ The customer wants hyperlinks within the report.
- ❑ The customer wants real-time access to data, without lag.
- ❑ The customer wants info graphics associated with the data, not just tabular data.

The team might look at this product backlog and decide to convert the first two bullet items into a series of tasks:

1. Create views to display the report.
2. Create models to connect to data sources.
3. Create a controller to identify and separate different destinations.
4. Implement a security model.

The real task list would probably be longer than that, but you get the idea. Because the team is self-organizing, the HTML/CSS expert would tackle the views, the database expert would construct the models, and the security expert would implement the security model. If no security expert is on the team, perhaps someone remembers that a security module was written for another project — might it not be useful in this context?

The sprint is set at 2 weeks, and the team takes on the tasks, meeting every day for a standup meeting that lasts no more than 10 minutes. At each meeting, the ScrumMaster asks three basic questions of each participant:

1. What have you done since the last time we saw you?
2. What are you going to do until the next time we see you?
3. What obstacles or barriers are in your way?

The first question focuses on **accomplishments**, the second on **to do's**, and the third on **risks or concerns**. The standup meeting allows the entire team to check in and understand how the project is going with a great deal of transparency. Very quickly, everyone gets a feeling for what's been accomplished, what is still left to do, and what's standing in the way.

Outsiders (other than developers, ScrumMaster, and product owner) are allowed to join the meetings, of course, but they aren't allowed to interfere directly in the project. What does "interfere" mean? Well, in many software development projects, you see many business managers or complete outsiders dictating requirements. These requirements don't come from the customers, they just arbitrarily live in the minds of senior management or outside stakeholders. Often, these arbitrary requirements impede schedules and complicate matters.

For example, there is rarely any real value to a requirement like "It must ship in Q1." In the mind of the person who brought it up, it has importance, but not to anyone else. What does that mean? Well, on somebody's strategic plan, such-and-such a product must ship in Q1, and the stakeholder's bonus depends on it. The customer doesn't care when the product comes out, just that it works the way they need it to when it does come out. (This is not to say that you should totally disregard a powerful stakeholder's concerns about schedules and money. After all, they will hopefully be rehiring you or referring you to another business in the future. Treat them seriously and with respect. Just don't let their concerns interfere with what you need to do to accomplish the project.)

What concepts are you going to take from Scrum? The idea of a backlog is key, as is the nature of sprints. You'll find that on many small projects, a sprint can last 1 or 2 days. You'll also find that you don't need to have a daily standup meeting, especially if it's just you working on things.

XP

The main thrust behind XP is to put in place daily practices that reconcile humanity and productivity. What this means in practice is that there is more weight given to face-to-face communication and feedback than to formal requirements' gathering.

Furthermore, XP proponents expound on the value of doing something simple and clean today rather than worrying about future problems that might entail complexity. For example, why worry about scaling to 50,000 customers when you only have 5 customers today? Wouldn't scaling out to 500 customers (or even 50!) be good enough to get something working now?

Another great thing from the XP movement involves the collegial respect between programmers. Contributions are made in a give-and-take environment, and in fact, many programmers pair up to tackle problems and work through issues. Finally, there is the matter of allowing programmers to take ownership of their code. It is not unusual to see programmers refactor code to simplify even when it isn't needed.

What are you going to take from XP? Definitely the simplicity and communication/feedback loops. It's important to incorporate good listening skills to any Agile approach. When working with a client one-on-one, you will need to interface often. Make sure that you allow a significant amount of time for the face-to-face contact, as it can create a powerful bond between you and the client.

Modifying Scrum and XP

Scrum and XP (extreme programming), like all methodologies, are wonderful things, but one immediate drawback for you right now, as you read this book, is that you're probably a lone programmer or work with a very small team. If so, you may be thinking that these approaches provide too much overhead even for you, and in some ways, you might be right. However, one of the great strengths of any Agile methodology is that it can be adapted to your needs.

The rest of this chapter is devoted to walking you through an Agile methodology for gathering requirements, planning your work, and getting started on the actual work. This basic modification has been refined by various "lone gun" programmers and has seen lots of success with typical web development projects. The example provided throughout the rest of this chapter assumes that you are working as a solo entrepreneur with a single small business owner. As you continue through this chapter, you should consider how you might tailor the information presented here to fit your specific needs. However, the basic approach to the methodology is applicable to many different-sized teams in various situations.

Because the goal of this book is to build a series of web tools (shopping cart, newsletter tool, others), there's no time like the present to start the process. Accordingly, the rest of this chapter focuses on gathering the requirements needed for the projects in the book.

Gather Your Requirements While You May

For the purposes of this book, you are working with a hypothetical customer who wants to build an eCommerce site. That's really all you know when you agree to meet with the customer. The customer's name is Claudia, and she runs a thriving retail store devoted to "all things kids." She only has a very basic web presence that gives the name of the store (*Claudia's Kids*) and some basic contact information. This is not a lot to go on, which is OK, because, unlike when using predictive methodologies, you want to adapt to the customer's needs.

The First Day

When you meet Claudia, she turns out to be an energetic 30-something who started her retail store 4 years before. The store was funded in part with credit cards, the severance from the high-tech job she was laid off from, and a loan from various friends and family. It took almost 2 years for her to claw out a decent profit in the store, but by catering to a specific market (moms who would pay anything to provide their kids with branded clothes and toys), Claudia has made a success of it.

Claudia's pretty sure it's time to expand. It didn't take long for her phenomenal growth to flatten out, but there isn't enough money coming in to expand to a second brick-and-mortar store. Nor does she feel comfortable with the costs associated with a mail order catalog. This is where you and CodeIgniter come in. Although she has no idea how to code an eCommerce site, she knows that a transactional site is the key to her success — she could, with the right site, expand her customer base and bring in lots of revenue beyond what comes in from walk-ins and the occasional long-time customer who phones in an order.

As you listen, you're taking notes, mostly about high-level nouns and verbs. You know already, for example, that you will need some kind of online catalog of products. You don't know what pieces of information you will need to track for each product, but you can be sure that each will have a price, a photo, a name, and some kind of unique identifier. Furthermore, they'll probably be organized into some kind of category scheme, such as toys or clothes. But that's all you know right now. You also know that there are customers involved, but you don't know if she wants to track each unique customer.

So now you have a place to start. There are only so many ways to attack the problem. With your previous experience building these kinds of systems, you know how to guide the discussion, which is fine, because that's what Claudia wants. She's the expert on her business and marketplace, and you're the expert coder. From here forward it's a partnership. She will eventually become the product owner in the process, the person who provides you, the developer, with the kind of necessary input to delineate tasks.

You can start anywhere, really, but you've learned from past experience not to start by asking bottom-up questions. In other words, trying to dissect every single possible field for a product or how categories interact would just confuse Claudia. Instead, you draw a big rectangle on a sheet of paper and label it "home page."

You tell Claudia that the best way to start is with a prototype mockup. That way the two of you can start figuring out the major components of each page and from there fill in the look and feel and other details.

As you talk, you draw a smaller horizontal rectangle near the top of the big rectangle. You explain that this is where the store's logo and main navigation will go — pages like Contact Us, About Us, and perhaps special features or deals. At the bottom of the big rectangle, you draw another smaller rectangle, and explain that this is the site's footer, which will contain a copyright notice, a link to the privacy policy, and other minutiae.

So far, what you've drawn looks a lot like Figure 2-1.

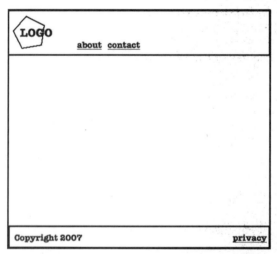

Figure 2-1

Now, you need to know what goes in the middle. You suggest some kind of featured item or point of focus or visual interest, but the page also needs to allow users to navigate quickly and easily to any point in the site.

Yes, Claudia says that a featured item is a good idea, perhaps something that could stay up for a week or so, something that she could control instead of something random. She wants a photo of the item, the item's name, a short description, and a link to some kind of detail page. You suggest that it might be good to have a "buy now" button as well, right on the home page, and she agrees. Claudia also thinks that something off to the right of the main feature might be a random list of other items, maybe one product from each major category. Each item in the list would feature a small thumbnail, a product name, and a link to a detail page. Again, you fill in a "buy now" link as well.

Your home page drawing now looks like Figure 2-2.

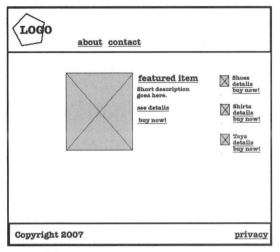

Figure 2-2

Speaking of categories, you decide to put a long vertical rectangle to the left of the main featured item, telling her, "This is where we'll list all the categories in your store. Let's talk about those for a bit."

Claudia nods and tells you that in her existing inventory, she has five or six major categories of products, each with their own subcategories. So far, her store only has two levels of categories, so you know that you will need to build a hierarchical category tree and a two-level navigation depending on what the user clicks on, as illustrated in Figure 2-3.

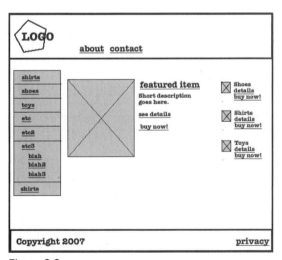

Figure 2-3

You both look at this mockup and decide that what you have is pretty good. You've been at it for about an hour, but instead of quitting just yet, you decide to push ahead to create two other page mockups: one for the Category view and one for the Detail view.

Claudia asks about the "buy now" page and the actual Shopping Cart. You tell her that this page can be mocked up tomorrow. After all, you need some time to assimilate everything you're learning from this meeting.

You decide to reuse your basic rectangle for your Category view. You explain that this is a generic view that shows any list of products and/or other categories. For example, if you had a clothing category, it might have certain subcategories associated with it: shirts, pants, skirts, and shoes.

A main category might even have individual products associated with it as well as subcategories, but at this point Claudia says, "no", that she wants to mirror the retail environment to some degree. In the store's inventory system, you would never see individual products associated with a high-level category like clothes. You make a note that only subcategories can have products associated with them.

The result is a fairly simple Category view, featuring all the subcategories associated with a main category or the products associated with a particular subcategory. The first type of view would list all subcategories alphabetically, with subcategory name, description, and a link to view products within that category.

When you ask if it's possible to have categories or subcategories removed or deleted from the online store, Claudia thinks long and hard and finally agrees to allow it. So now you know that you need to track some kind of status (active or inactive, live or in progress) and only show the ones that are active or live.

Next you ask if you should show some kind of image next to each category name and description. After some thinking, Claudia asks if it's possible to pull a random image from a product associated with a subcategory and use that. You tell her that, of course, it's possible, but something else just occurred to you: Is it possible for a product to be in more than one category at a time?

Claudia doesn't even have to think very long about it. She shakes her head, no, and says that she keeps things very organized in her store and intends to do the same online. So far, your diagrams for the category views (category and subcategory) look like Figure 2-4 and Figure 2-5.

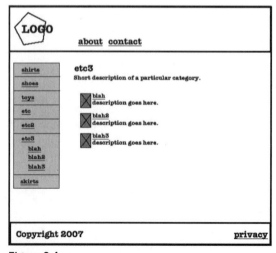

Figure 2-4

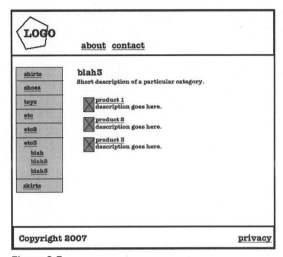

Figure 2-5

As you work, you take note that there really isn't that much of a difference between the two mockups. All you have to do is check to see where you are in the category hierarchy to show products or subcategories.

As Claudia reviews these mockups, she mentions that it would be nice to offer related items for any product. You take this as your cue to start the process of creating a mockup for the Product Detail page. Again, you use the shorthand rectangles that helped you create the home page, but this time you provide space for a large product image, image name, longer description, and a "buy now" button.

"It's not that simple," Claudia says, reacting to your mockup. "We also need to provide other information, such as colors and sizes. And I'd like to show related items off to the side."

"What do you mean by related items?"

"Well, if they're looking at a shirt, it would be nice to show some pants or shoes," she says.

When you ask if these would be random selections, she says, "no", that she would like to construct each page like she does her store. In the store, she will routinely put together outfits, as doing it this way increases her sales.

"Let's do this," you say, feeling a need to go away for a while to take better notes. "We'll do a related items sidebar, but it sounds like we need to figure out a way to group things together that doesn't involve categories. Something like a group number or something. Everything with the same group number stays together."

She nods and understands where you are going. She has other things to do, so she is also anxious to step away for a while. As she looks at the mockup for the Product Detail page (shown in Figure 2-6), she mentions how happy she is with the process so far.

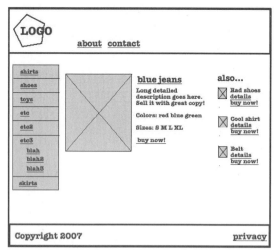

Figure 2-6

"This is a lot more relaxed and visual than I remember from my high-tech days," she says. "So far you haven't asked any scary questions, just about stuff that I know really well, like my business."

You thank Claudia for her time and set an appointment for the next day, in which you'll talk about a "buy now" page and fill in some other holes in your knowledge.

Assimilating What You've Learned

Congratulations, you've done a whole lot of work. Not only have you created four mockup pages (home page, category view, subcategory view, and Product Detail view), but you've also absorbed a great deal of information about categories and products.

Here's what you know about categories:

- ❑ Categories are hierarchical, but limited to two levels.
- ❑ Categories can be active or inactive.
- ❑ Categories have a name, a short description, and a long description.
- ❑ Images for categories are derived from the products assigned to them.

And this is what you know about products:

- ❑ A product can only belong to one category at a time.
- ❑ A product has a name, a large image, a thumbnail, a short description, a long description, and other possible metadata, such as sizes and colors.
- ❑ A product can be associated with other products to form groups or outfits.

❑   Although not mentioned yet, one could correctly deduce that products can be active or inactive.

❑   Something else not mentioned, but presumably a requirement, is that every product has a price expressed as a decimal number.

Converting what you know about categories into a query that would create a table in MySQL, you would have something like this:

```
CREATE TABLE 'categories' (
'id' INT NOT NULL AUTO_INCREMENT ,
'name' VARCHAR( 255 ) NOT NULL ,
'shortdesc' VARCHAR( 255 ) NOT NULL ,
'longdesc' TEXT NOT NULL ,
'status' ENUM( 'active', 'inactive' ) NOT NULL ,
'parentid' INT NOT NULL ,
PRIMARY KEY ( 'id' )
) TYPE = MYISAM ;
```

Similarly, converting what you know about products into a MySQL query, you would end up with the following:

```
CREATE TABLE 'products' (
'id' INT NOT NULL AUTO_INCREMENT ,
'name' VARCHAR( 255 ) NOT NULL ,
'shortdesc' VARCHAR( 255 ) NOT NULL ,
'longdesc' TEXT NOT NULL ,
'thumbnail' VARCHAR( 255 ) NOT NULL ,
'image' VARCHAR( 255 ) NOT NULL ,
'sizes' ENUM( 's', 'm', 'l', 'xl' ) NOT NULL ,
'colors' ENUM( 'red', 'blue', 'green', 'brown', 'white', 'black' ) NOT NULL ,
'grouping' VARCHAR( 16 ) NOT NULL ,
'status' ENUM( 'active', 'inactive' ) NOT NULL ,
'category_id' INT NOT NULL ,
'featured' ENUM ('true', 'false') NOT NULL,
'price' FLOAT( 4, 2 ) NOT NULL,
PRIMARY KEY ( 'id' )
) TYPE = MYISAM ;
```

At this point, using an enum for colors and sizes is a bit iffy, as there may be any number of size classifications (one for shoes, one for shirts, one for pants) and many different available color classes. But for right now, this will do.

Of course, having mockups and some idea of what your MySQL tables look like is a good thing, but before your next meeting with Claudia, you need to draw up a product backlog. The product backlog will serve as a list of all the features you want to have in the resulting eCommerce web site.

Remember in the following discussion that there is a fundamental difference between the product you are building (the eCommerce site) and the products in the actual store (shoes, clothes, etc.). As long as you keep the two concepts straight, you'll do fine.

Looking over your notes and mockups, you develop an initial product backlog based on successful stories. A good story usually follows the pattern "As an X, I want to do Y, so I can do Z." Here are a few stories you can put in the product backlog — and please note that normally the product owner would do this, but at this point it's faster for you to set a precedent:

1. As a user, I want to view a featured product on the home page so I can buy it.

2. As a user, I want to view other related products on the home page so I can buy them.

3. As a user, I want to view a list of categories so I can navigate to those parts of the site.

4. As a user, I want to be able to navigate to Product Detail pages so I can buy products.

5. As a user, I want to see related products on a Product Detail page so I can complete outfits or buy accessories.

6. As a user, I want to be able to see product thumbnails and images as often as possible to get an idea of what the products look like.

This is enough for now. Tomorrow, you'll meet with Claudia and she'll take over the product backlog.

The Second Day

When you see Claudia the next day, she looks concerned. You ask her what's wrong, and she starts right in.

"Well, I've been thinking a lot about the web site, and I think we're missing some key points. First of all, I want users of the site to be able to search for products. I also think that they need some way to check out. I'm also concerned that we haven't thought through the process of adding items to a Shopping Cart."

"That's fine. Let's walk through them all quickly and update our mockups. Then we'll update the product backlog I started last night and let you take it over from there, OK?"

With that, you're off and running, asking about search. Would it be better to have a link to a search page, or a search widget on each page? Claudia definitely thinks that a search widget on each page would be better.

What does the search operate on? In other words, what fields in the database does it search through? Claudia thinks for a moment and settles on category names and product names. You add that it wouldn't be that hard to also search through descriptions. While Claudia considers this, you update the home page mockup so that it looks like Figure 2-7. You show Claudia the new mockup and tell her that every page would have the search widget on the top.

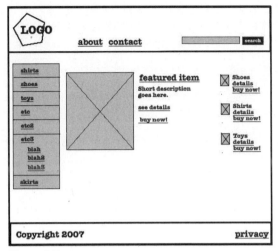

Figure 2-7

Accessibility and Usability

Two very important topics in modern web development involve usability and accessibility. The first, usability, is all about making a site as easy to use as possible — and not just easy to use for you the developer, but for the eventual user of the system. It means putting appropriate labels on buttons and links — in the language the user can understand.

It also means placing consistent global navigation on every page, and adding search features in places that users expect to find them (and that generate search results that are easy to understand).

Accessibility is about doing the best you can to make sure users with visual, auditory, cognitive, and motor-reflex impairments can use your site. It's about adding ALT tags to images, using UL lists for navigation, using CSS divs instead of tables for layout, and adding labels to form fields. Imagine trying to use a web site with the screen turned off, and only having a screen reader to guide you with audio instructions — instructions it gets from the site itself!

Usability and accessibility are each huge topics, but learning more about them and applying what you learn will make you a better web developer. Two great sources of information are www.useit.com *(Jakob Nielsen's usability site) and* www.knowbility.org *(an Austin-based accessibility consulting non-profit organization).*

Once you have that figured out, it's pretty easy to create a mockup of the Search Results page. You ask her how she wants the results to show up. Should it be just like the Category view, with a name, image, and short description for any products that come up?

"Yes," Claudia says, "but make it really clear when you're showing a product or a category."

You take a Category view mockup and quickly use it as a model for a Search Results mockup, which looks a lot like a Category view. You show her the results, which look like Figure 2-8.

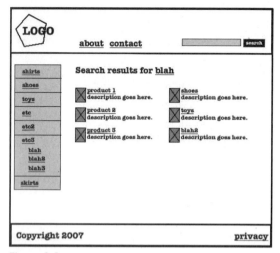

Figure 2-8

"That looks fine for now," Claudia says. "Perhaps we should list categories first, with their own headings, without thumbnails and descriptions." She thinks some more, and then shakes her head. "Let's leave it for now. Shall we tackle the 'buy now' and checkout areas?"

You hesitate momentarily because you really want to show her the product backlog you started, but Claudia is really caught up in the spirit of things, and you hate to break the flow. So you adapt your approach and spout out some ideas you have on the "buy now" pages.

"I think that when they click the 'buy now' link for a product, the underlying web site should simply add their information to a Shopping Cart," you say.

"Yes, that's like a lot of web sites you see today," Claudia agrees. "Just show them a quick note that confirms they've added a product to their cart."

"I also think we should show them a little icon of a shopping cart or a link they can click to view their Shopping Cart," you continue. "We can add the link to the top navigation bar, only showing it if the Shopping Cart has items in it."

You don't tell Claudia, but you plan on using a cookie to keep track of Shopping Cart items. You know that CodeIgniter has powerful functions for creating, editing, and deleting cookies. All you would need to do is keep track of the individual IDs associated with a product and maybe some other choices, like size or color.

"If we're doing that, then I would suggest we change the 'buy now' links to say 'add to cart' to keep the confusion to a minimum," Claudia says, and then smiles to herself because you've already updated various mockups, including the product detail, shown in Figure 2-9.

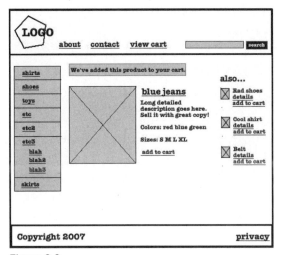

Figure 2-9

You mention that this mockup shows different states, including the confirmation message they talked about. Claudia immediately grasps what the mockup represents, but she wants to see a mockup of the Shopping Cart page.

"It needs to show every item in the Shopping Cart, grouped correctly by product," she says. "They should be able to check out immediately from the cart. In fact, you may want to update the confirmation message to allow folks to check out immediately."

You laugh because you can't help it — she's really getting into it, which is a big change from other projects you've been on. You realize, though, as you mock up the Shopping Cart page, that you'd better store the price in the Shopping Cart session — it wouldn't do to have a sudden price update affect users who are trying to check out. You make a note to yourself that before going live, you need to encrypt the cookie for an added measure of security. You confirm by asking Claudia about this issue.

"That's correct, although in practice, we would only make price changes very rarely, and even then on the weekends or late at night," she answers. "But still, there's a pretty good chance that someone could be online when I make a price change."

"What happens if someone tries to check out with a product that has been pulled after it's put in a user's Shopping Cart?"

"Oh, just check for anything like that at the last minute, during checkout," she says. While you and she have been talking, you've come up with a rough mockup of the Shopping Cart page, which looks a lot like Figure 2-10.

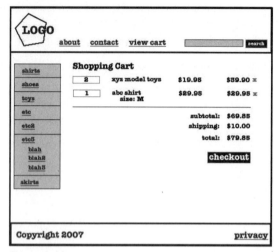

Figure 2-10

"The x's next to each line item allow the user to delete the item from their Shopping Cart," you explain.

Claudia points at the mockup. "There's something missing. There's no recalculate button. You know, when they decide they want two of the abc shirts instead of just one."

"We'll use AJAX to automatically recalculate the totals without having to do any of that," you explain, which seems to satisfy her. You know that this will make some things easier for you, but it will require users to have JavaScript enabled. You will need to put in some validation and error checking right before going live. But something else is still bothering her.

"What about calculating taxes and shipping? Some items are heavier than others. We can't just do a flat rate."

"Since I assume you're using Paypal or Google Checkout to handle payment, let's leave that part until later, as it's easy enough to integrate."

Claudia nods and says she's satisfied with the mockups. "Good", you say, because it's time to share the product backlog with her and make her a true product owner. Once she knows her way around the product backlog, it's time to plan the first sprint.

Revisiting the Product Backlog

You explain to Claudia that the product backlog is a prioritized list of requirements for her project. She is the product owner and, as such, creates and maintains the product backlog and uses it as the centralized, authoritative list of requirements, from which are derived all the tasks that are undertaken in any individual sprint.

Each sprint, furthermore, is any unit of time (typically 1 to 4 weeks) in which tasks are worked on. The goal is to have potentially shippable software at the end of each sprint, so it's important not to overcommit time and other resources.

You further explain that you've started the product backlog with six requirements:

1. As a user, I want to view a featured product on the home page, so I can buy it.

2. As a user, I want to view other related products on the home page, so I can buy them.

3. As a user, I want to view a list of categories, so I can navigate to those parts of the site.

4. As a user, I want to be able to navigate to Product Detail pages, so I can buy products.

5. As a user, I want to see related products on a Product Detail page, so I can complete outfits or buy accessories.

6. As a user, I want to be able to see product thumbnails and images as often as possible to get an idea of what the products look like.

"Each requirement is stated in general terms: As an X, I want to do Y, so I can do/achieve Z," you explain, as you go over every item in the list.

"It looks like we need to add a few more items to the list," Claudia says, and adds Items 7 and 8:

7. As a user, I want to search for products to find them quickly.

8. As a user, I want to be able to see my Shopping Cart, so I can check out more easily.

Once she is done, she thinks about the list for a long time before speaking. "There's really nothing in here about the administrator — me — and how I would manage the online store. I also don't see anything on here about keeping track of customers. And I haven't even told you all my ideas about wanting an online newsletter to help promote the site and communicate with my customers."

"This is why you're better suited to be the product owner," you respond. "All you have to do is put the information into the product backlog and then prioritize it. My job is to take the most important items — the ones on the top of the list — and create tasks that allow me to check off each requirement."

"How do you do that? Can you give me an example?"

"Of course," you reply. "I would look at the first two items, which have to do with the home page, and create a whole series of tasks. For example, I need to build the web page that represents what users see when they visit the site. I also need to create the models that allow your web site to interact with the database. I also need to build the database tables themselves. I also need to build all the special functions that organize items on the page."

You smile at Claudia's dismay. "You don't have to worry about all that. Just know that now that I have mockups that we've built together and a product backlog, I can create tasks that make sense. Also notice that a lot of the things I need to do for the first two requirements, like building database tables, also help me build the rest of the application quicker. They're one-time tasks, or at least, tasks that can be reused in different contexts."

"Furthermore," you continue, "I'll probably say right now that I'll tackle all these backlog items in the first sprint. I'm feeling pretty confident that I can tackle those items in a 4-week sprint, which means the first iteration of your web site should behave pretty much as we mocked up."

Claudia nods. "I feel pretty confident that you know what you're doing. My job is to sit down and think about all the things I want from this web site and capture all my ideas in this product backlog so you can keep working after the first backlog."

"One more thing," you say, holding up a hand. "This process allows you to change your mind, but let's try to limit major changes in direction for each sprint, while allowing minor course corrections throughout the process. That will make it easier for us to work faster and smarter."

You both decide that it's time to work separately. Although the team is very small (just you and Claudia), you decide to hold daily meetings starting the very next day, which means that you need to get started with some very basic tasks: installing CodeIgniter on a development server and creating the initial database tables. Without these tasks being complete, the rest of your task list isn't even doable.

Creating a Sprint Backlog

You've already committed to tackling all eight existing product backlog items in 4 weeks. You look over the list and start knocking out a sprint backlog:

1. Install and configure CodeIgniter on a development server.

2. Create the initial tables for products and categories.

3. Build a model for products, with functions for listing all products by category, listing product details for any given product, and listing other products that belong to the same group as a product.

4. Build a model for categories, with functions for listing all categories as a tree, listing subcategories for a category, and listing category details. The products' model already contains a function that allows you to list all products in a category.

5. Create a controller for all visible pages, with functions for the home page, About Us, Contact Us, Search Results, Product Detail, Shopping Cart, and Category view.

6. Create special controller functions for running the search and adding items to a Shopping Cart cookie.

7. Create other shopping cart functions that allow you to display everything in a Shopping Cart, recalculate prices with AJAX, and delete line items from a Shopping Cart.

8. Create all the views needed to display web pages. This will more than likely involve a master template with includes as needed to minimize your work later on.

This is about all the detail you'll need at the moment. If the team were larger, you might need more detail, but this backlog, combined with your mockups and the product backlog, should be more than enough to keep you on the right track.

Conclusion

Now that you've gone through the process, you can see how valuable this adaptive process is. You'll see later in the process how much Claudia changes her mind about certain details (such as the home page), but with Agile methodology and CodeIgniter tools, it'll be easy to adjust course and stay on schedule and within budget.

In the next chapter, you learn how to install and configure CodeIgniter on a LAMP (Linux-Apache-MySQL-PHP) server and get a quick overview of all the pieces involved (controllers, models, views, config files, libraries, helpers, and other built-in tools).

Keep the following points in mind as you continue on your journey:

❑   Agile methodologies are adaptive as opposed to predictive.

❑   Agile methodologies work best if you've got a small team working with a software project that is easily time-boxed. The team should meet regularly (daily if possible) and communicate about their achievements, to do's, and risks.

❑   It's almost always better to gather requirements by starting top-down and drawing mockups with the customer.

❑   It's important that the product owner (the customer) take charge of the product backlog as soon as possible. They've forgotten more about their business than you'll ever know.

❑   It's your job as developer to convert product backlog items into functional tasks in a sprint backlog.

❑   It is also your responsibility to estimate properly. Don't overcommit with too many tasks in any given sprint.

❑   Don't forget that many functional tasks can be leveraged across various areas of the current sprint (and even future sprints). For example, setting up good models for each database table allows you to quickly and easily work with those database tables for the rest of the project.

❑   The point of Agile is to break projects into manageable chunks. The emphasis is always on potentially shippable software at the end of any iteration or sprint. If a task can't be completed properly or on time, it's good and proper to try to reanalyze its importance and do something about it, instead of letting it fester and become a big problem.

❑   Because Agile projects tend to be iterative, it's sometimes hard to give accurate estimates to customers. Remember to think in terms of time spent on units of work and in iterations, and only give ranges. The further out the timeline, the less accurate you can be. The bigger the unit of work, the less accurate you can be. For example, if you are estimating a 2-week job, you might give an estimate that is plus-or-minus 5 percent. A 6-month job may be on the order of plus-or-minus 30 percent.

3

A 10,000-Foot View of CodeIgniter

Now that you've had your initial meeting with Claudia, your hypothetical client, and drawn up a task list for the first sprint, it's time to handle the first item on that task list, namely: "install and configure CodeIgniter on a development server." This one task requires you to acquire, download, install, and configure CodeIgniter.

The goal of this chapter is to give you the cook's tour of CodeIgniter. The tour covers the core basics that you need to understand to get up and running with CodeIgniter. After you learn this foundational information, you can use this chapter (and other resources, specifically `www.codeigniter.com`) as a future reference as you build on this knowledge. With any luck, most of the topics covered in this chapter will become part of your modus operandi from here on out as a CodeIgniter coder. Without further ado, let's dive in.

Downloading CodeIgniter

You can download the latest and greatest version of CodeIgniter by going to `www.codeigniter.com` and clicking the Download CodeIgniter button on the home page, as illustrated in Figure 3-1.

Figure 3-1

When you click the button, you'll get a dialog for downloading a ZIP archive, as shown in Figure 3-2. Either open it in your unzip utility (WinZip on Windows or StuffIt on Mac or another tool) or save it to your hard drive and then open it. You'll want to do a little bit of configuration before you push it to your development server.

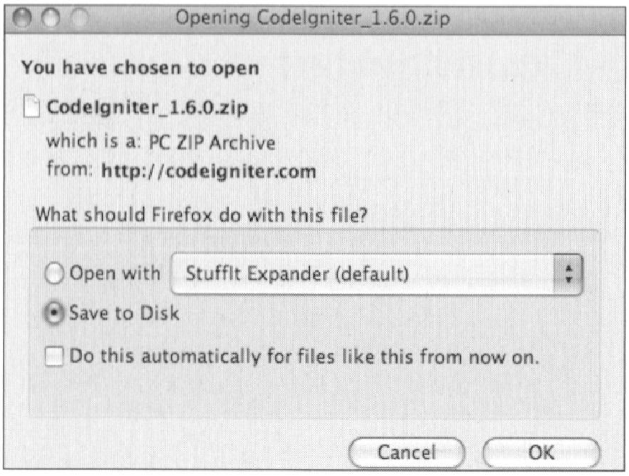

Figure 3-2

CodeIgniter at a Glance

Now that you have CodeIgniter downloaded and unzipped, take a minute to look at the file structure. The more familiar you are with it, the better off you'll be as you start to code. Figure 3-3 illustrates the initial folder structure you'll see. Take a quick look at it now.

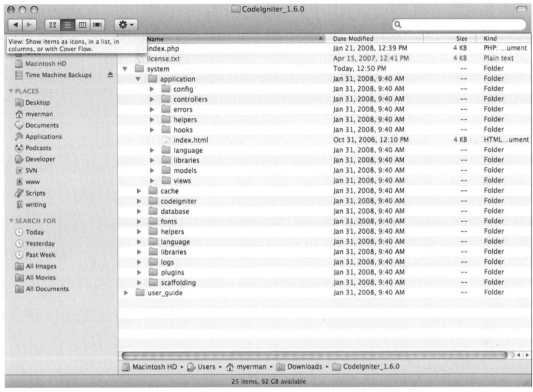

Figure 3-3

As received, the CodeIgniter root directory contains two files and two folders. The two files are index .php (which you want to keep there no matter what) and a license.txt file, containing CodeIgniter's license agreement. The two directories are user_guide/ (containing a version of the online documentation at www.codeigniter.com) and system/.

A quick note before you delve too much further into that all-important system/ folder: Approximately 100 percent of your web projects will require the use of custom CSS, JavaScript, and image files and folders. The best way to handle all of these assets is to create folders for them at the project root, as siblings to the system/ folder. This is as good a time as any to create your css/, js/, and images/ folders, so do that now. To make those folders accessible to CodeIgniter, you will also need to create a small .htaccess file in the root folder of your web site.

Here's what that .htaccess file would look like. It basically contains instructions that allows certain files and folders to be viewable on the web site:

```
RewriteEngine on
RewriteCond $1 !^(index\.php|images|captcha|css|js|robots\.txt)
RewriteRule ^(.*)$ /index.php/$1 [L]
```

If you are familiar with `mod_rewrite` in Apache, you will note that this rule ostensibly removes index .php from the URL of any destination. Below, when you're configuring CodeIgniter (and particularly the config.php file), you'll see why this is a good idea.

If you're not familiar with `mod_rewrite` in Apache, don't be too intimidated by this file. Basically, the .htaccess file sets forth a few rules, one of which removes index.php from all URLs. Other rules in the file allow the use of various other folders that you will need going forward (such as folders that contain CSS, JavaScript, Captcha files, and images).

The system/ Folder

The system/ folder is where all the action happens. This folder contains all the CodeIgniter code of consequence, organized into various folders:

- ❑ **application** — The *application folder* contains the application you're building. Basically, this folder contains your models, views, controllers, and other code (like helpers and class extensions). In other words, this folder is where you'll do 99 percent of your work.

- ❑ **cache** — The *cache folder* contains all cached pages for your application. In Chapter 9, you learn more about caching and how to turn your super-speedy development application into a blazingly fast live application.

- ❑ **codeigniter** — The *codeigniter folder* is where CodeIgniter's core classes live. You have almost no reason to go in here. All of your work will occur in the application folder. Even if your intent is to extend the CodeIgniter core, you would do it with hooks, and hooks live in the application folder.

- ❑ **database** — The *database folder* contains core database drivers and other database utilities. Again, there's no good reason for you to be in this folder.

- ❑ **fonts** — The *fonts folder* contains font-related information and utilities. Again, there's no reason to spend any time here.

- ❑ **helpers** — The *helpers folder* contains standard CodeIgniter helpers (such as date, cookie, and URL helpers). You'll make frequent use of helpers in your CodeIgniter career and can even extend helpers thanks to improvements introduced in CodeIgniter version 1.6.

- ❑ **language** — The *language folder* contains language files. You can ignore it for now.

- ❑ **libraries** — The *libraries folder* contains standard CodeIgniter libraries (to help you with e-mail, calendars, file uploads, and more). You can create your own libraries or extend (and even replace) standard ones, but those will be saved in the application/libraries directory to keep them separate from the standard CodeIgniter libraries saved in this particular folder.

- ❑ **logs** — The *logs folder* is the folder CodeIgniter uses to write error and other logs to.

❑ **plugins** — The *plugins folder* contains plugins. Plugins and helpers are very similar, in that they both allow developers to quickly address an issue or create content (like forms, links, etc.). However, the main difference between them is that plugins usually consist of one function, while helpers often have many functions bundled inside them.

The system/application Folder

The most important folder, the one that deserves most of your attention, is the /system/application folder and all of its subfolders. Ninety-nine percent of your work will be done right in this folder, so it deserves a bit of attention at this point. Learning "what goes where" now, will reduce confusion later.

The system/application folder is broken down into several folders:

❑ **config** — The *config folder* contains several important files that control your configuration options. There are files that manage your database setup and other variables that CodeIgniter needs to know about (such as the base URL, which libraries and helpers to autoload, etc.).

❑ **controllers** — The *controllers folder* contains the controllers you create for your application.

❑ **errors** — The *errors folder* comes with standard CodeIgniter error templates for 404 pages, PHP errors, and others. You are free to modify these templates to make them fit the look and feel of your application.

❑ **hooks** — The *hooks folder* contains any hooks you create for your application. Hooks, as mentioned above, are the best way to safely extend the CodeIgniter core.

❑ **libraries** — The *libraries folder* contains custom libraries you create for your application. Do not confuse this folder (which you use to store your own custom libraries) with the system/libraries folder (which contains the core CodeIgniter libraries).

❑ **models** — The *models folder* contains the models you create for your application.

❑ **views** — The *views folder* contains the views you create for your application.

In other words, the most important folders in /system/application are controllers/, models/, and views/. If you spend 99 percent of your time inside this folder, you'll spend 99 percent of that time with models, views, and controllers that you build.

The other very important folder is config/, which contains various important configuration files. You'll want to open them in an editor for tweaking before starting any project. Because these files are so important, you'll need to know about them in detail.

Initial Configuration

In this section, you learn the ins and outs of the files inside the system/application/config/ folder. This folder contains an assortment of files (including the index.html file). Of those files, four of them are important enough to warrant attention now. Those files, in order of importance for your project, are:

❑ config.php

❑ database.php

❑   autoload.php

❑   routes.php

The following sections go into more detail on each file. Please don't skip the information in these sections, as they contain instructions, hints, and tips that will make your CodeIgniter work much faster and easier. These instructions and tips are built upon trial and error and will keep the confusion and restarts down to a minimum.

config.php

The *config.php file* contains a series of configuration options (all of them stored in a PHP array called, appropriately enough, $config) that CodeIgniter uses to keep track of your application's information and settings.

The first configuration option you need to set inside config.php is the base URL of your application. You do that by setting the absolute URL (including the http:// part) for $config['base_url'], like so:

```
$config['base_url'] = "http://www.example.com/test/";
```

Once you've set this configuration option, you can recall it whenever you want using the CodeIgniter base_url() function, which can be a very handy thing to know. This one feature keeps you from having to rewrite hard-coded URLs in your application, when you migrate from development to test or from test to production.

The second thing you need to do is set a value for your home page by editing the $config['index_ page'] configuration option. CodeIgniter ships with a value of "index.php" for this option, which means that index.php will appear in all of your URLs. Many CodeIgniter developers prefer to keep this value blank, like so:

```
$config['index_page']  = '';
```

> To make this work, you need to include an .htaccess file to the CodeIgniter root directory, as was discussed previously, in the section "CodeIgniter at a Glance" in this chapter.

After you've set this option value, there's very little to do. For now, leave all the other values at their default settings:

```
$config['uri_protocol'] = "AUTO";
$config['url_suffix'] = "";
$config['language'] = "english";
$config['charset'] = "UTF-8";
$config['enable_hooks'] = FALSE;
$config['subclass_prefix'] = 'MY_';
$config['permitted_uri_chars'] = 'a-z 0-9~%.:_-';
$config['enable_query_strings'] = FALSE;
$config['controller_trigger'] = 'c';
$config['function_trigger'] = 'm';
$config['log_threshold'] = 0;
$config['log_path'] = '';
$config['log_date_format'] = 'Y-m-d H:i:s';
```

```
$config['cache_path'] = '';
$config['encryption_key'] = "enter_a_32_character_string_here";
$config['sess_cookie_name'] = 'ci_session';
$config['sess_expiration'] = 7200;
$config['sess_encrypt_cookie'] = TRUE;
$config['sess_use_database'] = FALSE;
$config['sess_table_name'] = 'ci_sessions';
$config['sess_match_ip'] = FALSE;
$config['sess_match_useragent'] = TRUE;
$config['cookie_prefix'] = "";
$config['cookie_domain'] = "";
$config['cookie_path'] = "/";
$config['global_xss_filtering'] = TRUE;
$config['compress_output'] = FALSE;
$config['time_reference'] = 'local';
$config['rewrite_short_tags'] = FALSE
```

For more details on each of these configuration options, simply read the comments embedded in /system/application/config/config.php. You will also get more detail on certain settings as you work through the sections of the book and tweak the configuration as needed. For example, at some point, you will want to use encryption for security purposes or set your logging threshold for debugging, and they both require making changes to this file.

CodeIgniter's Global XSS Filtering option is set to FALSE by default. The online User Guide suggests that setting this to TRUE adds a lot of performance overhead to the system. However, at this point, it is better to have some global protection put in place. That way you can be assured of some security precautions while you're in development. Chapter 9 discusses security issues in more depth, but for now, it's good to have something in place while you're developing.

In the same security vein, notice that sess_encrypt_cookie has been set to TRUE, and that you are to enter a 32-character encryption salt in encryption_key*. Doing these two things will encrypt any sessions and provide a salt for any hashing methods you use. Be sure to use a random string of upper- and lowercase letters and numbers. More information on encryption is covered in Chapter 9, but for now, it's good to incorporate this level of security awareness in your process.*

One final note before moving on: Make sure that you write down your encryption key and keep it safe somewhere, or, at least, maintain good backups. You'll need the key to retrieve other information, so if your site is compromised or erased (or if you lose your key any other way), you'll be glad you have a record of it.

database.php

The *database.php file* contains all the information required to connect to a database. Currently, CodeIgniter supports mysql, mysqli, postgres, odbc, and mssql connections. To connect to your database, simply enter valid information for your hostname, username, password, database name, and database driver.

Each of these is stored in the $db array under the "default" group, which means you could have numerous connection groups, each with their own unique name. For example, you could have one set of connection variables for your development environment and another for your production environment. As long as you've set the $active_group variable correctly, your application will keep connected.

```
$active_record = TRUE;
$active_group = "default";

$db['default']['hostname'] = "localhost";
$db['default']['username'] = "db_username";
$db['default']['password'] = "db_password";
$db['default']['database'] = "db_name";
$db['default']['dbdriver'] = "mysql";
$db['default']['dbprefix'] = "";
$db['default']['pconnect'] = TRUE;
$db['default']['db_debug'] = TRUE;
$db['default']['cache_on'] = FALSE;
$db['default']['cachedir'] = "";
$db['default']['char_set'] = "utf8";
$db['default']['dbcollat'] = "utf8_general_ci";
```

For now, keep the default values for options after `$db['default']['dbdriver']`. As needed, you will be introduced to them during upcoming projects (e.g., for setting up caching or running debug sessions).

autoload.php

The *autoload.php file* specifies which systems are automatically loaded by CodeIgniter. There's one school of thought that maintains that the autoloader should be kept as minimal as possible to keep the framework lightweight and nimble, but another school of thought maintains that certain frequently used systems should be autoloaded instead of called at the local level repeatedly.

You'll find your own balance as experience and local project needs warrant, but for now, set your options like this:

```
$autoload['libraries'] = array('database','session','email','validation');
$autoload['helper'] = array('url','form','text','date','security');
$autoload['plugin'] = array('captcha');
$autoload['model'] = array();
$autoload['config'] = array();
```

The first `$autoload` option, *libraries*, is a list of libraries that should be loaded. You're going to be using the database, session, e-mail, and form validation libraries a lot in this (and many other) CodeIgniter project(s), thus loading them now makes a good deal of sense. You learn more about these libraries later.

The second `$autoload` option, *helper*, is a list of helper collections that you will need to get work done. Almost every CodeIgniter project uses the URL, form, and text helpers frequently; it's not a bad idea to have date and security autoloaded as well, particularly as you'll need them to help you parse dates and handle security features.

For the time being, keep the third `$autoload` option, *plugin*, either blank or filled in with the CAPTCHA plugin, as you may have a need to use CAPTCHA devices in forms for your application for extra security.

The fourth $autoload option, *model*, allows you to autoload models. This is a new feature of CodeIgniter 1.6. You are going to create two basic models for Claudia's Kids below, one that handles product data and the other that handles category data. When you create those two models, you'll have the opportunity to come back to this file and autoload them.

Finally, the fifth $autoload option, *config*, is where you would list any custom configuration files. As it's unlikely that you've created any of those at this point, leave it blank.

routes.php

The *routes.php file* lets you remap URI requests to specific controller functions. For example, you may have a controller named *site* with a function named *index*. The URI for this controller/function combination might be:

```
http://www.example.com/site/index
```

Furthermore, if your site controller had a `pages` function that accepted a numeric ID for database lookup, the URI might look like this:

```
http://www.example.com/site/pages/4
```

In some cases, you might want to remap one or more of these default routes. For example, the second example might be better displayed as this:

```
http://www.example.com/about_us/
```

In that case, your routes.php file would contain a rule like this:

```
$route['about_us'] = "site/pages/4";
```

For right now, though, this kind of manipulation falls under "advanced usage," so don't worry too much about it. However, please do note that this kind of thing is possible. Also, be aware that two "reserved routes" exist: default_controller and scaffolding_trigger.

```
$route['default_controller'] = "welcome";
```

The default_controller route tells CodeIgniter which controller should be loaded if no controller is identified. For simplicity's sake, keep this setting at welcome, because you're going to create a welcome controller for the project associated with this book.

CodeIgniter Libraries

CodeIgniter libraries help you do your job faster and more efficiently. Each *library* is really a PHP class with various methods that you can use once the library is loaded by a controller. Some classes are so useful and so ubiquitous that you might as well autoload them (such as the database and session libraries).

CodeIgniter includes the following libraries:

❑ **Benchmarking** — The *Benchmarking library* is always active. Use it to determine the time difference between any two marked points in code and to calculate memory usage.

❑ **Calendaring** — The *Calendaring library* must be loaded by a controller. Use it to dynamically create calendars for given months and years, with some control over formatting and appearance.

❑ **Config** — The *Config library* is initialized automatically by the system. Use it to retrieve configuration information.

❑ **Database** — The *Database library* is a very powerful set of methods that must be loaded. You'll be using this library so much that the next subsection of this chapter focuses on it exclusively.

❑ **Email** — The *Email library* must be loaded. It includes a very powerful set of tools that simplifies the job of sending e-mails.

❑ **Encryption** — The *Encryption library* must be loaded. It provides you with powerful two-way encryption methods.

❑ **File Uploading** — The *File Uploading library* must be loaded. Use this library whenever you need to handle file uploads. It includes powerful validation features that can restrict a file by mime type, size (in kilobytes), or even image dimensions.

❑ **FTP** — The *FTP library* must be loaded. Use this library to transfer files to a remote server (only standard FTP is supported, by the way).

❑ **HTML Table** — The *HTML Table library* must be loaded. Use this very versatile library to autogenerate HTML tables from arrays or database result sets.

❑ **Image Manipulation** — The *Image Manipulation library* must be loaded. Use it to resize images, create thumbnails, crop or rotate images, and watermark images. Some functions require further PHP support (such as GD/GD2).

❑ **Input and Security** — The *Input and Security library* must be loaded. Use it to pre-process input data (from forms and URLs) and to handle some security functions (such as guarding against XSS attacks).

❑ **Language** — The *Language library* must be loaded. Use this library to load different sets of language files for internationalization.

❑ **Loader** — The *Loader library* is automatically loaded. You will use this library primarily to load views with your controller, but it is also used to load libraries.

❑ **Output** — The *Output library* is automatically loaded. This library has one main function: Send the finalized web page to the requesting browser. It is also used for caching.

❑ **Pagination** — The *Pagination library* must be loaded. Use this labor-saving library to paginate database results for performance and usability. You can control how many records to display per page, how many records to pull from the database, and the look and feel of different parts of the pagination.

❑ **Session** — The *Session library* must be loaded. Use CodeIgniter's Session library to maintain state information about a user. This library does not use PHP's built-in sessions — instead, it generates its own session data. Because this library is so important, a separate subsection of this chapter is devoted to it.

❑   **Template Parser** — The *Template Parser library* must be loaded. Use this library to create templates that contain parsable pseudo-templates. If you are familiar with Smarty, you'll find that CodeIgniter's templating isn't as feature-rich but is still very useful.

❑   **Trackback** — The *Trackback library* must be loaded. Use this library to send and receive Trackback data.

❑   **Unit Testing** — The *Unit Testing library* must be loaded. Use this class to unit test functions in your application. CodeIgniter provides an evaluation function and two result functions in this library.

❑   **URI Class** — The *URI Class library* is loaded automatically. You'll use this library a good deal, especially when you're parsing URLs, breaking them into segments that can then be passed to a controller or saved as variables.

❑   **User Agent** — The *User Agent library* must be loaded. Use this library to identify the browser, mobile device, or robot visiting your site. You can also use it to detect supported languages, character sets, and even referrers.

❑   **Validation** — The *Validation library* must be loaded. Use this library to validate form input in your applications. You get plenty of opportunities in this book to explore this library.

❑   **XML-RPC** — The *XML-RPC library* must be loaded. Use this library to set up XML-RPC clients and servers.

❑   **Zip Encoding** — The *Zip Encoding library* must be loaded. Use this library to create Zip archives of both text and binary data.

At this point in your CodeIgniter career, it would be pointless to cover each of these libraries in detail. Instead, as the projects in this book unfold, you are introduced to relevant libraries when the time is right.

However, there are two libraries that need some discussion now, both to make you more familiar with them and to give you an idea of how to work with them. The two libraries in question are Database and Session.

The Database Library

The *Database library* contains a series of helpful functions that make it easy for you to create and run queries and process the result sets from those queries.

The first thing to note about the Database library in CodeIgniter is that it allows you to pass in simple SQL queries. At the end of the day, many people who are new to CodeIgniter find this to be a great comfort. Although some of the built-in Active Record patterns provide helpful shortcuts, just knowing that you can bypass all of that and send in a complex query is worth its weight in gold:

```
$sql = "select a.name, a.id, b.groupname
        from persons a, groups b
        where a.group_id = b.id
        group by b.groupname, a.name";

$Q = $this->db->query($sql);
```

To loop over the result set of that query, you can use either the `result()` or `result_array()` methods, depending on whether you like to process your results as an object or as an array.

```
$sql = "select a.name, a.id, b.groupname
        from persons a, groups b
        where a.group_id = b.id
        group by b.groupname, a.name";

$Q = $this->db->query($sql);

foreach ($Q->result() as $row){
  echo $row->name;
  echo $row->id;
  echo $row->groupname;
}

//here's the alternative approach, with result_array
foreach ($Q->result_array() as $row){
  echo $row['name'];
  echo $row['id'];
  echo $row['groupname'];

}
```

There's really no discernible difference from a performance standpoint, but some developers prefer one over the other. It's your choice, really.

If you need a count of rows in a result set, use the `num_rows()` method:

```
$sql = "select a.name, a.id, b.groupname
        from persons a, groups b
        where a.group_id = b.id
        group by b.groupname, a.name";

$Q = $this->db->query($sql);

if ($Q->num_rows()){
  foreach ($Q->result() as $row){
    echo $row->name;
    echo $row->id;
    echo $row->groupname;
  }
}
```

Sometimes you may have a query that generates just one result row. In that case, use `row()` or `row_array()` (again, depending on your preference) to process that result set.

```
$sql = "select a.name, a.id, b.groupname
        from persons a, groups b
        where a.group_id = b.id
        limit 1";
```

```
$Q = $this->db->query($sql);

$row = $Q->row();
echo $row->id;

//alternative syntax
$row = $Q->row_array();
echo $row['id'];
```

Using this method allows you to pass any SQL query you want to the database, including inserts, updates, and deletes:

```
$sql = "insert into persons (name, gender, age)
        values ('Tom Myer', 'male',35)";

$this->db->query($sql);
```

A more secure way of handling this kind of query is to use query binding:

```
$sql = "insert into persons (name, gender, age)
        values(?,?,?)";

$this->db->query($sql, array("Tom","male",35));
```

Why is this method more secure? The query binding automatically escapes whatever data you pass through, eliminating potential security problems. In this book, however, very few raw queries are run, as most work is done via the Active Record class. In Chapter 9, where you learn more about security, database security is among the topics covered.

At some point, though, you'll want to take advantage of some of the Active Record patterns that CodeIgniter makes available to you. Each pattern allows you to interact with a database table with minimal scripting. This is good not only from a "conservation of typing" point of view; it also makes your database code more portable between database types.

For example, this is how you would retrieve all the database records from the persons table:

```
$Q = $this->db->get('persons');
```

If you want to limit how many records to retrieve from the persons table, you would do the following:

```
$Q = $this->db->get('persons',5,20);
//query would become:
//select * from persons limit 20, 5
//and would show five records after an offset of 20 (records 21 - 25)
```

If you want to limit which fields are selected in your query, use the select() method first:

```
$this->db->select('id, name, gender');
$Q = $this->db->get('persons');
```

You can even use the `from()` method to tell CodeIgniter which table to select from, like this:

```
$this->db->select('id, name, gender');
$this->db->from('persons');
$Q = $this->db->get();
```

Furthermore, you can list various `where` provisions using the aptly named `where()` clause:

```
$this->db->select('id, name, gender');
$this->db->from('persons');
$this->db->where('id', 14);
$this->db->where('status', 'live');
$Q = $this->db->get();

//query becomes:
//select id, name, gender from persons where id=14 and status='live'
```

You could also get fancy with the `where()` method, passing in operators, such as not equal (`!=`) or less than (`<`):

```
$this->db->select('id, name');
$this->db->from('persons');
$this->db->where('id >=', 3);
$Q = $this->db->get();

//query becomes:
//select id, name from persons where id >= 3
```

If you're impatient or need to pass in a custom `where` string, you can do that too:

```
$this->db->select('id, name');
$this->db->from('persons');
$this->db->where("name='Tom' and id > 3");
$Q = $this->db->get();

//query becomes:
//select id,name from persons where name='Tom' and id > 3
```

The `like()` method generates SQL LIKE clauses, which is extremely useful when building search functions:

```
$this->db->select('id, name');
$this->db->from('persons');
$this->db->like('name', 'Tom');
$Q = $this->db->get();

//query becomes:
//select id,name from persons where name like '%Tom%'
```

When doing an insert, first you build a data array and pass that array to the `insert()` method. In many cases, your data array consists of information from a form, but it could also contain data from a session or cookie.

```
$data = array(
  'name' => $_POST['name'] ,
  'gender' => $_POST['gender'],
  'age' => $_POST['age']
);

$this->db->insert('persons', $data);
```

Below you learn how to use the `update()` and `delete()` methods and a larger set of more specialized tools, but for now, you get the idea. The Database library offers a powerful feature set that lets you work with queries and result sets. You can use the Active Record patterns for their conciseness and power, or you can stick to more flexible SQL queries.

The Session Library

You may be familiar with PHP sessions already. CodeIgniter sessions are similar to PHP sessions (at least in the way they behave) but are separate from them altogether. For example, CodeIgniter stores session data in a cookie (by default, but it can also work with database tables) as opposed to PHP sessions, which save their session data on the server. You also have the option of saving CodeIgniter sessions in a database.

> *Here's a very important note if you are security conscious. Even if you choose to save CodeIgniter sessions in a database table, the same data are stored in a client-side cookie. That means that it is available to the end-user. Even if you use encryption, it is possible to tamper with the cookie and thereby cause problems. Therefore, in this book (and in your foreseeable CodeIgniter career), only use CodeIgniter sessions (and flashdata) to store data that are unimportant. If you need to have secure logins and authentication, use PHP sessions instead.*

By default, CodeIgniter sessions track a session ID, the user's IP address and user agent, and time stamps for the last activity and the last visit. For performance reasons, the time stamps are only updated every 5 minutes, so robots and multiple reloads of a page won't cause runaway load on your server.

One more thing to note — once the Session library has been initialized (or autoloaded), you don't have to take any further steps to start working with CodeIgniter session data.

Retrieving data from a CodeIgniter session is as easy as invoking that library's `userdata()` method. For example, to retrieve a CodeIgniter session's session_id, do it this way:

```
$sess_id = $this->session->userdata('session_id');
```

> *The `userdata()` function returns FALSE if the item you're trying to access doesn't exist.*

A very useful function of CodeIgniter sessions is to save data about a user and then access it at a later date. For example, you could create a login verification process that upon successful login adds the user's e-mail address to the CodeIgniter session:

```
//$username and $password are passed in from another process
//most likely a login form and then cleansed

$this->db->select('email');
$this->db->from('users');
$this->db->where('username', $username);
$this->db->where('password', $password);
$this->db->where('status', 'live');
$this->db->limit(1);
$Q = $this->db->get();

if ($Q->num_rows() == 1){
   $row = $Q->row();
   $this->session->set_userdata('user_email'], $row->email);
}
```

It would then be very simple to retrieve that e-mail if you ever wanted to print it in a view.

```
<?php
echo $this->session->userdata('email');
?>
```

Because CodeIgniter sessions are saved in a client-side cookie, many developers don't trust them for storage of sensitive information. Even with a 32-character salt for encryption, it's still possible that somebody might tamper with these data. In this book, you use encryption on sessions but restrict its usage to unimportant information. For the more sensitive things, like checking for a user login, you should use PHP sessions.

CodeIgniter Helpers

Helpers, as their name implies, help you with specific tasks. Unlike libraries, helpers are not object-oriented but procedural in nature. Each helper contains one or more functions, each focusing on a specific task, with zero dependence on other functions.

Helpers can either be loaded locally or autoloaded in /system/application/config/autoload.php. CodeIgniter ships with the following built-in helpers:

❑ **Array** — The *Array helper* contains functions that help you work with arrays. For example, the random_element() function takes an array as input and returns a random element from it.

❑ **Cookie** — The *Cookie helper* contains functions that help you set, read, and delete cookie data.

❑ **Date** — The *Date helper* contains functions that help you work with dates. For example, the now() function returns the current time as a UNIX time stamp.

❑ **Directory** — The *Directory helper* contains a single function that helps you work with directories. For example, the directory_map function reads a specified directory path and builds an array of it that contains all of its files and subdirectories.

❑ **Download** — The *Download helper* contains a single function that helps you download data easily. The `force_download()` function generates server headers that force data to be downloaded instead of viewed in a browser.

❑ **File** — The *File helper* contains functions that help you read, write, and delete files.

❑ **Form** — The *Form helper* contains functions that help you build forms. It is probably one of the most used helpers in the CodeIgniter toolbox.

❑ **HTML** — The *HTML helper* contains functions that help you create HTML blocks quickly and easily. For example, the `ul()` function can turn an array of items into a bulleted list.

❑ **Inflector** — The *Inflector helper* contains functions that help you to turn words into plural or singular form, to apply camel case, or to turn words separated by spaces into an underscored phrase. For example, the `singular()` function can turn the string "girls" into "girl."

❑ **Security** — The *Security helper* contains security-related functions like `xss_clean()`, which filters out any code that may be used in a cross site scripting hack.

❑ **Smiley** — The *Smiley helper* contains functions that help you manage emoticons. The functions in this helper might seem superfluous, but become invaluable if you are coding a bulletin board or chat application.

❑ **String** — The *String helper* contains functions that help you work with strings, like the `random_string()` function, which as its name implies, creates random strings based on type and length arguments.

❑ **Text** — The *Text helper* contains functions that help you work with text. For example, the `word_limiter()` function can limit a string to a certain number of words, which is useful if you're trying to limit user input on a form.

❑ **Typography** — The *Typography helper* contains a single function that helps you format text in appropriate ways. For example, the `auto_typography()` function wraps paragraphs with `<p>` and `</p>`, converts line breaks to `<br/>`, and converts quotes, dashes, and ellipses properly.

❑ **URL** — The *URL helper* contains functions that help you work with URLs. This is another helper that sees heavy use. You will use the `base_url()` and `anchor()` functions many times in any given project, but other functions, such as `safe_mailto()` and `anchor_popup()` are extremely useful as well.

❑ **XML** — The *XML helper* contains a single function that helps you work with XML. The `xml_convert()` function converts a given string into XML-ready text, converting ampersands and angle brackets (among other things) into entities.

You might be thinking to yourself, what's the point of using helpers? After all, if you know your PHP, you can use the `substr()` function instead of the `word_limiter()` or `character_limiter()` made available by the Text helper. Certainly, you're not forced to use helpers, but they're made available to you, and they do a fine job of saving time and effort.

As with libraries, there are simply too many helpers to cover here. Doing so would cause you to enter a level of detail that is close to mind-numbing. However, that being said, there is good reason to pay special attention to a pair of helpers that you will be using a lot in this and other CodeIgniter projects: Form and URL.

The Form Helper

One of the most useful helpers in the CodeIgniter toolbox is the *Form helper*. Forms represent a common HTML element that developers typically spend a lot of time building, maintaining, and debugging. The functions present in the Form helper help you keep things straight when working with forms.

To create a form, open a view file in your favorite editor and use the `form_open()` function to create a form element. Pass in the URI segment of the controller function that handles the POST data after the user clicks the Submit button. For example, if you were building a simple search form, you might open it this way:

```
echo form_open('welcome/search');
```

Many forms contain hidden form fields, which you can easily add with the `form_hidden()` function, like so:

```
echo form_hidden('id', '414');
echo form_hidden('searchtype', 'basic');
```

Adding form fields to your form is also easy, using the `form_input()` function. Although you can call the function by passing in a name-value pair, it's a good idea to get used to passing in a larger data array, in which a more complete data set can be organized.

```
$data = array(
   'name' => 'searchterm',
   'id' => 'search',
   'maxlength' => '100',
   'size' => '50',
   'style' => 'background-color:#f1f1f1'
)
echo form_input($data);
```

Similarly, you can create password fields with `form_password()`, file upload fields with `form_upload()`, and text areas with `form_textarea()`. Just set up an array and pass its values into the function.

Dropdowns are slightly different, in that they require you to pass in an array of choices for the dropdown, as well as a default value:

```
$values = array(
   'high' => 'high',
   'medium' => 'medium',
   'low' => 'low'
);

echo form_dropdown('priority', $values, 'medium');
```

Other elements, such as radio buttons and checkboxes, can be created with `form_checkbox()` and `form_radio()`. These two functions are covered later in this book.

Finally, you create a Submit button with `form_submit()`, and close a form with `form_close()`, like this:

```
echo form_submit('submit', 'search');
echo form_close();
```

Thus your entire search form looks like

```
echo form_open('welcome/search');
echo form_hidden('id', '414');
echo form_hidden('searchtype', 'basic');

$data = array(
   'name' => 'searchterm',
   'id' => 'search',
   'maxlength' => '100',
   'size' => '50',
   'style' => 'background-color:#f1f1f1'
)
echo form_input($data);

$values = array(
   'high' => 'high',
   'medium' => 'medium',
   'low' => 'low'
);

echo form_dropdown('priority', $values, 'medium');

echo form_submit('submit', 'search');
echo form_close();
```

The URL Helper

Another extremely useful helper is the *URL helper*. You will often be using three functions from this helper: `base_url()`, `anchor()`, and `redirect()`.

The `base_url()` function prints out the base URL configuration setting that you placed in the /system/application/config/config.php file. Its chief virtue is that it allows you to create more portable code. For example, if you need to reference an image in the root directory of the server, you can use `base_url()` to make sure that image is always found:

```
echo base_url() . '/images/logo.jpg';
```

Similarly useful, the `anchor()` function helps you create links that are portable from one environment to another. For example, to create a link to a contact_us page, you would simply pass two arguments to the `anchor()` function: the URI followed by the link text.

```
echo anchor('welcome/contact_us', 'Contact Us Today!');
```

Finally, the `redirect()` function allows you to create redirects in case of different problems. In the above example that involved the Session library, note the use of the `redirect()` function if an e-mail is not set correctly:

```
if ($this->session->userdata('email') != 'tom@example.com'){
    redirect('admin/logout', 'refresh');
}
```

The `refresh()` function takes two arguments. The first is the destination for the redirect, and the second argument can be either "location" or "refresh." Most of the time, you'll use the "refresh" option as the second argument.

Creating Models, Views, and Controllers

At this point, you're ready to start working with files that relate directly to your project — namely, the models, views, and controllers that make up the heart of the application you'll be building for Claudia.

Models and Database Tables

You received an extremely brief introduction to models, views, and controllers in Chapter 1, so in this section, you'll concentrate on the database tables and models you'll need for Claudia's project. Before you delve too deeply into constructing models for your tables, here's a quick reminder of the tables' structures from Chapter 2:

First, the categories table:

```
CREATE TABLE 'categories' (
'id' INT NOT NULL AUTO_INCREMENT ,
'name' VARCHAR( 255 ) NOT NULL ,
'shortdesc' VARCHAR( 255 ) NOT NULL ,
'longdesc' TEXT NOT NULL ,
'status' ENUM( 'active', 'inactive' ) NOT NULL ,
'parentid' INT NOT NULL ,
PRIMARY KEY ( 'id' )
) TYPE = MYISAM ;
```

Next, the products table:

```
CREATE TABLE 'products' (
'id' INT NOT NULL AUTO_INCREMENT ,
'name' VARCHAR( 255 ) NOT NULL ,
'shortdesc' VARCHAR( 255 ) NOT NULL ,
'longdesc' TEXT NOT NULL ,
'thumbnail' VARCHAR( 255 ) NOT NULL ,
'image' VARCHAR( 255 ) NOT NULL ,
'sizes' ENUM( 's', 'm', 'l', 'xl' ) NOT NULL ,
'colors' ENUM( 'red', 'blue', 'green', 'brown', 'white', 'black' ) NOT NULL ,
'grouping' VARCHAR( 16 ) NOT NULL ,
'status' ENUM( 'active', 'inactive' ) NOT NULL ,
'category_id' INT NOT NULL ,
```

```
'featured' ENUM ('true', 'false') NOT NULL,
'price' FLOAT( 4, 2 ) NOT NULL,
PRIMARY KEY ( 'id' )
) TYPE = MYISAM ;
```

The standard practice with CodeIgniter is to have one model for each database table, which gives you (and any other developer on the team) easy access to a well-organized library of functions that relate to a specific database table.

Because you're just at the very beginning of the project, the best thing to do right now is to initialize your models and put in the bare bones in each file. *Bare bones* in this context means adding two functions, one that allows you to select a particular category or product and another that allows you to list all of them.

The Categories Model

First, create the model for categories. You can name your models anything you want, as long as the names don't conflict with each other or the names of your controllers. Standard practice indicates putting some kind of prefix or suffix on a model filename to keep them distinct from controllers. Some programmers use a suffix of _model, others use a prefix of *m_*. In this book, you'll use a prefix of *m* on your model files to keep things straight (e.g., *mcats.php* or *mproducts.php*).

Once again, here's a very basic model called *MCats*, with its PHP 4 constructor. Notice that this model, like all models, extends the core CodeIgniter model.

```
class MCats extends Model{
    function MCats(){
        parent::Model();
    }
}
```

As promised, you will now add two simple functions to this model. The first will retrieve one category from the database:

```
function getCategory($id){
    $data = array();
    $options = array('id' => $id);
    $Q = $this->db->getwhere('categories',$options,1);
    if ($Q->num_rows() > 0){
        $data = $Q->row_array();
    }

    $Q->free_result();
    return $data;
}
```

This function passes in an $id variable that is used to select one (and only one) row matching that ID from the categories table. It then returns the data as an array for future use.

The second function retrieves all categories from the database:

```
function getAllCategories(){
  $data = array();
  $Q = $this->db->get('categories');
  if ($Q->num_rows() > 0){
    foreach ($Q->result_array() as $row){
      $data[] = $row;
    }
  }
  $Q->free_result();
  return $data;
}
```

This function is much simpler. All that's needed is a call to $this->db->get() with an argument of *categories* (the name of the database table), and all records from the database are retrieved as an array.

Your MCats model (stored in the /system/application/models/mcats.php file) should look like this now:

```
class MCats extends Model{
  function MCats(){
    parent::Model();
  }

  function getCategory($id){
    $data = array();
    $options = array('id' => $id);
    $Q = $this->db->getwhere('categories',$options,1);
    if ($Q->num_rows() > 0){
      $data = $Q->row_array();
    }

    $Q->free_result();
    return $data;
  }

  function getAllCategories(){
    $data = array();
    $Q = $this->db->get('categories');
    if ($Q->num_rows() > 0){
      foreach ($Q->result_array() as $row){
        $data[] = $row;
      }
    }
    $Q->free_result();
    return $data;
  }
}
```

As you progress through the project, you'll add more specialized functions (e.g., you will eventually need an easy way to grab categories that have a certain parentid), but for right now, this is good progress.

The Products Model

Now it's time to build your model for the products table: MProducts. Create a file called *mproducts.php* in the /system/application/models/ folder, and populate it with the following information:

```
class MProducts extends Model{
  function MProducts(){
    parent::Model();
  }

  function getProduct($id){
    $data = array();
    $options = array('id' => $id);
    $Q = $this->db->getwhere(products,$options,1);
    if ($Q->num_rows() > 0){
      $data = $Q->row_array();
    }

    $Q->free_result();
    return $data;
  }

  function getAllProducts(){
    $data = array();
    $Q = $this->db->get('products');
    if ($Q->num_rows() > 0){
      foreach ($Q->result_array() as $row){
        $data[] = $row;
      }
    }
    $Q->free_result();
    return $data;
  }
}
```

Structurally speaking, this model is very similar to the model you created for Categories. In fact, the only thing you've changed so far is the name of the model, the constructor call, and the name of the database table employed by the two functions.

As with the Categories model, you'll eventually create various specialized functions to get your work done (e.g., you'll need a function that will retrieve all products by `category_id`), but for now you have a good beginning.

Autoloading Your Models

Now that you have two bare-bones models built, open the /system/application/config/autoload.php file and add them both to the model $autoload option:

```
$autoload['model'] = array('MProducts', 'MCats');
```

Autoloading models makes them globally available to your entire application and saves time because you don't have to load them locally.

Controllers

For simplicity's sake, you're going to use the default controller, welcome.php, for the first part of this project. As things progress, you can create additional controllers as needed.

When you look at your project notes, you know that the following main destinations are required by your application:

- ❏ A home page
- ❏ A Category page, showing subcategories
- ❏ A subcategory page, showing products
- ❏ A Product Detail page
- ❏ A Shopping Cart page
- ❏ A Search Results page
- ❏ Various other minor pages, such as Contact Us, About Us, and Privacy Policy

Each of these destinations becomes a function of your controller. If you want users to visit an about_us page on your site, you need an `about_us` function in your controller. Right now you don't care about the details of what happens at those destinations; you just want to sketch them in, without regard to loading models, views, helpers, or anything else.

Your primary goal right now is to get an overview of the project space, so you open the default welcome .php controller in /system/application/controllers/ and get to work:

```php
class Welcome extends Controller {
  function Welcome(){
    parent::Controller();
  }

  function index(){
    //use this for your home page
  }

  function cat(){
    //use this for the category page
  }

  function subcat(){
    //use this for the subcategory view
  }

  function product(){
    //use this for the product view
  }

  function cart(){
    //use this for the shopping cart view
  }
```

```
function search(){
  //use this for the search results
}

function about_us(){
  //use this for the about_us page
}

function contact (){
  //use this for the contact page
}

function privacy(){
  //use this for the privacy page
}
}
```

As the project progresses, you'll spend more and more time in the controller, loading models, using libraries, and loading views as appropriate.

Before creating your views, you will need to do a bit of work on the `index()` function. Although you haven't created any views, you already have some design considerations in mind:

1. You need to load the navigation.

2. You need to load a template and reuse that template as often as possible.

3. At some point, you'll need to consider the use of subtemplates that are included in the master template.

You can't do anything about the third point at the moment, but you can do something about the other two. Create your `index()` function controller like this:

```
function index(){
  $data['title'] = "Welcome to Claudia's Kids";
  $data['navlist'] = $this->MCats->getAllCategories();
  $this->load->vars($data);
  $this->load->view('template');
}
```

Here's what will happen when you visit the home page of your site:

❑ `$data['title']` will be used as `$title` in the template view.

❑ The categories from the database are retrieved into `$data['navlist']` by the MCats model, and then passed along to the underlying view.

❑ The footer, header, and navigation subviews don't need to be loaded here, as they'll be loaded inside the template.php view.

❑ Right before the Template view is loaded, there's a call to `$this->load->vars()`, which makes the `$data array` available to not only the final view, but all the subviews as well. Running this command precludes the need to pass `$data` in as a second argument to `$this->load->view()`.

Since this is extremely basic, before you progress, it's time to create the views needed.

Views

At this point, you're only ready to start tackling views in a very limited way — specifically, creating reusable components for the project. Have a quick look at your mockup of the home page to plan out which components you'll need for the project (see Figure 3-4). As you work, you'll place these components into the /system/application/views/ folder.

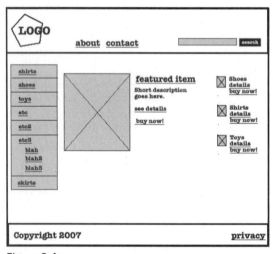

Figure 3-4

Any experienced web developer will tell you that a template of this nature has at least three reusable components:

❑ A wide horizontal header bar, containing the logo, global navigation, and search widget

❑ A wide horizontal footer bar, containing the copyright notice and a link to the privacy statement

❑ A narrow vertical navigation component that provides links to categories

The rest of the page real estate consists of content that changes from page to page. The home page may use this real estate to show a featured item, whereas the `search()` function might use that same real estate to display appropriate search results.

Again, the goal at the moment is not to understand every single aspect of how views work. What you want to do right now is create a general purpose Template view (made simple for this project because each page lives in the same square outline) and the three dynamic includes that you can load as needed with your controller.

This is also a good time to set up your initial CSS file (in the folder /css, which you created in Chapter 2 to hold your css) so that your views can reference it.

Setting Up a Simple CSS File

Create a file named *default.css*, and place it in the /css folder in your CodeIgniter root. Then place the following CSS into that file:

```
/* default css */

body{
    background-color:white;
    font-family: Arial, Verdana, sans-serif;
    margin:0;
    padding:0;
}

#wrapper{
    width:1000px;
    margin:10px auto;
    padding:10px;
    background-color:#f1f1f1;
    border:2px solid #ccc;
}

#nav{
    float:left;
    width:135px;
    height:auto;
}

#main{
    float:right;
    margin-left:150px;
    width:800px;
    height:auto;

}

#header{
    font-size:12px;
    margin-bottom:10px;
}

#footer{
    clear:both;
    padding-top:40px;
    font-size:9px;
}
```

This CSS file is undeniably simple (almost too simple!), but it will get you where you need to go. It establishes some basic structures you can use inside your templates, such as a wrapper div to contain your other containers (such as header, footer, main content, navigation, etc.).

As you refine the project, you'll have plenty of time to revisit this file and add more display rules (for links, bulleted lists, etc.).

Creating the Master Template

Now that you've established a simple CSS file, it's time to create a generic Template view that you can reuse throughout your application. In this master template, which you can name *template.php,* are a series of embedded PHP calls that load certain subviews, such as header, navigation, and footer.

These subviews contain the HTML and PHP that you will create in the next few sections. Notice in the following code that you're also trying to load a subview with $main. This variable will contain the name of a subview that is dynamically set within the controller and allows you a great deal of flexibility as you code your application. In Chapter 4, you learn how to use this functionality. For now, you can use a simple placeholder.

```
<!DOCTYPE html PUBLIC "-//W3C//DTD XHTML 1.0 Strict//EN"
        "http://www.w3.org/TR/xhtml1/DTD/xhtml1-strict.dtd">
<html xmlns="http://www.w3.org/1999/xhtml" xml:lang="en" lang="en">
<head>
  <meta http-equiv="content-type" content="text/html; charset=utf-8" />
  <title><?php echo $title; ?></title>
<link href="<?= base_url();?>css/default.css" rel="stylesheet" type="text/css" />
<script type="text/javascript">
//<![CDATA[
base_url = '<?= base_url();?>';
//]]>
</script>
</head>
<body>
<div id="wrapper">
  <div id="header">
  <?php $this->load->view('header');?>
  </div>

  <div id="nav">
  <?php $this->load->view('navigation');?>
  </div>

  <div id="main">
  <?php $this->load->view($main);?>
  </div>

  <div id="footer">
  <?php $this->load->view('footer');?>
  </div>
</div>
</body>
</html>
```

Save this file as template.php in the /system/application/views folder.

Creating the Header

The header file (header.php) is very simple, consisting of an image, some links to pages, and a form widget:

```
<a href="<?php echo base_url();?>">
<img src="<?php echo base_url();?>/images/logo.jpg" border="0"/>
</a>
<div><?php echo anchor("welcome/about_us","about us");?> 
<?php echo anchor("welcome/contact", "contact");?>
<?php
echo form_open("welcome/search");
$data = array(
  "name" => "term",
  "id" => "term",
  "maxlength" => "64",
  "size" => "30"
);
echo form_input($data);
echo form_submit("submit","search");
echo form_close();
?>
</div>
```

In this simple header, you're using the `anchor()` function to create links to the contact and about_us pages (remember the functions set up in the controller?), and then using a variety of form helper functions to create a simple search form.

Specifically, the `form_open()` function helps you create the form tag. The argument you pass to this function is the name of the controller and function that handles the form's input. This search form also uses a `form_input()` function to build the simple text field that accepts user input. In this case, you're setting up a simple array containing different values (the field's name, ID, maxlength, and size attributes) and then passing that into the `form_input()` function to create the form input.

Finally, you're also making use of the `form_submit()` and `form_close()` functions to finish the form.

Most beginning CodeIgniter developers always ask the same question when it comes to such helpers as `anchor()` and `form_open()`, and that is: Why use them? Most developers come to CodeIgniter with a certain level of comfort with HTML, so they feel that working with these helpers is somehow unnecessary. Rest assured, however, that once you start using these shortcuts, you will learn to appreciate them.

For example, any time you use the `anchor()` tag, the passed-in argument (representing a controller/function path) stays constant regardless of what server it may reside on. CodeIgniter takes care of figuring out all the paths.

Some things about this include aren't quite right (e.g., once you load it into your controller you'll see that the logo image isn't in quite the right place), but for right now, it's good enough to keep going. One of the beauties of iterative work is the ability to go back and tweak quickly as you need to.

Save this file as header.php in the /system/application/views folder.

Creating the Footer

The footer file (footer.php) is even simpler than the header file, as it contains some text and a link:

```
Copyright <?php echo date("Y");>
<?php echo anchor("welcome/privacy","privacy policy");?>
```

As with the header file, you can wait until the next iteration to address exact placement of HTML.

Save this file as footer.php in the /system/application/views folder.

Creating the Category Navigation

Of all the include files, the category navigation file (navigation.php) is probably the most complicated. This include file assumes the existence of an incoming array (named $navlist) that contains all the category names and IDs. This $navlist array will be created in the controller using the model (specifically, the model function you created above that extracts all the categories from the database).

As soon as you're done with this category include, you'll open the controller in an editor so you can see how all these pieces fit together:

```
if (count($navlist)){
   echo "<ul>";
   foreach ($navlist as $id => $name){
      echo "<li>";
      echo anchor("welcome/cat/$id",$name);
      echo "</li>";
   }
   echo "</ul>";
}
```

It will become extremely apparent to you, once you see this include in action for the first time, that it needs to be styled. You can do that in a separate look-and-feel pass by adjusting some elements in your default.css file.

Save this file as navigation.php in the /system/application/views folder.

Uploading Your Files

Different developers work differently, of course, but you'll find as you start out that frequently uploading files as you perform initial setup is pretty much mandatory. Once you get the process down, however, you'll find that you only need to upload a few times during initial setup. For example, many experienced CodeIgniter developers don't even bother to upload their initial CodeIgniter base until they've worked with configuration files and then set up rudimentary models and controllers.

Conclusion

The goal of this chapter is to walk you through the initial setup of CodeIgniter, explaining the key features that require your attention during configuration. As you continue working with CodeIgniter, keep the following points in mind:

- ❏ CodeIgniter files can be divided into main areas, to wit: a core that you shouldn't mess with, and everything else.

- ❏ If you have any doubts, the "everything else" usually resides within the /system/application/ folder. Just about anything you do to the files in this folder won't cause serious problems (unless of course, you have bugs in your own code!).

- ❏ If you absolutely must extend the core, do so with hooks and custom libraries placed safely within the confines of the /system/application/ folder. However, most of the time, you'll find that the CodeIgniter developers have provided you with most of what you need to get the job done.

- ❏ Certain configuration settings accomplish the basics that give you the peace of mind you need. For example, properly configuring your database settings (in /system/application/config/database.php) and autoload preferences (/system/application/config/autoload.php) will make your work go a lot more smoothly.

- ❏ You'll use certain libraries and helpers (particularly those dealing with databases, sessions, URLs, and forms) over and over again — having a good working knowledge of them will save you a great deal of time and energy.

- ❏ Depending on your project's needs, your models, views, and controllers will all have varying degrees of complexity. In most cases, though, having certain basic tools in place (such as basic querying functions in your models or base templates for your views) at the start of the project will save you a lot of time.

- ❏ Don't be afraid to work iteratively. If something doesn't work at first, tweak a configuration file or test a new view. CodeIgniter's setup is very forgiving and makes it easy to incorporate iterative development styles.

Creating the Main Web Site

If you've made it this far, congratulations! You've set up CodeIgniter and created the bare-bones models, views, and controllers that you'll need to work on the Claudia's Kids project. At this point, you're probably all done FTPing your CodeIgniter files to the development server. As soon as that process is done, it's time to take a quick look at your work so far.

Before you do that, please note that you are bound to see some errors. These have been left in intentionally so you can learn how to deal with them. By the time you're done with the first few pages of this chapter, you should be able to troubleshoot most common problems you'll encounter during development. With that in mind, load the home page of your nascent application in a browser window. You should see something similar to Figure 4-1.

You can't help but notice the three prominent PHP error blocks. Each error block comes with all the information you need to fix the problem. For example, each block is categorized by severity (two of these are notices) and message (undefined variables or array-to-string conversion). Finally, each error block gives you a file and line number.

In the case of the first error block, there's a problem with array-to-string conversion. What does that mean? Well, it's time to gather some clues. Here's what the `index()` function of the controller looks like:

```
function index(){
  $data['title'] = "Welcome to Claudia's Kids";
  $data['navlist'] = $this->MCats->getAllCategories();
  $this->load->vars($data);
  $this->load->view('template');
}
```

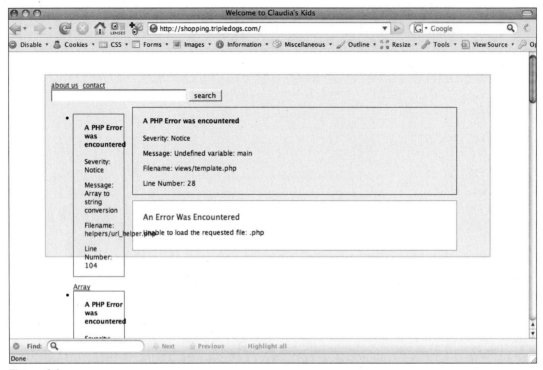

Figure 4-1

It appears that you're using the getAllCategories() model function to populate the $data['navlist'] in the controller. This, as noted in Chapter 3, gets processed as $navlist in the navigation view. The problem probably lies either in the model function or the way you're handling the data in the view.

Examining the model function, you should see:

```
function getAllCategories(){
  $data = array();
  $Q = $this->db->get('categories');
  if ($Q->num_rows() > 0){
    foreach ($Q->result_array() as $row){
    $data[] = $row;
    }
  }
  $Q->free_result();
  return $data;
}
```

The final output of the `getAllCategories()` function is a multidimensional array. Here's a snippet from that array as seen through the `print_r()` function, so you can visualize the discussion:

```
[0] => Array
    (
        [id] => 1
        [name] => shoes
        [shortdesc] =>
        [longdesc] =>
        [status] => active
        [parentid] => 0
    )

[1] => Array
    (
        [id] => 2
        [name] => shirts
        [shortdesc] =>
        [longdesc] =>
        [status] => active
        [parentid] => 0
    )

[2] => Array
    (
        [id] => 3
        [name] => pants
        [shortdesc] =>
        [longdesc] =>
        [status] => active
        [parentid] => 0
    )
```

Unfortunately, the view itself is looking for a flat array, with a key that corresponds to the category ID and a value that corresponds to the category name.

There are three possible solutions to this problem. The first is to rewrite the view to handle a multidimensional array. The second is to rewrite the model function to output the array as a flat list. The third is to create a different model function for your navigation and use that instead.

Of all the options, the third makes the most sense. Think about it: Why send the view more data than it needs? Why shouldn't you hand the view just what it needs, in a concise, neat package? Another thing to think about: Is it possible you may need the `getAllCategories()` function at some point? Of course! So it's good to keep it.

Go ahead and create a new model function called `getCategoriesNav()`. This new function will be dedicated solely to extracting category data needed for the navigation:

```
function getCategoriesNav(){
    $data = array();
    $Q = $this->db->get('categories');
    if ($Q->num_rows() > 0){
```

```
      foreach ($Q->result_array() as $row){
        $data[$row['id']] = $row['name'];
      }
    }
    $Q->free_result();
    return $data;
  }
```

As stated in Chapter 3, you can also get the result rows as objects by using the arrow syntax:

```
function getCategoriesNav(){
  $data = array();
  $Q = $this->db->get('categories');
  if ($Q->num_rows() > 0){
    foreach ($Q->result() as $row){
      $data[$row->id] = $row->name];
    }
  }
  $Q->free_result();
  return $data;
}
```

From a performance standpoint, it's *tomato–tomahto*.

Now call this new function instead of `getAllCategories()` in your controller function:

```
function index(){
  $data['title'] = "Welcome to Claudia's Kids";
  $data['navlist'] = $this->MCats->getCategoriesNav();
  $this->load->vars($data);
  $this->load->view('template');
}
```

When you reload your browser, you should still see two errors, as shown in Figure 4-2.

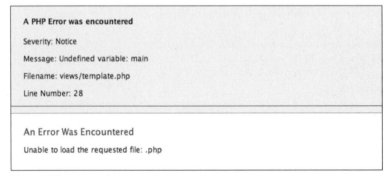

A PHP Error was encountered

Severity: Notice

Message: Undefined variable: main

Filename: views/template.php

Line Number: 28

An Error Was Encountered

Unable to load the requested file: .php

Figure 4-2

The reason for these two errors is simple. You haven't established a $data['main'] variable in your controller, and the view is expecting some kind of value so it can load an appropriate subview in that space. Why is it called *$data['main']*? It's called that because it will contain the "main" content for any given page, be it a Contact Us form, a home page listing, or a product page. Using a dynamic variable like this allows you to reuse templates.

The rest of this chapter focuses on how to create the content for this important variable. To do that, you will need to refer to the initial sketches created with Claudia. Starting with the next section of this chapter, you're going to be doing just that, working through each page of the application.

By the end of the chapter, you should know most of what you need to know to create an MVC web site. The last part, building the actual Shopping Cart application, is left for Chapter 5, only because the level of detail involved requires further attention.

Displaying the Home Page

So now you know what you have to do — populate the main variable in the template view. Before doing this, it's a good idea to look at the mockup you worked on with Claudia. As a reminder, it's shown in Figure 4-3.

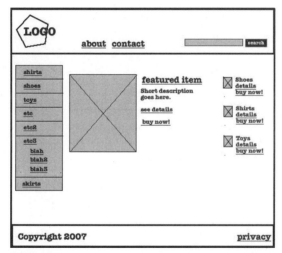

Figure 4-3

What Claudia wants on the home page is a main featured product with three other featured products to the right, each from a different category. The main featured product includes a large image and a short description, while the three others consist of a small thumbnail image and a title (no description). Both groups have appropriate links that allow the visitor to buy now or see more detail.

At the moment, you could spend a lot of time on display or look and feel issues, but you're going to take the MVC approach and work on the model first. Why? Because you need to have some data to work with first, and the model is where you do that.

Open the MProducts model (/system/application/models/mproducts.php). This model contains two bare-bones functions: getProduct() and getAllProducts(). At first glance, the getProduct() function looks promising, as you could call it four times and then check in each case for a featured designation of TRUE (or category IDs), but this approach feels too heavy-handed. In other words, it's like using a bulldozer where a shovel (or even a spoon) would suffice. It would be better for all involved to use a more specific query to get what we want and use that instead.

Instead, let's create two simple functions that will pull out the information needed to build the home page. The first new function, getMainFeature(),selects a random featured item for the home page. The second function, getRandomProducts(),selects random products from different categories (but never one that was chosen as the main feature on the same page).

Retrieving the Main Featured Product

Here's what the getMainFeature() function looks like. Notice the use of the built-in Active Record methods to get what you want, which is a random featured product from the products table:

```
function getMainFeature(){
  $data = array();
  $this->db->select("id,name,shortdesc,image");
  $this->db->where('featured','true');
  $this->db->where('status', 'active');
  $this->db->orderby("rand()");
  $this->db->limit(1);
  $Q = $this->db->get('products');
  if ($Q->num_rows() > 0){
    foreach ($Q->result_array() as $row){
      $data = array(
        "id" => $row['id'],
        "name" => $row['name'],
        "shortdesc" => $row['shortdesc'],
        "image" => $row['image']
      );
    }
  }
  $Q->free_result();
  return $data;
}
```

Pay special attention to the $this->db->orderby("rand()") directive. It builds an "order by rand()" SQL snippet. Combining this directive with $this->db->limit(1) retrieves exactly one random item. The query is further limited by the $this->db->where('featured', 'true') directive, which filters the result set to those records that have the featured field set to TRUE.

In other words, the resultant SQL query is:

```
select id, name, shortdesc, image
from products
where featured='true' and status='active '
order by rand()
limit 1
```

Retrieving Random Products for the Sidebar

The second function, `getRandomProducts()`, builds on the first function. It retrieves a variable number of products (you can pass in the number as an argument) from different categories (one per category, in fact). It also skips whatever product you tell it to skip, as you will pass in the product ID that was retrieved by the `getMainFeature()` function.

Have a look at the function, and then move on to the discussion below.

```
function getRandomProducts($limit,$skip){
  $data = array();
  $temp = array();
  if ($limit == 0){
    $limit=3;
  }
  $this->db->select("id,name,thumbnail,category_id");
  $this->db->where('id !=', $skip);
  $this->db->where('status', 'active');
  $this->db->orderby("category_id","asc");
  $this->db->limit(100);
  $Q = $this->db->get('products');
  if ($Q->num_rows() > 0){
    foreach ($Q->result_array() as $row){
      $temp[$row['category_id']] = array(
        "id" => $row['id'],
        "name" => $row['name'],
        "thumbnail" => $row['thumbnail']
      );
    }
  }

  shuffle($temp);
  if (count($temp)){
    for ($i=1;$i<=$limit;$i++){
      $data[] = array_shift($temp);
    }
  }

  $Q->free_result();
  return $data;
}
```

This function retrieves a maximum of 100 records, selecting fields like ID, name, thumbnail, and category_id, and places these data in a temporary array that is later shuffled (to ensure randomness; otherwise, the same categories are likely to be processed repeatedly) and then further processed by a simple `for` loop that creates a final data array.

Notice that the temporary array is keyed by category_id in the `foreach` loop:

```
if ($Q->num_rows() > 0){
   foreach ($Q->result_array() as $row){
      $temp[$row['category_id']] = array(
         "id" => $row['id'],
         "name" => $row['name'],
         "thumbnail" => $row['thumbnail']
      );
   }
}
```

This simple step ensures that the final step in the process, in which the function shifts however many items were specified by the `$limit` argument, gives you what you want: no more than one product per category in the returned data.

At the moment, there are no products or categories stored in the database tables, so now would be a good time to put in some sample data. For now, upload a few dummy images into the /images folder, and create a dozen dummy entries in the products table. The data don't have to be exactly like Claudia's inventory, nor do the pictures have to be anything more specific than a shot that has a watermark on it. It's all just for placement at the moment.

> Please note that there is a downloadable zip file available at www.wrox.com that contains some dummy data. The dummy data consist of sample categories, products, and uploadable images that you can use while you work. It's often easier to develop an application like this if you have something to work with.
>
> The dummy data aren't a work of literature. They merely contain product names like Dress 1 or Shoes 3 and descriptions like "This is a nice pair of shoes." The idea is to give you just enough differentiation that you can test your site. Your customers will blow it all away when they start entering real data.

> **phpMyAdmin**
>
> If you know about phpMyAdmin, you know that it's a powerful tool that allows you to administer your entire database. It allows you to add, drop, and modify databases; add, drop, and modify tables; add and remove fields to any table; add, modify, and remove data from any field; and much, much more. It even allows you to import and export data. It's an invaluable tool.
>
> If you have phpMyAdmin installed on your server (or if it's available as part of your hosting package), you'll be using it many times a day during development. If you don't have access to it, the only way you'll be able to manipulate the database is to work with the `mysql` command line. That may work OK for a short time, but eventually, you'll want to take the time to install phpMyAdmin.

Using the New Model Functions on the Home Page

As soon as you have some data and images loaded, open your controller file in a text editor and start making some quick changes. The first thing you want to do is call your new functions:

```
function index(){
   $data['title'] = "Welcome to Claudia's Kids";
   $data['navlist'] = $this->MCats->getCategoriesNav();
   $data['mainf'] = $this->MProducts->getMainFeature();
   $skip = $data['mainf']['id'];
```

```
    $data['sidef'] = $this->MProducts->getRandomProducts(3,$skip);
    $data['main'] = 'home';
    $this->load->vars($data);
    $this->load->view('template');
}
```

Running a `print_r()` on the data returned by the `getMainFeature()` function, you'll see something along the lines of the following little snippet:

```
[id] => 6
[name] => Shoes 1
[shortdesc] => This is a very good pair of shoes.
[image] => /images/dummy-main.jpg
```

Similarly, the data returned by the `getRandomProducts()` function would look like this via the `print_r()` function:

```
[0] => Array
  (
    [id] => 7
    [name] => Shoes 2
    [thumbnail] => /images/dummy-thumb.jpg
  )

[1] => Array
  (
    [id] => 8
    [name] => Shirt 1
    [thumbnail] => /images/dummy-thumb.jpg
  )

[2] => Array
  (
    [id] => 12
    [name] => Pants 1
    [thumbnail] => /images/dummy-thumb.jpg
  )
```

Setting `$data['main']` to home instructs the `$this->load->view()` command inside template.php to load the view called *home*. That's what you'll need to create next.

Creating the Home Page View

Now all you have to do is create some HTML based on these data. Your initial thought might be to put this logic directly in the main template view, but this is a bad idea. Why? Because you're going to be reusing the template view a lot, and if you have to maintain an ever-growing list of rules to govern the display of the `$main` variable, you're going to drive yourself (and everyone else) crazy trying to maintain it.

Instead, you're going to create a series of included templates, each dedicated to a different view. There are other ways to handle the problem, of course, including doing all this work in the models, creating a custom library, or using private functions, but the view approach is the purest when it comes to the MVC division of labor.

Since you're going to pass two arrays to the view, here's what that view, called *home*, looks like. Notice that it is processing an array called $mainf (which will hold the main featured item) and $sidef (which will contain a list of sidebar featured products).

```
<div id='pleft'>
<?php
  echo "<img src='".$mainf['image']."' border='0' align='left'/>\n";
  echo "<h2>".$mainf['name']."</h2>\n";
  echo "<p>".$mainf['shortdesc'] . "<br/>\n";
  echo anchor('welcome/product/'.$mainf['id'],'see details') . "<br/>\n";
  echo anchor('welcome/cart/'.$mainf['id'],'buy now') . "</p>\n";
?>
</div>

<div id='pright'>
<?php
  foreach ($sidef as $key => $list){
    echo "<img src='".$list['thumbnail']."' border='0' align='left'/>\n";
    echo "<h4>".$list['name']."</h4>\n";
    echo "<p>";
    echo anchor('welcome/product/'.$list['id'],'see details') . "<br/>\n";
    echo anchor('welcome/cart/'.$list['id'],'buy now') . "</p>\n";
  }
?>
</div>
```

Notice that the main feature is placed inside a div uniquely identified as *pleft*. The sidebar features are placed inside a div uniquely identified as *pright*. Doing things this way allows you to create the appropriate CSS rules for layout.

Before discussing anything else, it's good to talk about an alternative syntax using short tags. To use this alternative syntax, you must have short tag support enabled on your PHP installation. Some developers prefer this alternative syntax to what you see in the previous example. Some prefer the "old-fashioned way." There really is no difference other than your preference.

Here's what the previous example would look like with the alternative syntax:

```
<div id='pleft'>
  <img src='<?= $mainf['image']; ?>' border='0' align='left'/>
  <h2><?= $mainf['name']; ?></h2>
  <p><?= $mainf['shortdesc']; ?><br/>
  <?= anchor('welcome/product/'.$mainf['id'],'see details');?><br/>
  <?= anchor('welcome/cart/'.$mainf['id'],'buy now');?></p>
</div>

<div id='pright'>
<? foreach ($sidef as $key => $list) : ?>
  <img src='<?= $list['thumbnail'];?>' border='0' align='left'/>
  <h4><?= $list['name'];?></h4>
  <p><?= anchor('welcome/product/'.$list['id'],'see details');?><br/>
  <?= anchor('welcome/cart/'.$list['id'],'buy now');?></p>
<? endforeach; ?>
</div>
```

As you can see, there's practically the same number of lines and the same kinds of constructs. It's your choice.

Here's a reminder of how those two arrays ($mainf and $sidef) were called in the controller function index():

```
$home['mainf'] = $this->MProducts->getMainFeature();
$skip = $home['mainf']['id'];
$home['sidef'] = $this->MProducts->getRandomProducts(3,$skip);
$data['main'] = $this->load->view('home',$home,true);
```

You're not quite done with the home page; you will need to make some changes to the /css/default.css file you started in Chapter 3. Not only will you be adding new entries (for the new divs), but you'll also need to adjust some other layout rules. For example, you notice that the web site as a whole is much too wide for most monitors, so you decide to knock it down from 1,000 pixels (1000px) to 800 pixels (800px) in width.

Here is the complete CSS, with changes in bold:

```
/* default css */

body{
    background-color:white;
    font-family: Arial, Verdana, sans-serif;
    margin:0;
    padding:0;
}

#wrapper{
    width:800px;
    margin:10px auto;
    padding:10px;
    background-color:#f1f1f1;
    border:2px solid #ccc;
}

#nav{
    float:left;
    width:135px;
    height:auto;
}

#main{
    margin-left:150px;
    width:600px;
    height:auto;

}
```

```
#header{
   font-size:12px;
   margin-bottom:10px;
}

#footer{
   clear:both;
   padding-top:40px;
   font-size:9px;
}

#pleft{
   float:left;
   width:400px;
}

#pleft img{
   padding-right:10px;
}

#pright{
   float:right;
   height:auto;
   width:150px;
   text-align:left;
   padding-left:5px;
}

#pright img{
   padding-right:3px;
}
```

Now isn't the time to make everything perfect — you'll have at least two or three passes available for look and feel. For now, you're much more worried about functionality.

When you reload the home page in the browser, it should look like Figure 4-4.

The top still doesn't look right, nor is the page very pleasing to the eye (fonts are too big, link colors are standard, and much more), but the page is fairly close to the spirit of the original diagram. Refresh the browser a few times, and different products should be featured with each refresh. Notice that only one sidebar feature for any given category is allowed on the right, and that none of those products is the same as the main featured product.

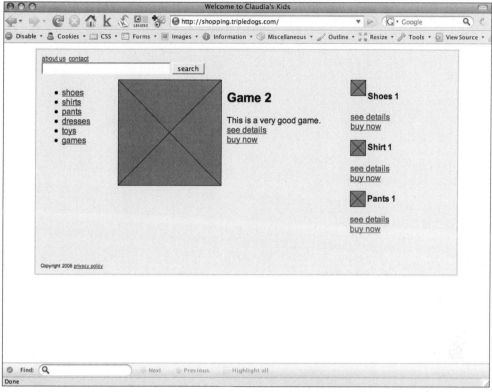

Figure 4-4

Displaying Product Categories

Now that you've figured out the home page view, the category view should go pretty fast. Remember the discussion with Claudia? The category view is actually two views, and the original notes involved a cat() controller function and a separate subcat() function.

There may be a better way to handle the differences between these two states. What's involved in these two states? The first is a category view that only displays subcategories, and the second is a subcategory view that shows actual products.

To make all this work, you need to make a slight change involving the creation of a clothes category. The clothes category will be the parent category of various other subcategories, namely, shoes, shirts, pants, and dresses. Once the clothes category is created, set the parentid value for the shoes, shirts, pants, and dresses category to match the ID of the new clothes category. While you're at it, create a category named *fun*, and place toys and games under it.

As soon as you're done, open the MCats model in an editor and make a slight change to the getCategoriesNav() function, limiting the query to retrieve only those categories that don't have a parentid value set. This will retrieve all top-level categories. While you're at it, order the results alphabetically by category name, and limit the list to active categories:

```
function getCategoriesNav(){
  $data = array();
  $this->db->where('parentid <', 1);
  $this->db->where(status', 'active');
  $this->db->orderby('name','asc');
  $Q = $this->db->get('categories');
  if ($Q->num_rows() > 0){
    foreach ($Q->result_array() as $row){
      $data[$row['id']] = $row['name'];
    }
  }
  $Q->free_result();
  return $data;
}
```

These two simple changes in the getCategoriesNav() function result in a much simplified navigation, as illustrated in Figure 4-5.

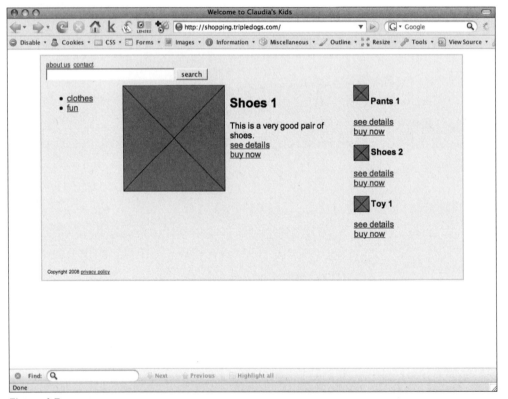

Figure 4-5

Now all you have to do to build the right view for categories (displaying either associated categories or products) is to check for the existence of a parentid value.

Here is a bare-bones look at the controller function cat(). Notice the use of the if statement looking for a parentid value. In a moment, you'll be able to fill it in, but this should give you an idea of what's going to happen:

```
function cat(){
  $cat = $this->MCats->getCategory($this->uri->segment(3));
  if (!count($cat)){
    redirect('welcome/index','refresh');
  }
  $data['title'] = "Claudia's Kids | ". $cat['name'];

  if ($cat['parentid'] < 1){
    //show other categories
  }else{
    //show products


  }
  $data['category'] = $cat;
  $data['main'] = 'category';
  $data['navlist'] = $this->MCats->getCategoriesNav();
  $this->load->vars($data);
  $this->load->view('template');
}
```

The first thing the function does is use the `getCategory()` function to retrieve the category in question. How does it know to do that? Because you're passing in a category ID inside the URI. Specifically, the third URI segment contains the category ID, and you use the `$this->uri->segment()` method to do that.

If you have security on your mind, you might have noticed that no validation is being done when the URI segment is grabbed. At the very least, you should be making sure this value is an integer of a certain length. Never fear, this site won't go live without some kind of validation at this level. In Chapter 9, you learn more about these kinds of security issues. Here, just learn how to use the tools.

A simpler way of grabbing the URI segment is to simply pass in the expected ID as an argument to the function, as:

```
function cat($id){
  $cat = $this->MCats->getCategory($id);
  if (!count($cat)){
    redirect('welcome/index','refresh');
  }
  $data['title'] = "Claudia's Kids | ". $cat['name'];

  if ($cat['parentid'] < 1){
    //show other categories
  }else{
    //show products


  }
  $data['category'] = $cat;
  $data['main'] = 'category';
  $data['navlist'] = $this->MCats->getCategoriesNav();
  $this->load->vars($data);
  $this->load->view('template');
}
```

This approach is much cleaner and makes it easier to map incoming URI segments to functional pieces of your code. You use this syntax throughout the project.

Because you're saving the retrieved category in a variable named $cat, you can do a quick check of $cat['parentid'] and make the right decision. If that value is less than 1, you're dealing with a category page, so you have to list subcategories. If not, you're dealing with a subcategory page, and you must list products.

Other things to note on this page: the $data['main'] variable is set to "category." In just a few pages, you'll be creating this category view. As usual, you're using $this->load->vars() to register the $data array and make it available to all your views.

Creating New Model Functions

Now it is time to build some new functions. You'll need a function to retrieve subcategories in the MCats model first. Here's one named getSubCategories(), accepting a category ID as an argument, which is used to match records with the right parentid:

```
function getSubCategories($catid){
    $data = array();
    $this->db->where('parentid', $catid);
    $this->db->where(status', 'active');
    $this->db->orderby('name','asc');
    $Q = $this->db->get('categories');
    if ($Q->num_rows() > 0){
        foreach ($Q->result_array() as $row){
            $data[] = $row;
        }
    }
    $Q->free_result();
    return $data;
}
```

The second function you need to create belongs in the MProducts model. This function retrieves all available products that match a category ID. As with the getSubCategories() function, you're going to pass in a category ID and then order the result set by product name:

```
function getProductsByCategory($catid){
    $data = array();
    $this->db->select('id,name,shortdesc,thumbnail');
    $this->db->where('category_id', $catid);
    $this->db->where(status', 'active');
    $this->db->orderby('name','asc');
    $Q = $this->db->get('products');
    if ($Q->num_rows() > 0){
        foreach ($Q->result_array() as $row){
            $data[] = $row;
        }
    }
    $Q->free_result();
    return $data;
}
```

Building out the `cat()` *Controller Function*

Now all you have to do is run the right function in the right context and then pass the result set to a single view. In the following code listing, the essential `if` statement is bold. Notice how the simple check for parentid transforms this controller function into a multipurpose tool that allows you to build the appropriate listing with the same set of views.

While you're at it, include a few lines of code to redirect users back to the home page if the category page being loaded is somehow bogus. You can do that very quickly with a simple PHP `count()` function:

```php
function cat($id){
  $cat = $this->MCats->getCategory($id);
  if (!count($cat)){
    redirect('welcome/index','refresh');
  }
  $data['title'] = "Claudia's Kids | ". $cat['name'];

  if ($cat['parentid'] < 1){
    //show other categories
    $data['listing'] = $this->MCats->getSubCategories($id);
    $data['level'] = 1;
  }else{
    //show products
    $data['listing'] = $this->MProducts->getProductsByCategory($id);
    $data['level'] = 2;
  }
  $data['category'] = $cat;
  $data['main'] = 'category';
  $data['navlist'] = $this->MCats->getCategoriesNav();
  $this->load->vars($data);
  $this->load->view('template');
}
```

Creating the Category View

Before coding the category view, it would be worth the time to revisit the diagrams for the category and subcategory views developed with the client. Here is the category view, illustrated in Figure 4-6.

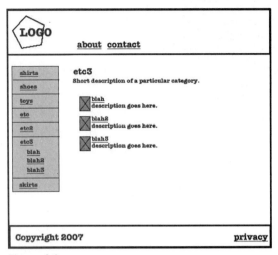

Figure 4-6

It's a very simple template, showing the category name and description, followed by a list of subcategories. The subcategory list features thumbnails from appropriate products, which you can add to the established function in a next pass.

The diagram for the subcategory view is very similar to that for the category view, the only difference being in the listing, which is a list of products in that subcategory. See Figure 4-7.

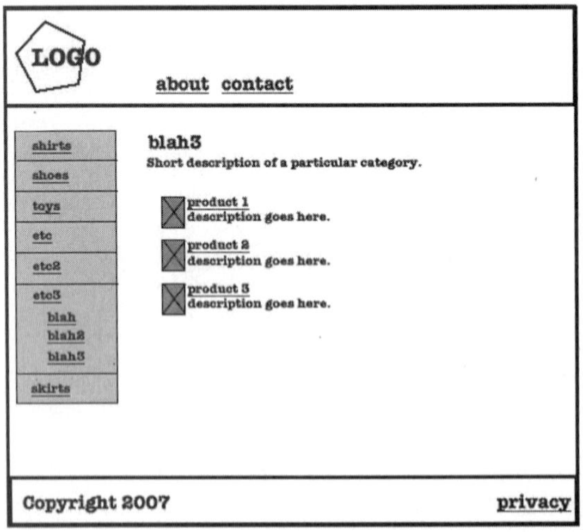

Figure 4-7

What all this means is some reworking of the `getSubCategories()` function. It will need to pull out a random thumbnail from a product within the category being listed. This may seem like a very complicated thing, but all that's required is a subquery within the main query.

As long as you create and run this second query with a different object instantiation (say, `$Q2` instead of `$Q`), then you'll be fine. In the following code listing, the subquery is bold to bring attention to it:

```php
function getSubCategories($catid){
   $data = array();
   $this->db->select('id,name,shortdesc');
   $this->db->where('parentid', $catid);
   $this->db->where(status', 'active');
   $this->db->orderby('name','asc');
   $Q = $this->db->get('categories');
   if ($Q->num_rows() > 0){
    foreach ($Q->result_array() as $row){

      $Q2 = $this->db->query("select thumbnail as src from products
          where category_id=".$row['id']. "
          order by rand() limit 1");

      if($Q2->num_rows() > 0){
         $thumb = $Q2->row_array();
         $THUMB = $thumb['src'];
      }else{
         $THUMB = '';
      }

      $Q2->free_result();

      $data[] = array(
        'id' => $row['id'],
        'name' => $row['name'],
        'shortdesc' => $row['shortdesc'],
        'thumbnail' => $THUMB
      );
    }
  }

  $Q->free_result();

  return $data;
}
```

As the subquery runs, any thumbnail path retrieved in the process gets stored in a variable, then passed down to the `$data` array that is being collated. What you end up with is a complete packet of information for the view, one that contains category information and product thumbnails rolled into one.

See how easy it is to make changes to CodeIgniter models in the face of requirements? You can start out complex, or you can grow from simple to complex, but never would anyone characterize the process as complicated. That's the beauty of a good MVC framework.

Finally, it's time to work directly on the category view. Luckily, you've already built a similar view for the home page, so you can use it as a rough model. Essentially, what you need to do is display the category and listing information properly. Because you're passing in an array with three distinctive parts (the category information, the listing, and what level the category lives on), you can easily create a listing:

```php
<div id='pleft'>
<?php
  echo "<h2>".$category['name']."</h2>\n";
  echo "<p>".$category['shortdesc'] . "</p>\n";

  foreach ($listing as $key => $list){
    echo "<img src='".$list['thumbnail']."' border='0' align='left'/>\n";
    echo "<h4>";

    switch($level){
      case "1":
      echo  anchor('welcome/cat/'.$list['id'],$list['name']);
      break;

      case "2":
      echo anchor('welcome/product/'.$list['id'],$list['name']);
      break;
    }
    echo "</h4>\n";
    echo "<p>".$list['shortdesc']."</p><br style='clear:both'/>";
  }
?>
</div>
```

All in all, you just need a quick `switch()` statement to help build the proper links (to either the category or product pages), and the result is something very close to Figure 4-8 (the category view) and Figure 4-9 (the subcategory view). Again, these views aren't perfect, and they certainly won't win any prizes at an award ceremony, but they get the job done, and that's the focus of this section.

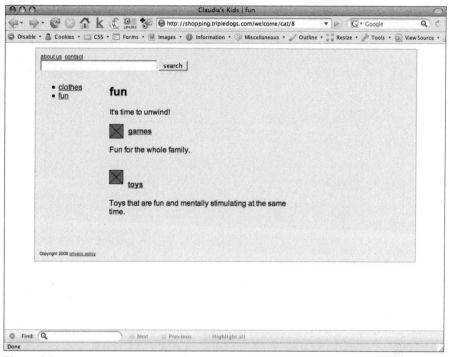

Figure 4-8

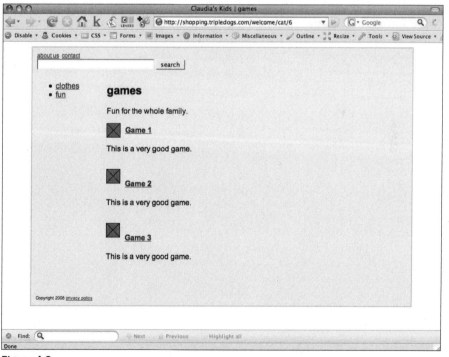

Figure 4-9

Displaying Product Details

In just a very short amount of time (less than a few hours, really), you've made a great deal of progress. The home page and both category views are now roughed in. It is time to create the product view. Before creating that view, it's a good idea to revisit the diagram for that page, so it's shown in Figure 4-10.

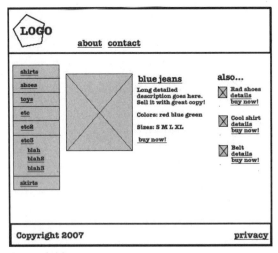

Figure 4-10

In many ways, this is a very similar interface to the home page, except that the sidebar items are in the same grouping as the product with central billing. So far, the discussion around the "grouping" concept has been a bit general, but it makes sense conceptually. The idea is to show not just a pair of jeans, but also the shirt and shoes that go with those jeans. In other words, the grouping is an easy way to display related items regardless of their home categories.

Therefore, before you can start coding, take a moment to group together different product records in your database. You need to do this in order to test out the algorithm you're going to write. It doesn't really matter if Pants A actually goes with Shirt B or Shoes D, all you need is a set of matching items to run the algorithm against.

A good idea might be to group different clothing items, with just enough affinity to keep your coding fast and iterative at this stage. Remember the Agile way — it's very likely that Claudia will make all manner of changes once she sees your work, so do just enough to make it work, and worry about all the details later. The same can be done with toys and games. Don't worry at the moment what the groups should be named, as at this point any arbitrary string (like "abc" or even "toyset 1") will do.

Updating the MProducts Model

Before you work with the controller, you'll need to create a new function in the MProducts model, one that will allow you to extract a variable number of products that match a grouping. Here is that new function, called getProductsByGroup(). It accepts three arguments: The first limits the result set, the second passes in a grouping string to match against, and the third tells the function which product ID to skip (in this case, the product you're skipping is the one that has been displayed on the page).

```php
function getProductsByGroup($limit,$group,$skip){
  $data = array();
  if ($limit == 0){
    $limit=3;
  }
  $this->db->select('id,name,shortdesc,thumbnail');
  $this->db->where('grouping', $group);
  $this->db->where('status', 'active');
  $this->db->where('id !=', $skip);
  $this->db->orderby('name','asc');
  $this->db->limit($limit);
  $Q = $this->db->get('products');
  if ($Q->num_rows() > 0){
    foreach ($Q->result_array() as $row){
      $data[] = $row;
    }
  }
  $Q->free_result();
  return $data;
}
```

Building the `product()` Controller Function

Now it's time to build the controller. By now the pattern should be pretty established in your mind. Your controller function for `product()` looks like this:

```php
function product($id){
  $product = $this->MProducts->getProduct($id);
  if (!count($product)){
    redirect('welcome/index','refresh');
  }
  $data['grouplist'] = $this->MProducts-
      >getProductsByGroup(3,$product['grouping'],$id);
  $data['product'] = $product;
  $data['title'] = "Claudia's Kids | ". $product['name'];
  $data['main'] = 'product';
  $data['navlist'] = $this->MCats->getCategoriesNav();
  $this->load->vars($data);
  $this->load->view('template');
}
```

First, use the third URI segment (which represents a product ID) to extract information about that product with the `getProduct()` model function.

If no product is retrieved (because it isn't active or it doesn't exist), then redirect the user back to the home page. This is a very simple way to ensure that only active (or extant) products are shown. In Chapter 9, you learn how to further defend against various kinds of attacks involving user input like URIs.

Otherwise, retrieve other products with the same group, and use `$this->load->vars()` to load the `$data` array for use by all the views. Along the way, set the `$data['main']` variable to "product," as you'll be using the product view in this context.

Creating the Product View

The view for products, called product.php, is very similar to the home page in form, function, and output. It accepts two arrays, one called `$products` and the other called `$grouplist`, and outputs the information in `pleft` and `pright` divs:

```
<div id='pleft'>
<?php
   echo "<img src='".$product['image']."' border='0' align='left'/>\n";
   echo "<h2>".$product['name']."</h2>\n";
   echo "<p>".$product['longdesc'] . "<br/>\n";
   echo "Colors:<br/>\n";
   echo "Sizes:<br/>\n";
   echo anchor('welcome/cart/'.$product['id'],'buy now') . "</p>\n";
?>
</div>


<div id='pright'>
<?php
   foreach ($grouplist as $key => $list){
      echo "<img src='".$list['thumbnail']."' border='0' align='left'/>\n";
      echo "<h4>".$list['name']."</h4>\n";
      echo "<p>";
      echo anchor('welcome/product/'.$list['id'],'see details') . "<br/>\n";
      echo anchor('welcome/cart/'.$list['id'],'buy now') . "</p>\n";
   }
?>
</div>
```

With this view built and uploaded, reload your browser to see the results. You should see something similar to Figure 4-11. Again, it won't win any awards, but it functions. Navigate the site to other products within the same group (and even different groups) to check the validity of your code.

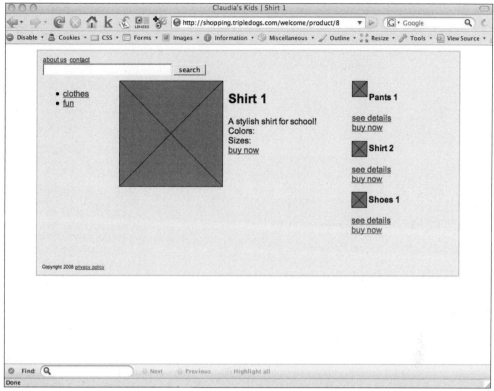

Figure 4-11

Leaving out the colors and sizes is intentional at this point. There wasn't much discussion about these database fields during discovery, and you suspect that Claudia will fill you in once she reviews your work so far. That's OK, because in Agile the idea is to iterate.

Displaying Search Results

Writing a search engine in CodeIgniter, and especially for this project, is pretty straightforward. As you'll see, it's all about judiciously using the built-in wildcard-matching methods in your model to pull it off.

Without further ado, here's a search() function you can add to the MProducts model. You pass it a single argument, a search term, which is then used to match across the name, shortdesc, and longdesc fields of the products table. For now, this search function returns a maximum of 50 rows in the result set:

```
function search($term){
    $data = array();
    $this->db->select('id,name,shortdesc,thumbnail');
    $this->db->like('name',$term);
    $this->db->orlike('shortdesc',$term);
    $this->db->orlike('longdesc',$term);
    $this->db->orderby('name','asc');
```

```
   $this->db->where('status','active');
   $this->db->limit(50);
   $Q = $this->db->get('products');
   if ($Q->num_rows() > 0){
     foreach ($Q->result_array() as $row){
       $data[] = $row;
     }
   }
   $Q->free_result();
   return $data;
}
```

Notice the use of $this->db->like() and $this->db->orlike()? These methods create wildcard matching on certain fields. The above code creates the following SQL statement:

```
select id, name, shortdesc, thumnail from products
where (name like '%$term%'
or shordesc like '%$term%'
or longdesc like '%$term%')
and status='active'
order by name asc
limit 50
```

Now that the search function is built, you can create the controller function called search(). Remember that this URL is loaded only when someone fills in a search term and clicks Search, so you'll need to check for form input.

In CodeIgniter, the way to check for form input is to use the $this->input->post() method. If there isn't a value for "term" in the form post, redirect the user to the home page. There are other security considerations to make, but most of those are covered in Chapter 9.

```
function search(){
  if ($this->input->post('term')){
    $search['results'] = $this->MProducts->search($this->input->post('term'));
  }else{
    redirect('welcome/index','refresh');
  }
  $data['main'] = 'search';
  $data['title'] = "Claudia's Kids | Search Results";
  $data['navlist'] = $this->MCats->getCategoriesNav();
  $this->load->vars($data);
  $this->load->view('template',$data);
}
```

Once again, you're going to use $data['main'] to pass along the name of the view you want loaded in the main area of the page. This time, you're also passing in an array called $search['results'] and looping over the array called $results in the view.

The search view looks like the following code listing. Notice that you're only using the pleft div, instead of both pleft and pright. The reason you're not going to use pright is that you don't need it — search pages don't have a right column that displays related products.

```
<div id='pleft'>
<h2>Search Results</h2>

<?php
if (count($results)){
  foreach ($results as $key => $list){
    echo "<img src='".$list['thumbnail']."' border='0' align='left'/>\n";
    echo "<h4>";
    echo anchor('welcome/product/'.$list['id'],$list['name']);
    echo "</h4>\n";
    echo "<p>".$list['shortdesc']."</p><br style='clear:both'/>";
  }
}else{
  echo "<p>Sorry, no records were found to match your search term.</p>";
}
?>
</div>
```

Upload your controller and new view, and then run a search on the site. You should see either search results or a message stating that no records matched the search term. Figure 4-12 illustrates this page.

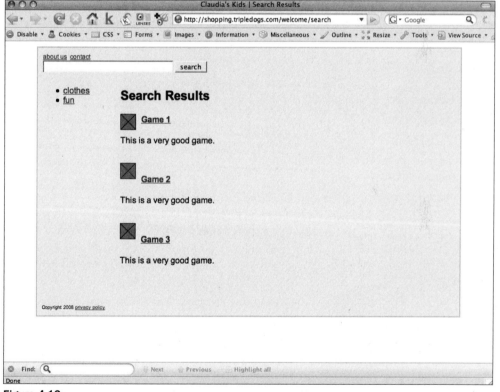

Figure 4-12

What about the Shopping Cart?

You've created a great deal of functionality in just a few hours. You have a working home page, category and subcategory pages, product detail pages, and a rudimentary search engine. You have specialized model functions to retrieve the data that you need, including navigation, featured products, and related products. Your main view, called *template*, is smart enough to load all the other subviews it needs and can accept a dynamically set view name from the controller.

What's left? Well, there isn't a real shopping cart on the site. There's no way for the site visitor to add a product to the shopping cart or to view the contents of that shopping cart. In Chapter 5, you create this shopping cart system using CodeIgniter sessions and the help of a new model that is dedicated to the shopping cart data in those sessions.

At this point in the project, you deserve a break. You've completed more with CodeIgniter in just a few hours than most other PHP developers could complete in several weeks. Your code is minimal, easy to understand, and easy to update. It's time to look at the sprint backlog to see what kind of progress you've made.

Revisiting the Sprint Backlog

At the end of Chapter 2, you created an initial sprint backlog. As you look over it now, you realize that you've made progress on more than half the items on that list.

Here's the list again:

1. Install and configure CodeIgniter on a development server. **DONE.**

2. Create the initial tables for products and categories. **DONE.**

3. Build a model for products, with functions for listing all products by category, listing product details for any given product, and listing other products that belong to the same group as a product. **DONE.**

4. Build a model for categories, with functions for listing all categories as a tree, listing subcategories for a category, and listing category details. The products model already contains a function that allows you to list all products in a category. **DONE.**

5. Create a controller for all visible pages, with functions for the home page, About Us, Contact Us, Search Results, Product Detail, Shopping Cart, and Category view. **80 percent DONE (need shopping cart).**

6. Create special controller functions for running the search and adding items to a Shopping Cart cookie. **50 percent DONE.**

7. Create other Shopping Cart functions that allow you to display everything in a Shopping Cart, recalculate prices with Ajax, and delete line items from a Shopping Cart.

8. Create all the views needed to display web pages. This will more than likely involve a master template with includes as needed to minimize your work later on.

Chapter 5 is where you dig into the Shopping Cart details. For now, take a well-deserved break!

Conclusion

In this chapter, you built the vast majority of a working web site in just a few days. The major controller functions, models, and views enable you and the client to see what's happening and iterate quickly.

As you continue your CodeIgniter career, keep the following points in mind:

❑ In most cases, it's useful to work incrementally. Creating bare-bones controllers and models, and then changing them as requirements and needs dictate, is perfectly OK.

❑ It's always helpful to think logically about the division of labor within your application. If you're dealing with data, create a model (remember that session data are data — they don't have to live in a database table!). If you're dealing with application flow or logic, make sure it's handled in the controller. If it involves something the user can touch, see, or interact with, put it in the view.

❑ When in doubt, always remember that things should never get complicated, even if the problem at hand is complex. If you find yourself repeating functions in code, then it's time to abstract it into a model or even a private function in the controller. In the following chapters, you are introduced to private functions, helpers, and libraries.

Displaying Product Details

In just a very short amount of time (less than a few hours, really), you've made a great deal of progress. The home page and both category views are now roughed in. It is time to create the product view. Before creating that view, it's a good idea to revisit the diagram for that page, so it's shown in Figure 4-10.

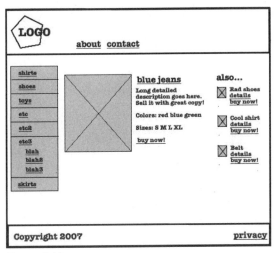

Figure 4-10

In many ways, this is a very similar interface to the home page, except that the sidebar items are in the same grouping as the product with central billing. So far, the discussion around the "grouping" concept has been a bit general, but it makes sense conceptually. The idea is to show not just a pair of jeans, but also the shirt and shoes that go with those jeans. In other words, the grouping is an easy way to display related items regardless of their home categories.

Therefore, before you can start coding, take a moment to group together different product records in your database. You need to do this in order to test out the algorithm you're going to write. It doesn't really matter if Pants A actually goes with Shirt B or Shoes D, all you need is a set of matching items to run the algorithm against.

A good idea might be to group different clothing items, with just enough affinity to keep your coding fast and iterative at this stage. Remember the Agile way — it's very likely that Claudia will make all manner of changes once she sees your work, so do just enough to make it work, and worry about all the details later. The same can be done with toys and games. Don't worry at the moment what the groups should be named, as at this point any arbitrary string (like "abc" or even "toyset 1") will do.

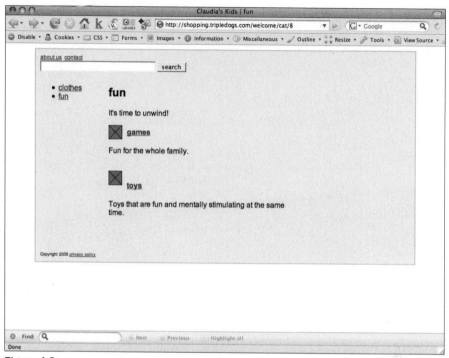

Figure 4-8

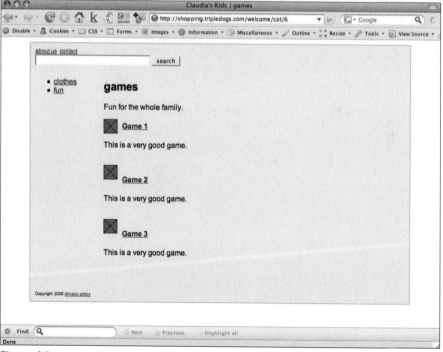

Figure 4-9

5

Building a Shopping Cart

In Chapter 4, you learned how to use CodeIgniter's MVC framework to create a basic eCommerce site, with its home page, category views, and product detail pages. In this chapter, you'll learn how to create the Shopping Cart. You'll also get feedback from the client on how to polish the site and then implement those changes inside your CSS and PHP files.

Displaying the Shopping Cart

At some point in any eCommerce site, site visitors add products to their shopping carts and then try to check out. By the end of the chapter, you'll have a working shopping cart (but no checkout function, as you'll need to confer with the client about this).

The approach you're going to take with Claudia's Kids is a simple, straightforward approach that makes use of both CodeIgniter's session object and native PHP sessions. If you're used to working with PHP sessions, you might be tempted to think that CodeIgniter's session object is the same thing. CodeIgniter sessions are different from PHP sessions, acting just like cookies. They can be encrypted and can store serialized data that are automatically created or updated as needed.

To use CodeIgniter sessions, all you need to do is load the library. In this case, you've already loaded the Session library in the autoloader.php file (in Chapter 2), so all you have to do now is use the appropriate functions.

Because CodeIgniter sessions are cookies, you have the same limitations as you do with cookies in general. For example, cookies can be tampered with by the end-user. This makes CodeIgniter sessions (even if the data in them are encrypted) hard to trust. Another limitation is the fact that a session cookie only holds 4 KB (kilobytes) of data. It is possible for someone to fill up their session cookie either accidentally or with malicious intent.

You're going to combine the two approaches. Your more sensitive data are going to go into PHP sessions. Other data, like a flag that indicates whether there are any items in the Shopping Cart, will go into the CodeIgniter session.

Before going any further, it's a good idea to review what the expectations are concerning the Shopping Cart.

The first thing to notice when reviewing the diagrams is that you need to change the "buy now" links in your views to "add to cart." If you recall, early in the diagramming process, Claudia asked you to change the potentially confusing "buy now" links with a more accurate "add to cart". Making this change is easy enough, implemented with a simple search and replace in any text editor.

The second thing is that the process of adding a product to a shopping cart doesn't really involve a view. Instead, it can simply use a status message to provide the user with visual confirmation, as pictured in Figure 5-1.

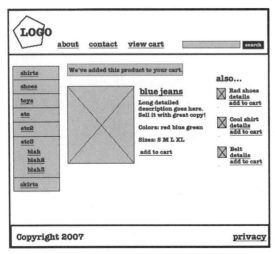

Figure 5-1

This status message can be achieved with very little effort in the controller `cart()` function.

Finally, the third thing to consider (and this is also illustrated in Figure 5-1) is that once a user has added items to her cart, a third navigation option (called "view cart") is dynamically added to the main navigation. When the user clicks this link, she can view and manipulate items in her Shopping Cart, as illustrated in Figure 5-2.

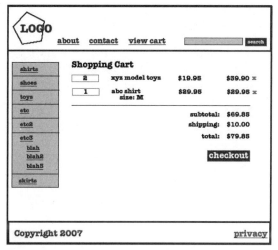

Figure 5-2

There's a lot of functionality to build, but the job can be broken down into major tasks. First things first: Allow users to add products to their Shopping Carts.

First Things First

Before doing anything else, open your Welcome controller and add the following line to the constructor:

```
function Welcome(){
  parent::Controller();
  session_start();
}
```

The `session_start()` line initializes the PHP sessions that you will need to make the Shopping Cart work. Without this command, you will just get error messages whenever you try to write to or read from a PHP session.

Adding Products to a Shopping Cart

Adding products to a user's Shopping Cart is fairly easy. What you need to store is the ID, price, and number of each product. Why store the price? Because you don't want any back-end product updates (like price increases) to change the price of products in active Shopping Carts.

The first bit of information, the product ID, is very easy to determine, as in all views you pass in the product ID to the `cart()` controller function:

```
echo anchor('welcome/cart/'.$product['id'],'add to cart');
```

Once again, to build the controller function, you're going to take advantage of smart coding to minimize your work. The `cart()` controller function should be able to handle not only adding products to the

109

Shopping Cart, but displaying all products in the cart as well. All you have to do is check for the presence of a product ID in the URI segment.

Once you have that information, you can extract the product from the database into an array, and if that array has values in it, extract what you need and drop the data from the array into a custom session variable called *cart*. Of course, the session variable itself has to be checked to make sure you're not overwriting data, and that requires some looping and decision trees.

It would be very easy to put all of this data wrangling directly in the controller, but since it's likely that you'll need this kind of data handling in other parts of your application, it's best to create a new model (call it *MOrders* because it is the Model for Orders — it's the naming convention adopted in Chapter 3). Although no database table exists at the moment for this information (it's all handled with PHP sessions), you might expand the Shopping Cart to include cookies, database tables, or even flat files at a later date. It doesn't matter. In an MVC context, if you're processing data, do as much as you can in the model.

First, create a new model called *MOrders* (save it as /system/application/models/morders.php). Then create an `updateCart()` function. The `updateCart()` function takes two arguments: the product's ID and the full database record for a product. You're going to use `$productid` as the name of the first argument (because you're passing in a product ID) and `$fullproduct` for the second argument (again, because you're passing in the full product information). The function's first task is to make a copy of the PHP session array named *cart*. Then it loops through this copy of the data, looking to see if this particular product already exists.

If the product doesn't already exist, then add it to the array. If it does exist, increment the product's count by one. Finally, the entire thing (along with a running total count) is updated in the PHP session, and a confirmation message is created using CodeIgniter's `set_flashdata()`. The `set_flashdata()` method is new to CodeIgniter 1.6, and it allows you to create a temporary variable that is used immediately and then discarded. You're going to use it to store a confirmation message and then show it on the very next page.

```php
<?php

class MOrders extends Model{
   function MOrders(){
     parent::Model();
   }

function updateCart($productid,$fullproduct){
   //pull in existing cart first!
   $cart = $_SESSION['cart'];
   $totalprice = 0;
   if (count($fullproduct)){
     if (isset($cart[$productid])){
        $prevct = $cart[$productid]['count'];
        $prevname = $cart[$productid]['name'];
        $prevname = $cart[$productid]['price'];

        $cart[$productid] = array(
          'name' => $prevname,
          'price' => $prevprice,
          'count' => $prevct + 1
        );
```

```
    }else{
      $cart[$productid] = array(
        'name' => $fullproduct['name'],
        'price' => $fullproduct['price'],
        'count' => 1
      );
    }

    foreach ($cart as $id => $product){
      $totalprice += $product['price'] * $product['count'];
    }
    $_SESSION['totalprice'] = $totalprice;
    $_SESSION['cart'] = $cart;
    $this->session->set_flashdata('conf_msg', "We've added this product to your
        cart.");
    }
  }

}//end class
?>
```

The beauty of this setup lies in the fact that if the product isn't in the user's Shopping Cart, then it is added along with whatever price is currently available from the database. If the product is already in the Shopping Cart, then it simply updates the count, but nothing else.

All of this processing may seem like a lot of work, but it will save you lots of processing in the view.

Now for the controller function named cart(). All you have to do to keep things running smoothly is pass in an argument that corresponds with the product ID. In other controller functions, you've been using $id as the name of this argument, but in this case, it makes sense to use $productid.

Please note that this $productid bears absolutely zero resemblance to the $productid used in the model. All you're trying to do is use nomenclature that is semantically valid. You could have passed in a variable named $buffyTheVampire or $myproduct or simply $id. In this case, you've opted for $productid. In any case, if the product ID passed to the function has an associated value, then run the updateCart() function in MOrders, and redirect users back to the product page. If the passed in product ID is less than 0, display everything that's saved in the user's Shopping Cart (this is discussed later, in the section, "Displaying the Shopping Cart to the User").

```
function cart($productid){
  if ($productid > 0){

    $fullproduct = $this->MProducts->getProduct($productid);
    $this->MOrders->updateCart($productid,$fullproduct);
    redirect('welcome/product/'.$productid, 'refresh');
  }else{
    $data['title'] = "Claudia's Kids | Shopping Cart";
    if (count($_SESSION['cart']) == true){
      $data['main'] = '';
      $nav['navlist'] = $this->MCats->getCategoriesNav();
      $this->load->vars($data);
      $this->load->view('template');
```

```
      }else{
         redirect('welcome/index','refresh');
      }
   }
}
```

The next thing you have to do is adjust your product view to read in the flash data saved in your CodeIgniter session:

```
<div id='pleft'>

<?php
if ($this->session->flashdata('conf_msg')){
  echo "<div class='message'>";
  echo $this->session->flashdata('conf_msg');
echo "</div>";
}
?>


<?php
  echo "<img src='".$product['image']."' border='0' align='left'/>\n";
  echo "<h2>".$product['name']."</h2>\n";
  echo "<p>".$product['longdesc'] . "<br/>\n";
  echo "Colors:<br/>\n";
  echo "Sizes:<br/>\n";
  echo anchor('welcome/cart/'.$product['id'],'add to cart') . "</p>\n";
?>
</div>


<div id='pright'>
<?php
  foreach ($grouplist as $key => $list){
     echo "<img src='".$list['thumbnail']."' border='0' align='left'/>\n";
     echo "<h4>".$list['name']."</h4>\n";
     echo "<p>";
     echo anchor('welcome/product/'.$list['id'],'see details') . "<br/>\n";
     echo anchor('welcome/cart/'.$list['id'],'add to cart') . "</p>\n";
  }
?>
</div>
```

Finally, add a message class to the CSS file to handle the new message you're creating. In the example below, you're creating a message class with red text inside a red-bordered box:

```
.message{
   border:1px solid red;
   background-color:#ccc;
   color:red;
   padding:5px;
   width:250px;
   font-size:12px;
   margin:5px;
}
```

What you should end up with is something that looks like Figure 5-3.

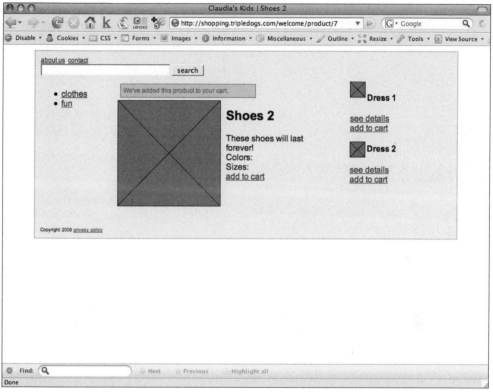

Figure 5-3

Adding the View Cart Link to the Navigation

The second part of the Shopping Cart is very simple. You simply add a link that says "view cart" to the main navigation if there are items in the customer's Shopping Cart.

To do this, simply adjust the header view to look for contents in the cart session variable. If the cart contains information, then show the link.

```
<a href="<?php echo base_url();?>">
<img src="<?php echo base_url();?>/images/logo.jpg" border="0"/>
</a>
<div><?php echo anchor("welcome/about_us","about us");?> 
<?php echo anchor("welcome/contact", "contact");?>
<?php
if (count($_SESSION['cart']) == true){
  echo " ". anchor("welcome/cart", "view cart");
}
?>
```

```php
<?php
echo form_open("welcome/search");
$data = array(
  "name" => "term",
  "id" => "term",
  "maxlength" => "64",
  "size" => "30"
);
echo form_input($data);
echo form_submit("submit","search");
echo form_close();
?>
</div>
```

Displaying the Shopping Cart to the User

Remember the check you did in the `cart()` controller function? If there wasn't a third URI segment, the code displays every item in the user's Shopping Cart? In this section, you learn how to do that. In essence, the task breaks down into two major parts:

❑   Display all items in the user's Shopping Cart.

❑   Create some JavaScript functions that allow the visitor to make changes to the Shopping Cart (i.e., delete items, add more of a certain item, etc.).

In the previous section, you set up `$data['main']` to be blank if you were just displaying the Shopping Cart for the user. Right now, you're going to set this variable to a value of `shoppingcart`, as the plan is to loop through the cart session variable in that view.

```php
$data['main'] = 'shoppingcart';
```

Because creating a useful Shopping Cart is a bit complicated, you're going to want to tackle the work in several major steps.

Creating the Display Table in the View

The shoppingcart view is entirely based on the contents of the user's Shopping Cart, which is stored in a CodeIgniter session. In this view, you want to generate the HTML necessary by looping through the session data. The idea is to create a form that contains a combination of text and only one column of user-changeable form fields.

To keep things from getting too complicated, you'll want to make good use of `form_input()` and other handy shortcuts provided by the form helper.

If you need to brush up on forms, see "The Form Helper" section of Chapter 3.

Notice that in the code below, the $TOTALPRICE variable is taken from the totalprice session variable. One more thing that's important to note: You may be wondering why there's a class assignment of "process" on each form field that contains the product count. In the upcoming sections, you're going to be adding some Ajax handlers to update the form, and you're going to filter the form fields by class name. It's a handy trick made available to you by the Prototype library — more on this in the section "Adding Update Functionality to the Shopping Cart" later in this chapter.

```php
$TOTALPRICE = $_SESSION['totalprice'];
if (count($_SESSION['cart'])){
  foreach ($_SESSION['cart'] as $PID => $row){
    $data = array(
        'name' => "li_id[$PID]",
        'value'=>$row['count'],
        'id' => "li_id_$PID",
        'size' => 5,
        'class' => 'process'
      );
      echo "<tr valign='top'>\n";
      echo "<td>". form_input($data)."</td>\n";
      echo "<td id='li_name_".$PID."'>". $row['name']."</td>\n";
      echo "<td id='li_price_".$PID."'>". $row['price']."</td>\n";
      echo "<td id='li_total_".$PID."'>".$row['price'] * $row['count']."</td>\n";
      echo "</tr>\n";
  }

  $total_data = array('name' => 'total', 'id'=>'total', 'value' => $TOTALPRICE);
  echo "<tr valign='top'>\n";
  echo "<td colspan='3'> </td>\n";
  echo "<td>$TOTALPRICE ".form_hidden($total_data)."</td>\n";
  echo "</tr>\n";

  echo "<tr valign='top'>\n";
  echo "<td colspan='3'> </td>\n";
  echo "<td>".form_submit('submit', 'checkout')."</td>\n";
  echo "</tr>\n";

}else{
  //just in case!
  echo "<tr><td>No items to show here!</td></tr>\n";
}//end outer if count
?>
</table>
</form>
</div>
```

At this point, you should have something similar to the view illustrated in Figure 5-4.

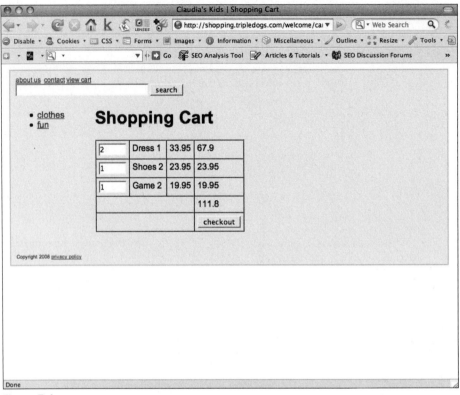

Figure 5-4

You may be looking at the code and wondering how all of this is going to work. After all, right now, if a user makes a change to the form fields on the left, nothing changes. That's where the next task comes in.

Also, you may note that the Shopping Cart display has a few items missing, such as a working checkout button or a row that indicates shipping. As these are rules not yet provided by the client, they can be addressed in the next two chapters, which are focused on building out the administrative panels.

Adding Update Functionality to the Shopping Cart

Once a web site visitor gets to the Shopping Cart page, he may or may not check out immediately. He may make changes to his Shopping Cart line items and then go back to perusing the site. Any changes made on the Shopping Cart page will have to be tracked in the session.

The way you're going to handle this problem is very simple. You're going to add an Update button to the Shopping Cart interface, then use it to call a custom Scriptaculous Ajax function that will interact with a new controller function you're going to write. Therefore, you'll need to install the Scriptaculous framework, which includes Prototype, as it isn't included with CodeIgniter.

You can download the Scriptaculous libraries from `http://script.aculo.us/`.

Updating the template and shoppingcart Views

Once you've uploaded all the necessary files for the Scriptaculous framework, make a simple change to your main template view, adding calls to those files so that they're universally available:

```
<script type="text/javascript" src="<?php echo
        base_url();?>js/prototype.js"></script>

<script type="text/javascript" src="<?php echo base_url();?>js/scriptaculous.js"
        ></script>
```

Furthermore, while you're at it, add a call to a third file, one called customtools.js. For now, this file will be empty, but it will contain all your custom JavaScript code.

```
<script type="text/javascript" src="<?php echo base_url();?>js/customtools.js" >
</script>
```

Next, you're going to add an Update button to the shoppingcart view that calls a custom JavaScript function called jsUpdateCart(). Just be sure to put this new button before the submit code:

```
echo "<tr valign='top'>\n";
echo "<td colspan='3'> </td>\n";
echo "<td><input type='button' name='update' value='update'
        onClick='javascript:jsUpdateCart()'/></td>\n";
echo "</tr>\n";
```

There is one more thing you need to do with the shoppingcart view. At the very end of the file, add a <div> tag with an ID of ajax_msg. As you'll see in the next section, this is the <div> tag your Ajax function will use to print status messages.

```
<div id='ajax_msg'></div>
```

Creating the Custom JavaScript Functions

Now open the /js/customtools.js file you created above and add two new JavaScript functions to it.

The first is jsUpdateCart(), which you'll use to parse the Shopping Cart form and send information to a custom controller function. In this function, use getElementsByClassName to grab all form elements with the class name of *process*. Extract the ID assigned to each class, and then split that ID on the underscore character (_) to get the real numeric ID for the product. Finally, grab the value from the field itself (i.e., how many of a particular product), and then send all of these data in a neat comma- and colon-delimited bundle to the ajax_cart() controller function (which you'll build momentarily).

The second function is showMessage(), which becomes the Ajax response. This is where any messages or return values actually display in the browser. Notice that the function is sending the request output to the ajax_msg div, then reloading the browser.

```
function jsUpdateCart(){
  var parameter_string = '';
  allNodes = document.getElementsByClassName("process");
  for(i = 0; i < allNodes.length; i++) {
    var tempid = allNodes[i].id;
    var temp = new Array;
    temp = tempid.split("_");
    var real_id = temp[2];
    var real_value = allNodes[i].value;
    parameter_string += real_id +':'+real_value+',';
  }

  var params = 'ids='+parameter_string;
  var ajax = new Ajax.Updater(
  'ajax_msg', '/welcome/ajax_cart',
          {method:'post',parameters:params,onComplete:showMessage}
  );

}

function showMessage(req){
  $('ajax_msg').innerHTML = req.responseText;
  location.reload(true);
}
```

Creating the `ajax_cart()` Controller Function

The controller function `ajax_cart()` is incredibly simple. All it has to do is load the MOrders model and then call a new function, `updateCartAjax()`, passing in as an argument the list of data supplied by the `jsUpdateCart()` JavaScript function:

```
function ajax_cart(){
  $this->load->model('MOrders','',TRUE);
  return $this->MOrders->updateCartAjax($this->input->post('ids'));
}
```

Expanding the MOrders Model

The final step in this process is to write a function called `updateCartAjax()` in the MOrders model. This function steps through the provided list of IDs and counts and then updates the cart as needed.

If the count for a given product ID is 0, then remove it from the Shopping Cart array altogether. If the count is the same as it was before for a given item, then don't bother to change it. If it's different, change it. This will help you keep track of all changes as you go, so you can keep track of activity accurately.

When the process ends, it will return one of three messages. If no data were sent to the function (unlikely, but possible), then it returns "No records to update." If changes were made (i.e., the user raised or lowered the number of items in the Shopping Cart), it returns the number of records that were changed. If data were sent in, but no changes were made (i.e., the user simply hit the update button without making any changes), it returns "No changes detected."

```php
function updateCartAjax($idlist){
  $cart = $_SESSION['cart'];
  //split idlist on comma first
  $records = explode(',',$idlist);
  $updated = 0;
  $totalprice = $_SESSION['totalprice'];
  if (count($records)){
    foreach ($records as $record){
      if (strlen($record)){
        //split each record on colon
        $fields = explode(":",$record);
        $id = $fields[0];
        $ct = $fields[1];
        if ($ct > 0 && $ct != $cart[$id]['count']){
          $cart[$id]['count'] = $ct;
          $updated++;
        }elseif ($ct == 0){
          unset($cart[$id]);
          $updated++;
        }
      }
    }
  }

    if ($updated){
      $totalprice =0; //with changes, must reset this value!
      foreach ($cart as $id => $product){
        $totalprice += $product['price'] * $product['count'];
      }
      $_SESSION['totalprice'] = $totalprice;

      $_SESSION['cart'] =$cart;
      echo $updated . " records updated!";
    }else{
      echo "No changes detected!";
    }
  }else{
    echo "No records to update!";
  }
}
```

Give it a try by changing a few items in the Shopping Cart and hitting Update. What you should see is something similar to Figure 5-5.

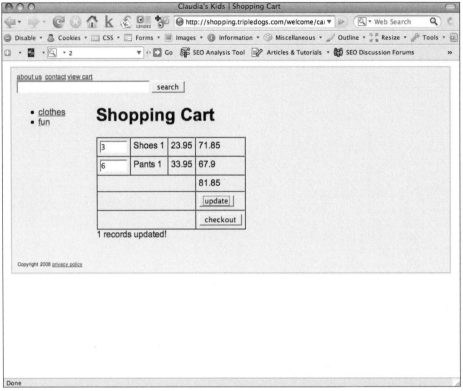

Figure 5-5

Please note the use of "1 records updated" in the status message. In Chapter 10, you learn how to present users with grammatically correct messages. For here, the status message works well enough to keep you on track.

The beauty of this approach is not just that the interface has been updated by the user, but now the session has been too, asynchronously. If the user were to leave this page to continue shopping, the session would be updated as well.

Adding a Delete Function to the Shopping Cart

The original mockup for the Shopping Cart view included a simple way for users to delete an item they no longer wanted. At this point, if any user sets a product amount to 0, the item gets dropped, but that isn't very obvious.

So it's time to add a simple delete function. You'll do this in four steps:

1. Update the shoppingcart view.
2. Add a JavaScript handler.
3. Update the Controller.
4. Update the Model.

Updating the shoppingcart View

The first thing you have to do is update the view, because you'll want to add a column to the far right to include a "delete" link. You'll also want to adjust all the following rows that contain totals and buttons. In the example below, the changed markup is bold:

```
<h1>Shopping Cart</h1>
<div id='pleft'>

<?php echo form_open(); ?>
<table border='1' cellspacing='0' cellpadding='5'>
<?php
$TOTALPRICE = $_SESSION['totalprice'];

if (count($_SESSION['cart'])){
   foreach ($_SESSION['cart'] as $PID => $row){
     $data = array(
        'name' => "li_id[$PID]",
        'value'=>$row['count'],
        'id' => "li_id_$PID",
        'class' => 'process',
        'size' => 5
     );

     echo "<tr valign='top'>\n";
     echo "<td>". form_input($data)."</td>\n";
     echo "<td id='li_name_".$PID."'>". $row['name']."</td>\n";
     echo "<td id='li_price_".$PID."'>". $row['price']."</td>\n";
     echo "<td id='li_total_".$PID."'>".$row['price'] * $row['count']."</td>\n";
     echo "<td><a href='#' onclick='javascript:jsRemoveProduct($PID)'>
             delete</a></td>\n";
     echo "</tr>\n";
   }

   $total_data = array('name' => 'total', 'id'=>'total', 'value' => $TOTALPRICE);
   echo "<tr valign='top'>\n";
   echo "<td colspan='3'> </td>\n";
   echo "<td colspan='2'>$TOTALPRICE ".form_hidden($total_data)."</td>\n";

   echo "</tr>\n";

   echo "<tr valign='top'>\n";
   echo "<td colspan='3'> </td>\n";
   echo "<td colspan='2'><input type='button' name='update'
             value='update' onClick='javascript:jsUpdateCart()'/></td>\n";
   echo "</tr>\n";
   echo "<tr valign='top'>\n";
   echo "<td colspan='3'> </td>\n";
   echo "<td colspan='2'>".form_submit('submit', 'checkout')."</td>\n";
```

```
    echo "</tr>\n";
}else{
    //just in case!
    echo "<tr><td>No items to show here!</td></tr>\n";
}//end outer if count
?>
</table>
</form>
<div id='ajax_msg'></div>
</div>
```

If you were to update your browser now, you'd see something very similar to Figure 5-6.

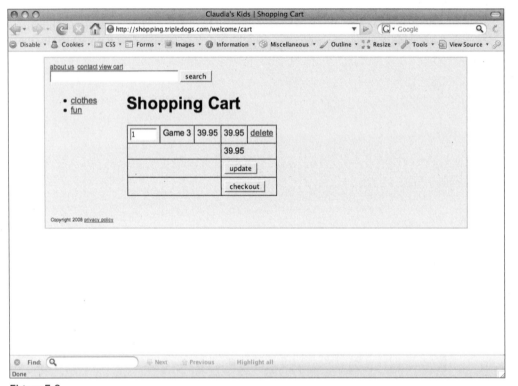

Figure 5-6

Adding a JavaScript Handler

In the shoppingcart view, you added a call to a JavaScript function called `jsRemoveProduct()`, passing in a product ID. It's now time to create this function, adding it to the customtools.js you created previously in the chapter.

This particular function will be a lot simpler than the `jsUpdateCart()` one. In fact, all it will do is accept the incoming product ID and call a new controller function called `ajax_cart_remove()`:

```
function jsRemoveProduct(id){
  var params = 'id='+id;
  var ajax = new Ajax.Updater(
    'ajax_msg','/welcome/ajax_cart_remove',
    {method:'post',parameters:params,onComplete:showMessage}
  );
}
```

Notice that you'll be reusing the `showMessage()` function from above.

Updating the Controller

All you have to do in the controller is add a new function called `ajax_cart_remove()`. This function will simply call a function in the MOrders model that will remove the product represented by the incoming product ID.

```
function ajax_cart_remove(){
  return $this->MOrders->removeLineItem($this->input->post('id'));
}
```

Updating the Model

Finally, create a `removeLineItem()` function in the MOrders model. This function tries to delete the incoming product ID from the Shopping Cart. If the Shopping Cart contains the product ID, it runs `unset()` on that particular part of the Shopping Cart and then updates the totalprice. The last thing the function does is report back whether a product was, indeed, removed.

```
function removeLineItem($id){
  $totalprice = 0;
  $cart = $_SESSION['cart'];
  if (isset($cart[$id])){
    unset($cart[$id]);
    foreach ($cart as $id => $product){
      $totalprice += $product['price'] * $product['count'];
    }
    $_SESSION['totalprice'] = $totalprice;
    $_SESSION['cart'] = $cart;
    echo "Product removed.";
  }else{
    echo "Product not in cart!";
  }
}
```

After loading all of this new code, run through the process of adding items to your Shopping Cart. If you delete a product, you should see something similar to what is pictured in Figure 5-7.

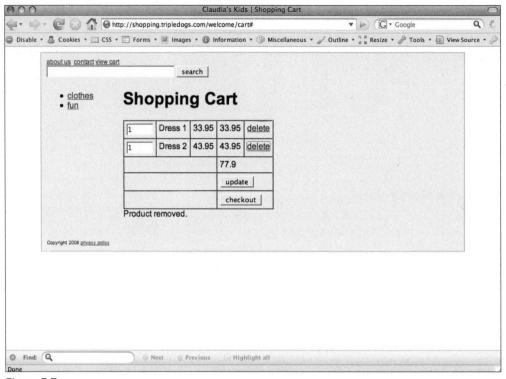

Figure 5-7

Revisiting the Sprint Backlog

At the end of Chapter 1, you created an initial sprint backlog, and then updated it at the end of Chapter 4. As you look over it now, you realize that everything from that initial list has been completed.

Here's the list again:

1. Install and configure CodeIgniter on a development server. **DONE.**

2. Create the initial tables for products and categories. **DONE.**

3. Build a model for products, with functions for listing all products by category, listing product details for any given product, and listing other products that belong to the same group as a product. **DONE.**

4. Build a model for categories, with functions for listing all categories as a tree, listing subcategories for a category, and listing category details. The products model already contains a function that allows you to list all products in a category. **DONE.**

5. Create a controller for all visible pages, with functions for the home page, About Us, Contact Us, Search Results, Product Detail, Shopping Cart, and Category views. **DONE**.

6. Create special controller functions for running the search and adding items to a shopping cart cookie. **DONE**.

7. Create other shopping cart functions that allow you to display everything in a shopping cart, recalculate prices with Ajax, and delete line items from a shopping cart. **DONE**.

8. Create all the views needed to display web pages. This will more than likely involve a master template with includes as needed to minimize your work later on. **DONE**.

It's time to meet with Claudia. You're sure that she'll have lots of feedback.

Meeting with Claudia

You meet with Claudia at her store. Her employees are quietly taking care of customers as you step Claudia through what you've built. You let her know from the very beginning that what she needs to concentrate on is functionality, and not look and feel, but even though she agreed to this, she still winces at every page.

"What's wrong?" you ask her, concerned that perhaps what you've built isn't passing muster.

"Well, I can see how we have just about everything we put on the backlog," she says, "But the entire thing looks a bit amateurish. It needs polish."

"Exactly what I was saying about functionality versus look and feel," you explain. "Think of web-site development as building a house. You always put in the foundation first, then the frame and electrical and plumbing, then the drywall and flooring. Later on we can worry about picking out the nice stuff, like the furniture and paint colors."

Claudia laughs. "I guess I want all the nice stuff now!"

"Well, you're in luck, because we're just about ready for all the nice things. We just need to go through the site and make an inventory of what needs changing."

Claudia looks a bit skeptical. "This is the easy part," you reassure her. "With CodeIgniter's help, I've built a fully functional eCommerce site in just a few days."

"Well, I don't see any place where I can add products myself," Claudia says, arching an eyebrow.

"OK, fully functional as far as the web-site visitor is concerned. I'll build the administrative panels in the next go-around."

"OK, well, I've been taking notes. Can I share those with you?" Claudia asks, and you tell her to share.

Here's what Claudia has noticed as you walk through the site:

- ❑ Logo is missing.
- ❑ Top part of the web page needs serious work.
- ❑ Search field is too wide.
- ❑ Product images and thumbnails are all missing.
- ❑ Real products and categories need to be added to the site.
- ❑ Product descriptions and prices are all wrong.
- ❑ Navigation on the left site is too simple, needs to show categories and subcategories.
- ❑ Gray color is too depressing. What other colors can we have?
- ❑ Way too many clicks to add a product to the cart.
- ❑ It's not obvious how to get back home once you're inside the site.

"This is a great list," you say. "We can address every single one of these very quickly."

You explain to Claudia that if she provides a logo, you can add it to the site without too many problems. You can also adjust the look and feel of the header portion of the site without too much trouble, including the search field. The same goes for the colors and general look and feel of the site.

As for the navigation, that's an easy rewrite of the model. The same goes for the number of clicks you have to go through before you can add a product to a cart.

As for putting in real content, you suggest to her that she wait until the next sprint, because that's when you're going to build the administrative panels. At that point, she can upload her own pictures and maintain her product and category listings.

"In fact, once we clean up the web-site look and feel a bit, you'll get a chance to tell me everything you want in an administrative panel, just like you did with the public side of the site. We'll just repeat the process on the back end!"

Claudia promises to send you a logo, and you agree to meet in another day or two to review your new look and feel. By the time you get back to your office, the Claudia's Kids logo is waiting for you in your e-mail inbox.

You leave the meeting feeling good about completing the first sprint backlog and knowing that because there are new changes, you'll likely need a new sprint backlog to handle those changes. Before you take that step, though, you know that you need to address a few things about the web site's look and feel.

Remember, it's vital to be agile (lowercase *a*) rather than Agile (uppercase *A*). Just because Agile methodology says "create a sprint backlog now," that doesn't mean that you need to do it right this second. Sometimes it's important to handle important things as they come up.

Polishing the Look and Feel

At the very beginning of this project, some choices were made to use a very bland template and bland CSS to get the ball rolling. The emphasis of this book is on web-site *development* as opposed to *design*, but you'll have to address look and feel at some point, even if you hire a freelance designer to come to your aid. Now it's time to spice things up. This is your opportunity as a web developer to start expressing a little more aesthetic taste and artistic sensibility in creating the site.

Uploading the Logo

The first thing you need to do is add the Claudia's Kids logo (naming it logo.jpg) into the /images folder. The logo has a "beach feel" with a color palette inspired by the sand and surf. It's illustrated as in Figure 5-8.

Figure 5-8

When you drop the logo file into a picture editor, you see that it is using the following color values:

- ❏   The word *Claudia's* is #14B8B8.

- ❏   The word *Kids* is #EFDDA8.

- ❏   The background gradient runs from #D4F7F7 to #14B8B8.

Updating the CSS

You decide to use this palette throughout the rest of the site, adding in a few darker variants on the sandy color (like #C98C21), and dutifully update the CSS. In the code listing below, the changed CSS is in bold. Notice that even the message class, which is used to give the visitor important information, is also updated. There are also new rules for headers, paragraphs, and links.

```
/* default css */

body{
  background-color:white;
  font-family: Arial, Verdana, sans-serif;
  margin:0;
  padding:0;
}

#wrapper{
  width:800px;
```

```css
    margin:10px auto;
    padding:10px;
    background-color:#e4deae;
    border:2px solid #efdda8;
}

h1 {
    font-size:1.2em;
    color:#14b8b8;

}

h2{
    font-size:1em;
    color:#14b8b8;
}

h3{
    font-size:.9em;
    color:#14b8b8;
}

h4{
    font-size:.8em;
    color:#14b8b8;
}

p,li,td{
    font-size:.8em;
}

a,a:link{
    color:#c98c21;
    text-decoration:underline;
}

a:hover{
    color:#14b8b8;
}


#nav{
    float:left;
    width:135px;
    height:auto;
}

#main{
    margin-left:150px;
    width:600px;
    height:auto;
}
```

```
#header{
  font-size:12px;
  margin-bottom:10px;
}

#footer{
  clear:both;
  padding-top:40px;
  font-size:9px;
}


#pleft{
  float:left;
  width:400px;
}

#pleft img{
  padding-right:10px;
}

#pright{
  float:right;
  height:auto;
  width:150px;
  text-align:left;
  padding-left:5px;
}

#pright img{
  padding-right:3px;
}

.message{
  border:1px solid #c98c21;
  background-color:#efdda8;
  color:#c98c21;
  padding:5px;
  width:250px;
  font-size:12px;
  margin:5px 0px 5px 0px;}
}
```

When you load your updated CSS on the site, you should see something like Figure 5-9 when you update your browser.

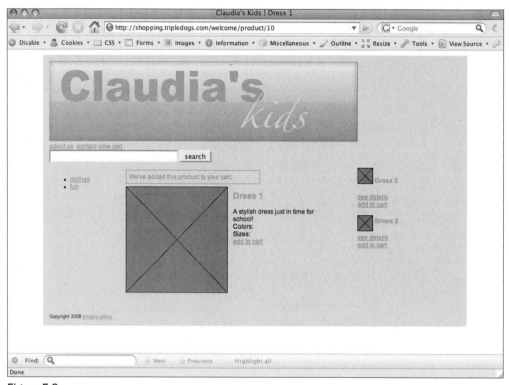

Figure 5-9

Fixing the Header

The header portion of the site is currently maintained in the header view. From a design perspective, there are a few design and usability problems with the items in that view. For example, the search widget is too wide, and the links don't particularly look like navigation items. They just look like a list of words. In this section, you remedy these problems.

First, though, open the /system/application/views/header.php in your editor. The first thing you're going to do is wrap the entire contents of the file (except for the image) into a `<div>` tag with ID `globalnav`. Inside that div, you're going to put in a `<ul>` tag, and wrap each of your links in an `<li>` tag. That goes for the search form as well!

Once every item in the navigation is in an `<li>` tag, you can reduce the width of the search field by setting the size variable of the `$data` array to something like 15.

Finally, you can add a very simple bit of code to detect whether you're on the home page by using `$this->uri->segment()`. If you're on the home page, don't show a link to Home. If you're not, then show the visitor a link he can click to go Home.

> Why are you suddenly using `$this->uri->segment()` when you were simply assigning incoming segments to an argument in the controller? First of all, you're working inside the view, not the controller, and thus it makes sense to use this function in this context. Second of all, you're looking at

the second segment (as in "welcome/index") to see if it matches "index" or not. Before, you were possibly looking at the third segment, which would serve as an argument to a controller function (i.e., the 5 would serve as an argument to `category()` *in /welcome/category/5).*

```
<a href="<?php echo base_url();?>">
<img src="<?php echo base_url();?>images/logo.jpg" border="0"/>
</a>

<div id='globalnav'>
<ul>
<?php
if ($this->uri->segment(2) != "index"){
  echo "<li>".anchor("welcome/index","home")."</li>";
}
?>
<li><?php echo anchor("welcome/about_us","about us");?></li>
<li><?php echo anchor("welcome/contact", "contact");?></li>
<?php
if (count($_SESSION['cart'])){
  echo "<li>". anchor("welcome/cart", "view cart") . "</li>";
}
?>

<li>

<?php
echo form_open("welcome/search");
$data = array(
  "name" => "term",
  "id" => "term",
  "maxlength" => "64",
  "size" => "15"
);
echo form_input($data);
echo form_submit("submit","search");
echo form_close();
?>
</li>
</ul>
</div>
```

Now all you have to do is update the CSS by adding a series of rules to handle the globalnav `<div>` and its `<ul>` list.

The first thing you need to do is set the rules for the globalnav `<div>` itself. You want a box with a dark background, 600 pixels wide by 30 pixels high (using this width value will make the navigation bar as wide as the logo):

```
/* navigation */

#globalnav {
  width: 600px;
  height:30px;
```

```
    margin: 2px 0 10px 0;
    padding: 0;
    background: #31363E;
}
```

Next, establish the rules for the `<ul>` list. You don't want any margin or padding on it, and you also don't want any bullets on any of the list items. Why not? Because you're about to create a horizontal list, and bullets would make the list look confusing and muddled. Stripping the bullets out of the list items leaves you with a clean look.

```
#globalnav ul {
   margin: 0;
   padding: 0;
   list-style: none;
}
```

Next, establish the rules for the `<li>` elements and the links within them. In this case, the links will be a light color that changes to a sandy tan when someone rolls over them.

```
#globalnav li {
   float: left;
   margin: 0;
   padding: 0;
   font-size: 80%;
   letter-spacing: 2px;
   text-transform: uppercase;
}

#globalnav li a {
   float: left;
   padding: 10px 12px;
   text-decoration: none;
   color: #e7e3d9;
   border: none;
}

#globalnav li a:hover {
   color: #e4deae;
}
```

Finally, as you'll be including the search form instead of an `<li>`, you want to make sure it is placed well within the list item, so add a bit of padding to offset it from the top and bottom.

```
#globalnav li form{
   padding:3px 0px;
}
```

What you should end up with so far is something that looks like Figure 5-10.

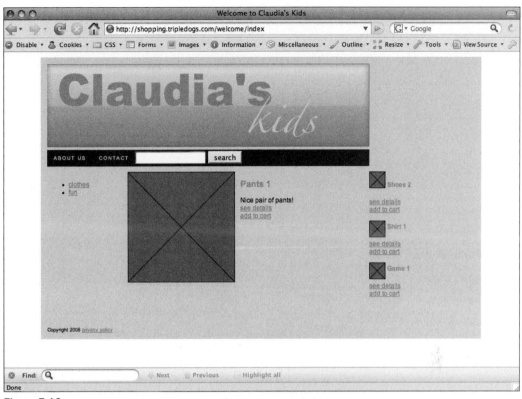

Figure 5-10

Fixing the Side Navigation

The side navigation work will be similar to the global navigation. You need to rework the CSS to show two levels of category, but in order to do that, you need to extract two layers of category from your model and process them all correctly in your view.

Updating the model isn't a problem. You already have a good working function in the MCats model called `getCategoriesNav()`. All you have to do to make it output the categories properly is add a new order by clause (making the list come out in asc parentid order) as well as an asc name order clause, and add a group by clause to group the database output by parentid and ID.

As you loop through each record, check to see if the parentid extracted is greater than 0. If it is, then save the resulting ID and name in an array that is a child of that parentid. If the parentid is not greater than 0, save just the name, using the ID as the parentid. Key the entire array by 0 (which is the topmost number allowed in the hierarchy), and you have a multidimensional array that represents the category tree.

```
function getCategoriesNav(){
  $data = array();
  $this->db->select('id,name,parentid');
  $this->db->where('status', 'active');
  $this->db->orderby('parentid','asc');
  $this->db->orderby('name','asc');
  $this->db->groupby('parentid,id');
  $Q = $this->db->get('categories');
  if ($Q->num_rows() > 0){
    foreach ($Q->result() as $row){
      if ($row->parentid > 0){
        $data[0][$row->parentid]['children'][$row->id] = $row->name;
      }else{
        $data[0][$row->id]['name'] = $row->name;
      }
    }
  }
  $Q->free_result();
  return $data;
}
```

Running a `print_r()` on the data from this function reveals the structure of your new navigation array. As you can see, everything is neatly packed away in three levels. First there is level 0, or the top of the tree. Then come levels 7 and 8 (the categories "clothes" and "fun"), each with their own children. The children each have their own IDs and names stored properly.

```
Array
(
    [0] => Array
    (
        [7] => Array
        (
            [name] => clothes
            [children] => Array
            (
                [4] => dresses
                [3] => pants
                [2] => shirts
                [1] => shoes
            )
        )

        [8] => Array
        (
            [name] => fun
            [children] => Array
            (
                [6] => games
                [5] => toys
            )
        )
    )
)
```

Knowing what the structure is like, changing your navigation view is easy. Loop through the list of categories to the appropriate level. If you see a name, print it with the proper ID. If you see children, descend one level and print the IDs and names you encounter there.

```
if (count($navlist)){
   echo "<ul>";
   foreach ($navlist as $key => $list){
      foreach ($list as $topkey => $toplist){
         echo "<li class='cat'>";
         echo anchor("welcome/cat/$topkey",$toplist['name']);
         echo "</li>\n";
         if (count($toplist['children'])){
         foreach ($toplist['children'] as $subkey => $subname){
            echo "\n<li class='subcat'>";
            echo anchor("welcome/cat/$subkey",$subname);
            echo "</li>";
         }
       }
      }
    }
   }
   echo "</ul>\n";
}
```

Now that all the hard work has been done in the model and view, all you have to do is update your CSS. In the view, you specified a class of cat for the top-level categories and a class of subcat for the subcategories. Since the entire <ul> is contained within the nav div, you can create some nice effects easily within your CSS file.

First things first: add a border around the existing #nav rule. You can use the same color as the background on your global nav component:

```
#nav{
    float:left;
    width:135px;
    height:auto;
    border:2px solid #31363E;
}
```

When you setup the <ul> for the nav div, remove all margin, padding, and list styling. You don't want any bullets to show! You're not really building a bullet list. You're just using the <ul> list to build a navigation list. (This time, it's vertical, but the idea is the same as with the horizontal navigation.)

```
#nav ul{
   margin: 0;
   padding: 0;
   list-style: none;
}
```

Next, create the look and feel for the cat and subcat <li> classes. A good suggestion is to make the cat class a different background color with slightly bigger text. Another good idea is to indent the subcat class more to show a hierarchy.

```
#nav ul li.cat{
    background-color:#31363e;
    font-size:1em;
    padding-left:5px;
}

#nav ul li.subcat{
    padding-left:15px;
    font-size:.9em;
}
```

Next, set up the look and feel for the cat and subcat links. Again, reuse the border color as the background color for the cat <li> elements, but use no background color for the subcat <li> elements. Note the different colors used for the links.

```
#nav li.cat a {
    text-decoration: none;
    color: #e4deae;
    border: none;
}

#nav li.subcat a {
    text-decoration: none;
    color: #000;
    border: none;
}
```

Finally, establish color changes for hover states. Reuse that blue you used with the rest of the site.

```
#nav li.subcat a:hover {
    text-decoration:none;
    color:#14b8b8;
}
#nav li.cat a:hover {
    text-decoration:none;
    color:#14b8b8;
}
```

The final result should look like Figure 5-11.

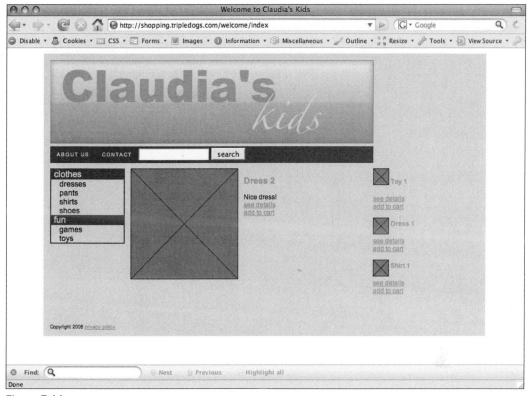

Figure 5-11

Placing the Add to Cart Links

The next issue that needs addressing is adding "add to cart" links throughout the site. Currently, a visitor can add a product to her cart on the home page and any product detail page. However, she can't do that on a subcategory page or a search results page.

First, open the search view (/system/application/views/search.php), and add an anchor after the description that allows the user to add the product to her cart (bold in the following code):

```
<div id='pleft'>
<h2>Search Results</h2>

<?php
if (count($results)){
  foreach ($results as $key => $list){
    echo "<img src='".$list['thumbnail']."' border='0' align='left'/>\n";
    echo "<h4>";
    echo anchor('welcome/product/'.$list['id'],$list['name']);
    echo "</h4>\n";
    echo "<p>".$list['shortdesc']. "<br/>".
```

```
         anchor('welcome/cart/'.$list['id'],'add to cart').
 "</p><br style='clear:both'/>";
     }
}else{
   echo "<p>Sorry, no records were found to match your search term.</p>";
}
?>
</div>
```

Do the same thing on the category view (/system/application/views/category.php), adding an anchor() after the description text.

```
<div id='pleft'>
<?php
  echo "<h2>".$category['name']."</h2>\n";
  echo "<p>".$category['shortdesc'] . "</p>\n";
  foreach ($listing as $key => $list){
     echo "<img src='".$list['thumbnail']."' border='0' align='left'/>\n";
     echo "<h4>";
     switch($level){
        case "1":
        echo anchor('welcome/cat/'.$list['id'],$list['name']);
        break;

        case "2":
        echo anchor('welcome/product/'.$list['id'],$list['name']);
        break;
     }
     echo "</h4>\n";
     echo "<p>".$list['shortdesc'].
        "<br/>" . anchor('welcome/cart/'.$list['id'],'add to cart').
        "</p><br style='clear:both'/>";
  }
?>
</div>
```

Cleaning up Thumbnail and Text Positioning

The last bit of cleanup you're going to do involves how the thumbnails and text lay out on the home, category, product, and search views. This will involve quite a bit of nudging in both CSS and the views.

The first step is adjusting the CSS rule for H4s, which is the header level you've assigned for thumbnails. Simply zero out the top and bottom margins.

```
h4{
   margin-top:0px;
   margin-bottom:0px;
   font-size:.8em;
   color:#14b8b8;
}
```

While you're in the CSS file, create two new classes, one called `productlisting` and the other called `thumbnail`. The `productlisting` class will be used to encapsulate the text and the thumbnail, and the `thumbnail` class will be assigned to each thumbnail image, giving it its own unique margin properties.

```css
img.thumbnail{
    clear:both;
    float:left;
    margin-right:5px;
    margin-bottom:15px;
}

.productlisting{
    float:left;
    width:70%;
    font-size:.8em;
    margin-bottom:30px;
}
```

Next, go through the home, category, product, and search views, and do the following to each thumbnail and product description:

❏   Remove the align=left property on each thumbnail image.

❏   Add a class of `thumbnail` to each thumbnail.

❏   Wrap the entire block (thumbnail and text) in a div with a class of `productlisting`.

❏   Remove any `<br style='clear:both'/>` tags you may find. Your new `thumbnail` class replaces these.

❏   Remove any `<p>` elements.

Here's what the home view should look like after you're finished (changes in bold):

```php
<div id='pleft'>
<?php
    echo "<img src='".$mainf['image']."' border='0' align='left'/>\n";
    echo "<h2>".$mainf['name']."</h2>\n";
    echo "<p>".$mainf['shortdesc'] . "<br/>\n";
    echo anchor('welcome/product/'.$mainf['id'],'see details') . "<br/>\n";
    echo anchor('welcome/cart/'.$mainf['id'],'add to cart') . "</p>\n";
?>
</div>

<div id='pright'>
<?php
    foreach ($sidef as $key => $list){
        echo "<div class='productlisting'>
            <img src='".$list['thumbnail']."' border='0' class='thumbnail'/>\n";
        echo "<h4>".$list['name']."</h4>\n";
        echo anchor('welcome/product/'.$list['id'],'see details') . "<br/>\n";
        echo anchor('welcome/cart/'.$list['id'],'add to cart') . "\n</div>";
    }
?>
</div>
```

139

Here's the category view:

```
<div id='pleft'>
<?php
  echo "<h2>".$category['name']."</h2>\n";
  echo "<p>".$category['shortdesc'] . "</p>\n";

  foreach ($listing as $key => $list){
    echo "<div class='productlisting'>
        <img src='".$list['thumbnail']."' border='0' class='thumbnail'/>\n";
    echo "<h4>";

    switch($level){
      case "1":
      echo anchor('welcome/cat/'.$list['id'],$list['name']);
      break;

      case "2":
      echo anchor('welcome/product/'.$list['id'],$list['name']);
      break;
    }
    echo "</h4>\n";
    echo $list['shortdesc'].
      "<br/>" . anchor('welcome/cart/'.$list['id'],'add to cart').
      "</div>";
  }
?>
</div>
```

Here's the product view:

```
<div id='pleft'>

<?php
if ($this->session->flashdata('conf_msg')){ //change!
  echo "<div class='message'>";
  echo $this->session->flashdata('conf_msg');
  echo "</div>";
}
?>
<?php
  echo "<img src='".$product['image']."' border='0' align='left'/>\n";
  echo "<h2>".$product['name']."</h2>\n";
  echo "<p>".$product['longdesc'] . "<br/>\n";
  echo "Colors:<br/>\n";
  echo "Sizes:<br/>\n";
  echo anchor('welcome/cart/'.$product['id'],'add to cart') . "</p>\n";
```

```
?>
</div>


<div id='pright'>
<?php
  foreach ($grouplist as $key => $list){
    echo "<div class='productlisting'>
        <img src='".$list['thumbnail']."' border='0' class='thumbnail'/>\n";
    echo "<h4>".$list['name']."</h4>\n";
    echo anchor('welcome/product/'.$list['id'],'see details') . "<br/>\n";
    echo anchor('welcome/cart/'.$list['id'],'add to cart') . "\n</div>";
  }
?>
</div>
```

Finally, here's the search view:

```
<div id='pleft'>
<h2>Search Results</h2>

<?php
if (count($results)){
  foreach ($results as $key => $list){
    echo "<div class='productlisting'>
        <img src='".$list['thumbnail']."' border='0' class='thumbnail'/>\n";
    echo "<h4>";
    echo anchor('welcome/product/'.$list['id'],$list['name']);
    echo "</h4>\n";
    echo $list['shortdesc']."<br/>".
      anchor('welcome/cart/'.$list['id'],'add to cart')."</div>";
  }
}else{
  echo "<p>Sorry, no records were found to match your search term.</p>";
}
?>
</div>
```

The home page of Claudia's Kids should now look something like Figure 5-12.

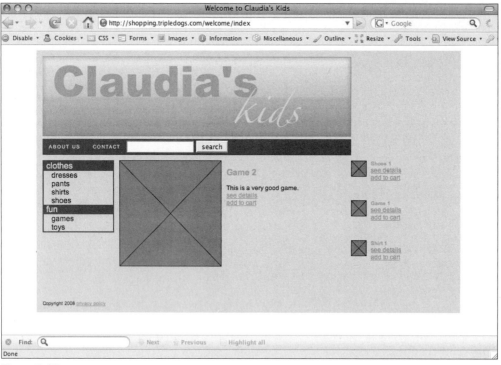

Figure 5-12

It isn't perfect, but you now have a skinned site that can be updated easily via CSS.

Conclusion

In this chapter, you expanded the original site with a shopping cart and polished the final product. In the next two chapters, you'll build out the administrative panels for this site and add any custom features that the client wants.

As you continue your CodeIgniter career, keep the following points in mind:

❏   When in doubt, work incrementally. It's OK to start simple and work your way to a complex solution.

❏   When updating look and feel, it's sometimes useful to think about what controller and model updates are needed to support the UI changes.

❏   It's always helpful to think logically about the division of labor within your application. If you're dealing with data, create a model (Remember that session data are data, they don't have to live in a database table!). If you're dealing with application flow or logic, make sure it's handled in the controller. If it involves something the user can touch, see, or interact with, put it in the view.

❑ Although CodeIgniter doesn't come with any native Ajax support built-in, there are plenty of Ajax-capable frameworks available. This chapter featured the use of Scriptaculous and Prototype, but you could easily go with any of the others. CodeIgniter is very flexible this way.

❑ Work on what's easiest for you first. In this chapter, you were guided through the process by working out the intricacies of the model and controller first, and then moving on to the view, and then to the CSS to support the HTML in the view. If you feel more comfortable with another approach, feel free to explore.

6

Creating a Dashboard

In Chapters 4 and 5, you completed most of the work needed to build a functional (if rudimentary) eCommerce site. You created models for extracting category and product data and handling orders. You also built controllers and views that presented users with well-organized home pages, category pages, and product pages. You even created a shopping cart mechanism.

In this chapter, you concentrate on building some administrative tools. The first step in this process is to visualize what Claudia wants, but you can make quite a few good guesses even before talking to her. You can assume, for example, that she wants some way to manage products and categories. You can also assume that she will need some way to track orders and export data. Before you make too many assumptions, though, it's time to meet with Claudia.

Gathering Requirements

When you meet with Claudia, she is in good spirits. In less than a week, she has been given a good working site that's easy for customers to use. Now she wants to concentrate on making the site easier to use on the administrative side.

"The first thing that I need to do," she says, "is easily manage categories and products."

"Yes," you answer, "Let's talk about administering categories first."

In 20 minutes, Claudia spells out what she needs:

- ❏ A secure way to log in to the administrative panel
- ❏ A dashboard that allows administrative users to manage categories and products
- ❏ A way to create, edit, and delete categories
- ❏ A way to create, edit, and delete products (including images and thumbnails)

❑ A way to easily assign a product to a category

❑ A way to assign products to categories in batch mode

❑ A way to assign products to groups in batch mode

❑ A way to export category and product listings

The first order of business has to do with the admins. Are there going to be more than one? Do they need to have different access levels to the different components?

Claudia thinks about it for a few seconds and shakes her head. "In the future, we may have a need for more administrator logins and privileges, but I don't think we need it now."

"Point taken," you answer, "but it may be easier to put something rudimentary in now. Perhaps a simple way to keep track of users and which parts of the system they can enter — categories, products, orders, and export functions."

"As long as it stays simple," Claudia says. "I guess I can see a need for giving one of my store clerks the ability to do limited things, such as update product information or export a list of products."

The next question you ask is about the dashboard. What does Claudia want to see there?

"The usual information — just allow me to navigate easily to categories, products, and other sections of the site. Oh, and maybe a way to administer some of the web pages we have on the site, like About Us or the Privacy Policy page."

"What about viewing popular products or other kinds of analytics information?"

"Maybe something like that, but I'm not too clear on that. What might be more useful is some kind of indication of how many ongoing orders there are, or how much traffic each category or product has. It doesn't have to be complex."

Next, you ask about exporting. "What kinds of formats do you want to export information in?"

"Definitely Excel or comma-separated values. That's what I need."

What about importing data into products and categories?

"That would be terrific! It would save a lot of time, especially in the beginning."

"What about backups? For example, if you need to make a pretty big change to your product listing?"

Claudia nods her head. "Can't we use the export feature for that? It seems that if I'm exporting information, I should be able to use it as a backup."

Finally, you tell her that the look and feel of the administrative panel will be simpler than those of the public pages. There would be some global navigation along the top, as well as a dashboard area that contains important information, like product listings or informational forms.

Claudia seems to approve, and you ask her to send in her notes on the conversation you've just had. She smiles knowingly and shows off her detailed notes. "I've learned something from the first go-around," she says.

By the time you get back to your office, you have an e-mail containing a list of all the topics you covered in the meeting. It's time to create a sprint backlog.

Creating a Sprint Backlog

Because it's time for a new sprint, it's time to create a new backlog for it. Based on your conversation with Claudia, you come up with the following backlog:

1. Create a series of admin controllers (in their own folder).

2. Secure those controllers and build a login form on the public side.

3. Create a new model for admin users.

4. Create controllers and views to administer those users.

5. Expand, as needed, the models for orders, products, and categories.

6. Create a dashboard view.

7. Create CRUD (create, review, update, delete) screens for products and categories.

8. Create import and export functions for products and categories.

9. Add an easy way to assign products to categories and groups in batch mode.

There's a lot to do, but now that you understand how models, views, and controllers work, there isn't anything too complicated about any of it.

The first step is creating a secure set of controllers, a model for users, and a login form to access it all.

Creating a Rudimentary Admin Framework

One of the great things about CodeIgniter controllers is that they can be organized into folders. This adds only one more URI segment to your activity but keeps related controllers together. In the following sections, you build out some administrative controllers related to orders, products, categories, and admin users, all of which reside in a folder called *admin*.

This way, once a user logs in, he will be directed to work in the admin/products controller or the admin/categories controller (depending on his task), and each set of controller tasks can be kept separate and organized.

The best thing about this arrangement is that you can continue to work with the same models as before, extending them as needed (although you'll find that many of the models you wrote for the public side of the site are just as useful in the admin context).

The first step in working up a series of admin controllers is to organize your work into folders and controllers, followed by thinking about an administrative framework you can employ. This framework needs to be fairly secure and should involve a new model and database table (for users) and a login form and verification process that sets some kind of global variable needed to access the admin controllers and views.

Before you get too involved with all that, it's time to organize your admin controllers.

Using Folders to Organize Controllers

When you're building a more complex series of interrelated controllers, it's often a good idea to organize those controllers into folders. In your case, you want to create an admin subfolder in the /system/ application/controllers folder, as illustrated in Figure 6-1.

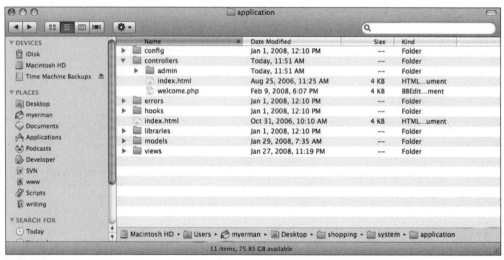

Figure 6-1

In this folder, you'll create several placeholder controllers:

❑   dashboard.php

❑   products.php

❑   categories.php

❑   admins.php

Just make them bare-bones controllers for now. You'll get back to them presently. Remember to use session_start() in each of them, as you'll be using PHP sessions for authentication when administrators log in.

Here's a basic controller stub for admin/dashboard:

```
class Dashboard extends Controller {
  function Dashboard(){
    parent::Controller();
    session_start();
  }
}
```

And here's the basic controller stub for admin/products:

```
class Products extends Controller {
  function Products(){
    parent::Controller();
    session_start();
  }
}
```

Next is the basic controller stub for admin/categories:

```
class Categories extends Controller {
  function Categories(){
    parent::Controller();
    session_start();
  }
}
```

Finally, this is the basic controller stub for admin/admins:

```
class Admins extends Controller {
  function Admins(){
    parent::Controller();
    session_start();
  }
}
```

Creating the Login Mechanism

Before you can continue building out the administrative controllers, it's a good idea to create a login and verification process to allow admins access to the secure area.

The process is pretty simple. All you need to do is create a `login()` function in the Welcome controller and then tie it to a view and a model that will check for the proper administrative privileges. The model will, of course, need to be tied to a database table with information stored for each admin.

So before doing anything else, create a simple database table called *admins* that has ID, username, e-mail, password, and status fields. Make the status field an enum with two states, active and inactive. Also, make sure that both the username and e-mail fields are unique.

```
CREATE TABLE 'admins' (
'id' INT NOT NULL AUTO_INCREMENT ,
'username' VARCHAR( 16 ) NOT NULL ,
'email' VARCHAR( 255 ) NOT NULL ,
'status' ENUM( 'active', 'inactive' ) NOT NULL ,
'password' VARCHAR( 16 ) NOT NULL ,
PRIMARY KEY ( 'id' ) ,
UNIQUE (
'username' ,
'email'
)
);
```

At this point, you're noticing that the password field in the admins table is storing plaintext passwords. You also notice that the login feature in this chapter is created without a bit of encryption or other protections.

Although you are introduced to a lot of this in Chapter 9, in this chapter, you build out the user admin area of the dashboard and incorporate some security measures there to keep passwords secure.

Once you have the database table built, use phpMyAdmin or another tool to create an administrative account for Claudia. You'll be using the account credentials to gain access, so keep it simple for now. A good suggestion would be to use a username of *admin* with a password of *kids*.

Now that the table is built, create a model for admins called *MAdmins* in the /system/application/ models/ folder. At this moment, all you need is a single function in that model — one that verifies the existence of an active admin with a certain username and password.

If a user successfully logs in, you want to set some PHP session data (like the user's ID and username) for use at a later time — for example, to display on the admin dashboard or for checking to make sure she has the right to be in the admin dashboard without having to requery the database.

```
class MAdmins extends Model{

  function MAdmins(){
    parent::Model();
  }


  function verifyUser($u,$pw){
    $this->db->select('id,username');
    $this->db->where('username',$u);
    $this->db->where('password', $pw);
    $this->db->where('status', 'active');
    $this->db->limit(1);
    $Q = $this->db->get('admins');
    if ($Q->num_rows() > 0){
      $row = $Q->row_array();
      $_SESSION['userid'] = $row['id'];
      $_SESSION['username'] = $row['username'];
    }else{
```

```
          $this->session->set_flashdata('error', Sorry, your username or password is
              incorrect!');
      }
   }

}
```

Notice that the `verifyUser()` function stores an error message in CodeIgniter's flash data if there is no match on the query. You'll use these flash data to display the error in case the user mistypes her username or password.

Don't forget to add MAdmins to the list of models that get autoloaded! Simply edit the list in /system/application/config/autoload.php.

```
$autoload['model'] = array('MCats','MProducts','MOrders','MAdmins');
```

Now that you have the table built and the corresponding model hooked up to it, it's time to create a basic `verify()` function in the Welcome controller.

You use the `verify()` function to do several things:

1. First, you check to see if there are any incoming POST data.

2. If there are incoming POST data, take the username and password field information and send it to the `verifyUser()` function of the MAdmins model.

3. Once that process has run, check to see if there is a value in the userID session variable that is greater than 0. If so, redirect the user to the admin/dashboard controller.

4. Otherwise, show the login view.

Here's the new controller function:

```
function verify(){
   if ($this->input->post('username')){
      $u = $this->input->post('username');
      $pw = $this->input->post('password');
      $this->MAdmins->verifyUser($u,$pw);
      if ($_SESSION['userid'] > 0){
         redirect('admin/dashboard','refresh');
      }
   }
   $data['main'] = 'login';
   $data['title'] = "Claudia's Kids | Admin Login";
   $data['navlist'] = $this->MCats->getCategoriesNav();
   $this->load->vars($data);
   $this->load->view('template',$data);
}
```

Next comes the login view. This will be just a simple form that prompts the user for a username and password and then posts to welcome/verify, where the entered credentials can be verified.

```
<div id='pleft'>
<h2>Please login to Access the Dashboard</h2>
<?php
if ($this->session->flashdata('error')){
   echo "<div class='message'>";
   echo $this->session->flashdata('error');
   echo "</div>";
}
?>
<?php
$udata = array('name'=>'username','id'=>'u','size'=>15);
$pdata = array('name'=>'password','id'=>'p','size'=>15);


echo form_open("welcome/verify");
echo "<p><label for='u'>Username</label><br/>";
echo form_input($udata) . "</p>";
echo "<p><label for='p'>Password</label><br/>";
echo form_password($pdata) . "</p>";
echo form_submit('submit','login');
echo form_close();
?>
</div>
```

When you're finished, you should have something similar to Figure 6-2.

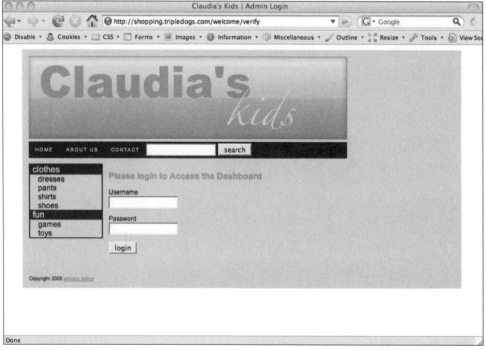

Figure 6-2

If you were to attempt to log in, you'd only see a blank page. That's because you still haven't built out the dashboard controller in the admin folder. That's in the next section. But before doing that, take a moment and add a "dashboard" link to the footer view, making it possible for admins to log in from anywhere on the site:

```
Copyright <?php echo date("Y"); ?>
<?php echo anchor("welcome/privacy","privacy policy");?>
   
<?php echo anchor("welcome/verify","dashboard");?>
```

Creating the Home Page of the Admin Panel

Now it's time to create a home page in the administrative dashboard. The process for creating this home page will be extremely similar to the process you underwent to create the pages on the public side.

The first step is to create an index() function in the admin/dashboard controller. Once you've got that in place, you will need some kind of admin template view that you can use to call all of your administrative subviews that are included within it.

Instead of reusing the templates that are used on the public side, it's probably a good idea to create a generic-looking administrative UI that has fewer moving parts — but you can decide all of that in a minute. The first step is to create the index() function.

```
function index(){
    $data['title'] = "Dashboard Home";
    $data['main'] = 'admin_home';
    $this->load->vars($data);
    $this->load->view('dashboard');
}
```

As you can see, the index() function here is nothing much to look at. It has a title, it loads a view called *dashboard*, and it looks like you're going to use a subview called *admin_home* at some point. There are no model functions called here, because nothing on the dashboard page is dynamic at this point. That may change, of course, but then all you have to do is call the model functions you need.

One more thing needs to be done before you can move on. Remember that you're setting a PHP session variable called userid if they successfully log in. You need to set a quick check for that variable at the top of the controller, like this:

```
function Dashboard(){
    parent::Controller();
    session_start();
    if ($_SESSION['userid'] < 1){
        redirect('welcome/verify','refresh');
    }
}
```

What about the views? The first is the dashboard view. This view will be very similar to the main template view you've been using on the public side, except that you won't use quite as much of the look and feel. In fact, you'll be using a different CSS file.

153

Here's what the dashboard view looks like, from an HTML markup and PHP code standpoint:

```
<!DOCTYPE html PUBLIC "-//W3C//DTD XHTML 1.0 Strict//EN"
        "http://www.w3.org/TR/xhtml1/DTD/xhtml1-strict.dtd">
<html xmlns="http://www.w3.org/1999/xhtml" xml:lang="en" lang="en">
<head>
  <meta http-equiv="content-type" content="text/html; charset=utf-8" />
  <title><?php echo $title; ?></title>
<link href="<?= base_url();?>css/admin.css" rel="stylesheet" type="text/css" />
<script type="text/javascript">
//<![CDATA[
base_url = '<?= base_url();?>';
//]]>
</script>
<script type="text/javascript" src="<?php echo
            base_url();?>js/prototype.js"></script>
<script type="text/javascript" src="<?php echo base_url();?>js/scriptaculous.js"
            ></script>
<script type="text/javascript" src="<?php echo base_url();?>js/customtools.js"
            ></script>
</head>
<body>
<div id="wrapper">
  <div id="header">
  <?php $this->load->view('admin_header');?>
  </div>

  <div id="main">
  <?php $this->load->view($main);?>
  </div>

  <div id="footer">
  <?php $this->load->view('admin_footer');?>
  </div>
</div>
</body>
</html>
```

There are a few things to note about this view.

1. You will need to create an admin.css file for use on the admin dashboard.

2. You will need to create an admin_header subview.

3. You will also need to create an admin_footer subview.

4. The dashboard view has no need for a navigation subview.

5. You will also need an admin_home subview to show anything on the dashboard index.

Creating the admin_header View

The easiest thing to do right now is to create the admin_header view. All you need is something similar to the global navigation on the public side (e.g., the horizontal UL list). Each item in the list contains a link to a different part of the administrative area, plus a link to allow the user to log out.

```
<div id='globalnav'>
<ul>
<li><?php echo anchor("admin/dashboard/index","dashboard");?></li>
<li><?php echo anchor("admin/categories/","categories");?></li>
<li><?php echo anchor("admin/products/", "products");?></li>
<li><?php echo anchor("admin/admins/", "users");?></li>
<li><?php echo anchor("admin/dashboard/logout/", "logout");?></li>
</ul>
</div>
```

Creating the admin_footer View

The admin_footer subview is even simpler: just a simple copyright notice. If more is needed later, you can easily update it.

```
Copyright <?php echo date("Y"); ?>
```

Creating the admin.css File

The admin.css file is just a much simpler version of the CSS instructions on the public side of the web site. You might notice that these CSS instructions create a "drab" look and feel. Some people feel that the admin side should look more like the public side. Others believe that the admin side should look as different as possible from the public side, so that no one is ever confused as to where he is, and what he's doing. For the purposes of this book, the latter approach is taken.

There's no need to have a #nav div or any of that category/subcategory navigation. Also, there's no need for flashy colors or complex div layouts. Grays and blacks are fine here, as are tables for data display, as you'll have a lot of that.

Here is the entire admin.css file:

```
body{
   background-color:white;
   font-family: Arial, Verdana, sans-serif;
   margin:0;
   padding:0;
}

#wrapper{
   width:800px;
   margin:10px auto;
   padding:10px;
   background-color:#fff;
   border:2px solid #ccc;
}
```

```
h1 {
   font-size:1.2em;
   color:#999;
}

h2{
   font-size:1em;
   color:#999;
}

h3{
   font-size:.9em;
   color:#999;
}

 h4{
  margin-top:0px;
  margin-bottom:0px;
  font-size:.8em;
  color:#999;
}

p,li,td{
   font-size:.8em;
}

 a,a:link{
   color:#999;
   text-decoration:underline;

}
a:hover{
   color:#ccc;
}

 #main{
    margin-left:10px;
    width:700px;
    height:auto;
}

#header{
    font-size:12px;
    margin-bottom:10px;
}
```

```
#footer{
    clear:both;
    padding-top:40px;
    font-size:9px;
}

.message{
  border:1px solid #c98c21;
  background-color:#efdda8;
  color:#c98c21;
  padding:5px;
  width:250px;
  font-size:12px;
  margin:5px 0px 5px 0px;
}

.floatleft{
  float:left;
}

.floatright{
  float:right;
}


/* navigation */

#globalnav {
  width: 700px;
  height:30px;
  margin: 2px 0 10px 0;
  padding: 0;
  background: #ccc;
}

#globalnav ul {
  margin: 0;
  padding: 0;
  list-style: none;
}

#globalnav li {
  float: left;
  margin: 0;
  padding: 0;
  font-size: 80%;
  letter-spacing: 2px;
  text-transform: uppercase;
}
```

```
#globalnav li a {
  float: left;
  padding: 10px 12px;
  text-decoration: none;
  color: #999;
  border: none;
}

#globalnav li form{
  padding:3px 0px;
}
```

Creating a Basic admin_home View

Now that the basic admin template is built along with the supporting header and footer subviews and the CSS, it's time to create a basic view that will allow the administrative user to quickly access all the tools available to them.

At first, this may seem a bit silly because links in the global nav seem to be doing the same thing. This is really an opportunity to provide some context on those links. For your purposes, a bullet list with bold links and a bit of explanation will do just fine. Again, you'll make good use of the anchor() function.

```
<ul>
<li><b><?php echo anchor("admin/categories/","Manage Categories");?>.</b>
<br/>
Create, edit, delete and manage product categories on your online store.
</li>
<br/>
<li><b><?php echo anchor("admin/products/","Manage Products");?>.</b>
<br/>
Create, edit, delete and manage products on your online store.
</li>
<br/>

<li><b><?php echo anchor("admin/admins/","Manage Users");?>.</b>
<br/>
Create, edit, delete and manage users who can access this dashboard.
</li>
<br/>

<li><b><?php echo anchor("admin/dashboard/logout/","Logout");?>.</b>
<br/>
Exit this dashboard when you're done.
</li>
<br/>
</ul>
```

When you're all done, upload your files and log in to the dashboard. You should see a home page that is similar to what's pictured in Figure 6-3.

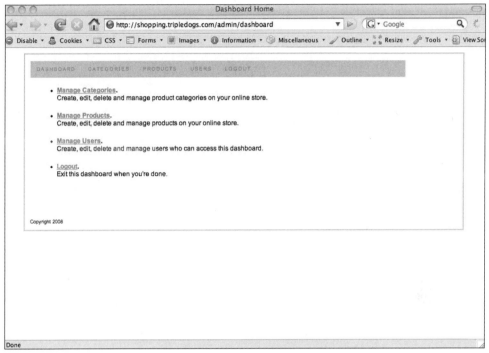

Figure 6-3

It's certainly not flashy, but it's functional and clean. Of course, if you were to click on any of those links, none of them would work, so it's time to start filling in the gaps in the system.

But before you do that, you will create a simple way to allow users to log out.

Creating a Logout Function

Creating a logout function is very easy. In this particular case, the logout links are pointed at admin/dashboard/logout. All you need to do then is create a `logout()` function in your admin/dashboard controller that destroys the CodeIgniter session and then redirects users back to the welcome/verify page.

```
function logout(){
  unset($_SESSION['userid']);
  unset($_SESSION['username']);
  $this->session->set_flashdata('error',"You've been logged out!");
  redirect('welcome/verify','refresh');
}
```

Now when an admin logs out, he or she should see an error message similar to the one pictured in Figure 6-4.

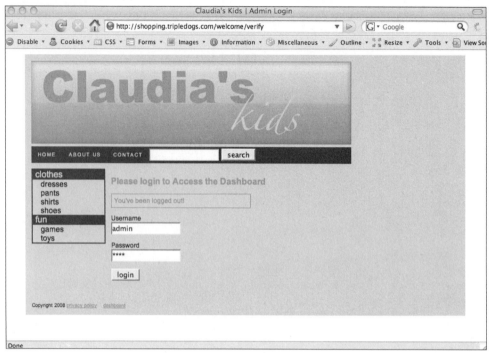

Figure 6-4

That's one bit of work that is out of the way. Now you can concentrate on the other parts of the admin tool.

Creating the Category Management Tools

In this section, you create all the pages that Claudia needs to manage categories. This involves adding some new functions to the admin/categories controller, adding a handful of functions to the existing MCats model, and creating three new views.

Creating the Category Home Page

The first step is creating the Category home page. In the admin/categories controller, create an index() function:

```
function index(){
    $data['title'] = "Manage Categories";
    $data['main'] = 'admin_cat_home';
    $data['categories'] = $this->MCats->getAllCategories();
    $this->load->vars($data);
    $this->load->view('dashboard');
}
```

There's nothing surprising here. You're merely calling up a list of categories using `getAllCategories()` and feeding it to a subview called admin_cat_home.

The admin_cat_home subview is also very simple. It loops through the category listing provided by the controller and prints out an ID, name, status, and a list of actions (edit and delete) for each one. Notice that this isn't anything terribly exciting or even complicated.

```php
<h1><?php echo $title;?></h1>
<p><?php echo anchor("admin/categories/create", "Create new category");?></p>
<?php
if ($this->session->flashdata('message')){
  echo "<div class='message'>".$this->session->flashdata('message')."</div>";
}
if (count($categories)){
  echo "<table border='1' cellspacing='0' cellpadding='3' width='400'>\n";
  echo "<tr valign='top'>\n";
  echo "<th>ID</th>\n<th>Name</th><th>Status</th><th>Actions</th>\n";
  echo "</tr>\n";
  foreach ($categories as $key => $list){
    echo "<tr valign='top'>\n";
    echo "<td>".$list['id']."</td>\n";
    echo "<td>".$list['name']."</td>\n";
    echo "<td align='center'>".$list['status']."</td>\n";
    echo "<td align='center'>";
    echo anchor('admin/categories/edit/'.$list['id'],'edit');
    echo " | ";
    echo anchor('admin/categories/delete/'.$list['id'],'delete');
    echo "</td>\n";
    echo "</tr>\n";
  }
  echo "</table>";
}
?>
```

At the top of the page there is a link that allows users to create a new category if needed. The use of flashdata is again in evidence. You'll use it very soon to display information from actions taken by the admin.

Before moving on to create that part of the application, take a look at your new page. It should look like Figure 6-5.

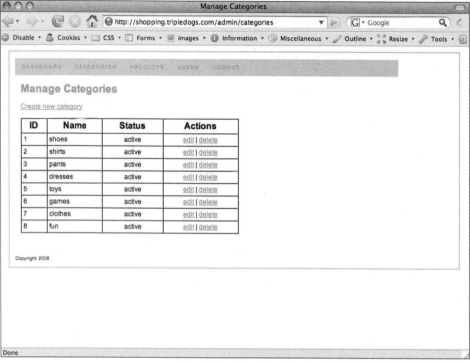

Figure 6-5

Creating the Category Create View

Now it's time to create a simple form that will allow Claudia to create a new category whenever she wants. Before jumping into the code, you have to know that this new create() function will pull double duty.

> If you need a quick reminder of how to build forms in CodeIgniter, refer to "The Form Helper" section in Chapter 3.

First, it checks to see if there are any incoming POST data (and specifically, a name field). If there are POST data, it runs the addCategory() function in the MCats model. You haven't created that function yet, but you will.

If no POST data are detected, it displays the dashboard view, loading the admin_cat_create view into $data['main']. Also, it loads the top-level categories using getTopCategories(). Don't worry — you haven't created this function yet.

Before you start working in the model to create those two functions, create your create() function:

```
function create(){
    if ($this->input->post('name')){
        $this->MCats->addCategory();
        $this->session->set_flashdata('message','Category created');
```

```
            redirect('admin/categories/index','refresh');
      }else{
        $data['title'] = "Create Category";
        $data['main'] = 'admin_cat_create';
        $data['categories'] = $this->MCats->getTopCategories();
        $this->load->vars($data);
        $this->load->view('dashboard');
      }
  }
```

OK, now it's time to create your two new functions in your model. The easiest one to deal with at the moment is the getTopCategories() function. Basically, you want to end up with an array that contains the topmost category (category 0, which represents the root of the category tree) and every category whose parentid is equal to 0.

```
function getTopCategories(){
    $data[0] = 'root';
    $this->db->where('parentid',0);
    $Q = $this->db->get('categories');
    if ($Q->num_rows() > 0){
      foreach ($Q->result_array() as $row){
        $data[$row['id']] = $row['name'];
      }
    }
    $Q->free_result();
    return $data;
}
```

The second function, addCategory(), is much more straightforward. All you have to do to add data to a table is load up a data array and then pass that array to $this->db->insert() along with a table name. Presto, your information is inserted.

Don't worry about database security at the moment. You'll be doing a pass in Chapter 9 that will take care of most of the problems you might encounter.

```
function addCategory(){
    $data = array(
      'name' => $_POST['name'],
      'shortdesc' => $_POST['shortdesc'],
      'longdesc' => $_POST['longdesc'],
      'status' => $_POST['status'],
      'parentid' => $_POST['parentid']
    );

    $this->db->insert('categories', $data);
}
```

A quick note here about security and validation. Normally, at this point, you would run each of these fields from the form through a validation process (to make sure they are the right length or hold the right data). In Chapter 9, you learn how to implement different methods for cleaning up this kind of user input. For now, with XSS Global Filtering turned on, you should rest easy enough.

Now that the controller and model have been updated, simply create the view with a form in it. The following code snippet uses the Form helper functions extensively. First, include a header so you pull in your title, and then open the form. Remember to post to admin/categories/create, as you're checking for POST data in that function. In other words, if there are no POST data, show this form. Otherwise, run the addCategory() function you just added to the model.

```
<h1><?php echo $title;?></h1>

<?php
echo form_open('admin/categories/create');
```

Then it's just a matter of adding form_input() fields for category name and shortdesc, and a form_textarea for longdesc.

```
echo "<p><label for='catname'>Name</label><br/>";
$data = array('name'=>'name','id'=>'catname','size'=>25);
echo form_input($data) ."</p>";

echo "<p><label for='short'>Short Description</label><br/>";
$data = array('name'=>'shortdesc','id'=>'short','size'=>40);
echo form_input($data) ."</p>";

echo "<p><label for='long'>Long Description</label><br/>";
$data = array('name'=>'longdesc','id'=>'long','rows'=>5, 'cols'=>'40');
echo form_textarea($data) ."</p>";
```

For status, feed in an array that holds the two available statuses (active and inactive).

```
echo "<p><label for='status'>Status</label><br/>";
$options = array('active' => 'active', 'inactive' => 'inactive');
echo form_dropdown('status',$options) ."</p>";
```

For parentid, use the incoming $categories array as the possible choices in the dropdown.

```
echo "<p><label for='parent'>Category Parent</label><br/>";
echo form_dropdown('parentid',$categories) ."</p>";
```

Finally, use form_submit() to add a Submit button, and close the form with form_close().

```
echo form_submit('submit','create category');
echo form_close();
?>
```

Your Category Create form should look a lot like Figure 6-6.

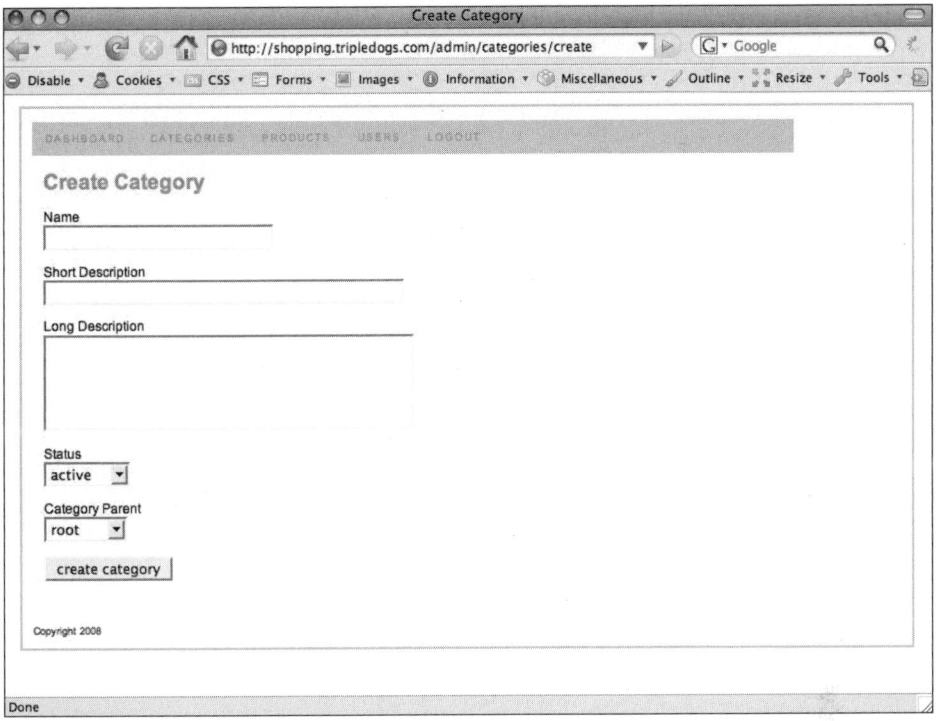

Figure 6-6

Go ahead and test the form by creating a new category. You should see a success message when you add the category.

Creating the Category Edit View

The edit category is pretty much just like the create category view, except you have to load the existing category information into the form and you perform an update on the table instead of an insert.

Taking it step-by-step, first update the controller with an `edit()` function:

```
function edit($id=0){
  if ($this->input->post('name')){
    $this->MCats->updateCategory();
    $this->session->set_flashdata('message','Category updated');
    redirect('admin/categories/index','refresh');
  }else{
    $data['title'] = "Edit Category";
    $data['main'] = 'admin_cat_edit';
    $data['category'] = $this->MCats->getCategory($id);
    $data['categories'] = $this->MCats->getTopCategories();
    $this->load->vars($data);
    $this->load->view('dashboard');
  }
}
```

Notice that the category ID is passed to the function as an argument. Also notice that its default state is 0. Why? Because this function does double duty, sometimes working off a URI segment and sometimes working from POST data. Since you've already built the `getTopCategories()` and `getCategory()` functions, there's nothing to do there. All you have to do is add an `updateCategory()` function to the MCats model.

In form and function, this function is very similar to the previous `addCategory()` function, except for the last two lines, where you set a `where` clause (limiting the forthcoming update to a certain category ID) and use `$this->db->update()` instead of `$this->db->insert()`.

```php
function updateCategory(){
  $data = array(
    'name' => $_POST['name'],
    'shortdesc' => $_POST['shortdesc'],
    'longdesc' => $_POST['longdesc'],
    'status' => $_POST['status'],
    'parentid' => $_POST['parentid']

  );

  $this->db->where('id', $_POST['id']);
  $this->db->update('categories', $data);

}
```

Next, build the Edit form. All you really have to do is use the Create form as your model, but remember that you have to make three small changes. First, make sure it posts to the admin/categories/edit path. Second, make sure that you embed a hidden field with the category ID in it to make `updateCategory()` work right. Third, make sure that you load all the data from `$category` into the form fields.

```php
<h1><?php echo $title;?></h1>

<?php
echo form_open('admin/categories/edit');
echo "<p><label for='catname'>Name</label><br/>";
$data = array('name'=>'name','id'=>'catname','size'=>25, 'value' =>
            $category['name']);
echo form_input($data) ."</p>";

echo "<p><label for='short'>Short Description</label><br/>";
$data = array('name'=>'shortdesc','id'=>'short','size'=>40, 'value' =>
            $category['shortdesc']);
echo form_input($data) ."</p>";

echo "<p><label for='long'>Long Description</label><br/>";
$data = array('name'=>'longdesc','id'=>'long','rows'=>5, 'cols'=>'40', 'value' =>
            $category['longdesc']);
echo form_textarea($data) ."</p>";

echo "<p><label for='status'>Status</label><br/>";
$options = array('active' => 'active', 'inactive' => 'inactive');
echo form_dropdown('status',$options, $category['status']) ."</p>";
```

```
echo "<p><label for='parent'>Category Parent</label><br/>";
echo form_dropdown('parentid',$categories,$category['parentid']) ."</p>";

echo form_hidden('id',$category['id']);
echo form_submit('submit','update category');
echo form_close()
?>
```

Your Edit form should look something like Figure 6-7.

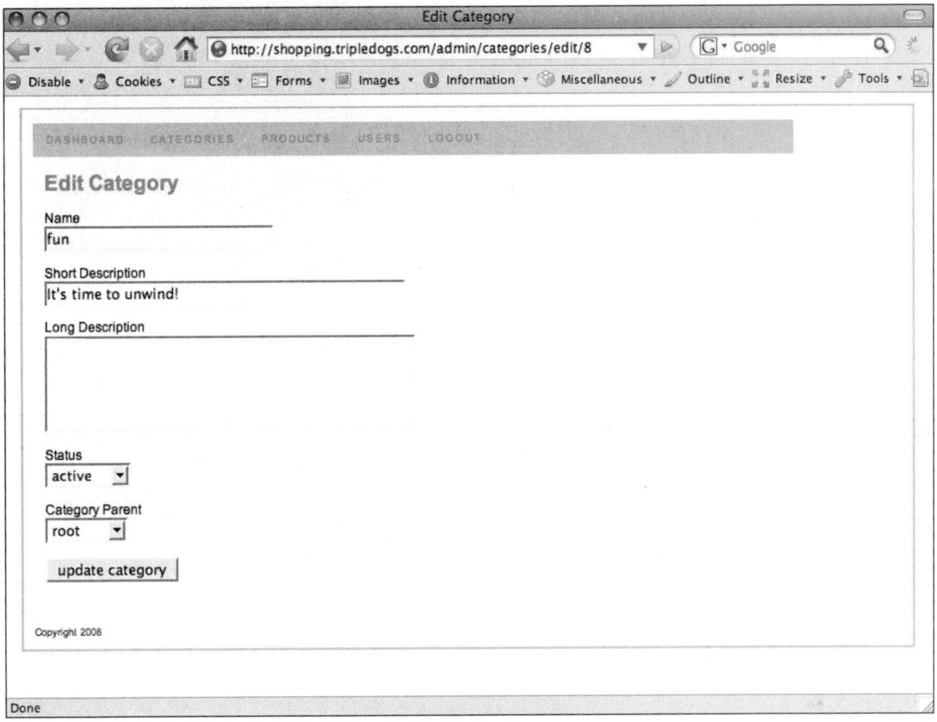

Figure 6-7

Creating the Category Delete Function

Deleting categories in the administrative tool is very simple: You're not really going to let admins delete categories, as this could cause all sorts of problems with products that are suddenly orphaned. Instead, you're only going to allow categories to be *inactivated*.

Deleting categories and possibly making orphans out of products deserves a richer discussion. Most of that discussion occurs in Chapter 7, in which we address possible orphans. For now, the code in this section will keep you moving down the path to your goal.

Start with the controller by creating a simple `delete()` function:

```
function delete($id){

    $this->MCats->deleteCategory($id);
    $this->session->set_flashdata('message','Category deleted');
    redirect('admin/categories/index','refresh');
}
```

Once more, you're pulling the category ID you need as an argument to the function, passing that ID to the `deleteCategory()` function in your MCats model, then redirecting the user back to the category index page.

Here's the `deleteCategory()` function. It is very simple — consisting of a query that sets a given category's status to inactive.

```
function deleteCategory($id){
    $data = array('status' => 'inactive');
    $this->db->where('id', $id);
    $this->db->update('categories', $data);
}
```

There's no view involved in this, but you should still see a status message, as pictured in Figure 6-8.

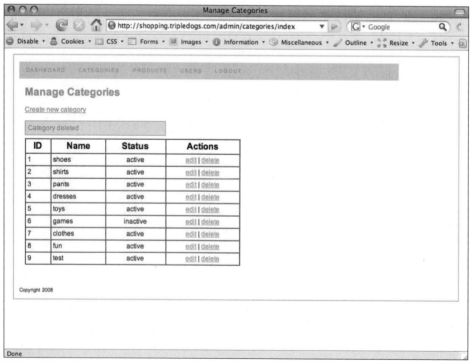

Figure 6-8

That's it! Claudia now has a working administrative tool that will let her manage her categories. Yes, there are some questions that have gone unanswered at this point (especially surrounding deleted categories and how to handle orphaned products), but it's good enough for now. Chapter 7 is where you figure out how to handle those little details.

It's time to create some Product management tools in the same vein.

Creating the Product Management Tools

By now you understand how to build out administrative screens with CodeIgniter, so it won't come as any surprise to you that by and large you'll be able to reuse the Category code you just wrote to expedite the creation of the products section.

Indeed, the only thing different about the Product tools is that you have to allow for the uploading of an image and a thumbnail for each product, but other than that, you're dealing with pretty much the same kind of information.

Creating the Product Home Page

Here's the `index()` function, which makes use of the MProducts model to retrieve all products:

```
function index(){
  $data['title'] = "Manage Products";
  $data['main'] = 'admin_product_home';
  $data['products'] = $this->MProducts->getAllProducts();
  $this->load->vars($data);
  $this->load->view('dashboard');
}
```

The admin_product_home view is pretty much the same as the admin_cat_home view, except that you're looping through a $products array instead of a $categories array.

```
<h1><?php echo $title;?></h1>
<p><?php echo anchor("admin/products/create", "Create new product");?></p>
<?php
if ($this->session->flashdata('message')){
  echo "<div class='message'>".$this->session->flashdata('message')."</div>";
}

if (count($products)){
  echo "<table border='1' cellspacing='0' cellpadding='3' width='400'>\n";
  echo "<tr valign='top'>\n";
  echo "<th>ID</th>\n<th>Name</th><th>Status</th><th>Actions</th>\n";
  echo "</tr>\n";
  foreach ($products as $key => $list){
    echo "<tr valign='top'>\n";
    echo "<td>".$list['id']."</td>\n";
    echo "<td>".$list['name']."</td>\n";
    echo "<td align='center'>".$list['status']."</td>\n";
```

```
        echo "<td align='center'>";
        echo anchor('admin/products/edit/'.$list['id'],'edit');
        echo " | ";
        echo anchor('admin/products/delete/'.$list['id'],'delete');
        echo "</td>\n";
        echo "</tr>\n";
    }
    echo "</table>";
}
?>
```

Without a lot of effort, then, you've created a product index page that replicates the functionality of the category index page. You should have something that looks somewhat like Figure 6-9.

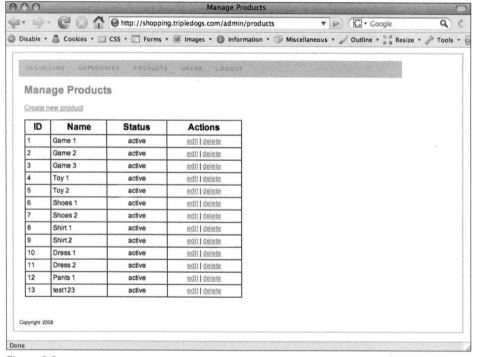

Figure 6-9

Creating the Product Create Page

The `create()` function of the admin/products controller is structurally similar to the `create()` function of the admin/categories controller. First, check for incoming POST data. If they exist, add the record to the database with an `addProduct()` model function, and return the user to the product home page.

If no POST data are detected, show the form, but along the way, gather up all subcategories eligible for product assignment with an MCats model function named `getCategoriesDropDown()`. You'll build this function and the other function you need in a minute. First, here's the `create()` function for your controller.

```
function create(){
  if ($this->input->post('name')){
    $this->MProducts->addProduct();
    $this->session->set_flashdata('message','Product created');
    redirect('admin/products/index','refresh');
  }else{
    $data['title'] = "Create Product";
    $data['main'] = 'admin_product_create';
    $data['categories'] = $this->MCats->getCategoriesDropDown();
    $this->load->vars($data);
    $this->load->view('dashboard');
  }
}
```

The `addProduct()` function in the MProducts model is a little more complicated than the `addCategory()` function you created in the last section, and for one good reason: You have to upload an image and a thumbnail.

The first part of the function is extremely straightforward, as you are expecting a series of POST fields from a form, fields like: name, shortdesc, and so on. These are extremely easy to gather and populate a data array with:

```
function addProduct(){
  $data = array(
  'name' => $_POST['name'],
  'shortdesc' => $_POST['shortdesc'],
  'longdesc' => $_POST['longdesc'],
  'status' => $_POST['status'],
  'grouping' => $_POST['grouping'],
  'category_id' => $_POST['category_id'],
  'featured' => $_POST['featured'],
  'price' => $_POST['price']

  );
```

Next, to enable file uploads, you need to do a bit of configuration work. Using a `$config` array, set values for upload_path (where you expect images to be stored), allowed_types (to restrict the types of files that can be uploaded), max_size, and so on, and then load the upload library.

Please note that you must set the upload_path folder to be writable for any of this to work! Checking on that and making sure it is writable will save you a lot of time.

```
$config['upload_path'] = './images/';
$config['allowed_types'] = 'gif|jpg|png';
$config['max_size'] = '200';
$config['remove_spaces'] = true;
$config['overwrite'] = false;
$config['max_width']  = '0';
$config['max_height']  = '0';
$this->load->library('upload', $config);
```

After you've configured and loaded the upload library, use the `do_upload()` method to upload whatever files are designated in the form fields named *image* and *thumbnail*. Once the files have been uploaded, add their path information into the `$data` array you've already started at the top of the function.

```
if(!$this->upload->do_upload('image')){
$this->upload->display_errors();
exit();
}
$image = $this->upload->data();

if ($image['file_name']){
$data['image'] = "/images/".$image['file_name'];
}

if(!$this->upload->do_upload('thumbnail')){
$this->upload->display_errors();
exit();
}
$thumb = $this->upload->data();

if ($thumb['file_name']){
$data['thumbnail'] = "/images/".$thumb['file_name'];
}
```

Now, use the `$this->db->insert()` method to add the data record to the products table.

```
$this->db->insert('products', $data);
}
```

All that's left to do now is to create a simple admin_product_create view, which is essentially a multi-part form. You will need to use the `form_open_multipart()` function to support file uploads.

```
<h1><?php echo $title;?></h1>

<?php
echo form_open_multipart('admin/products/create');
```

Next, step through the usual list of suspects to print out dropdowns and text fields for category_id, name, shortdesc, and longdesc.

```
echo "<p><label for='parent'>Category</label><br/>";
echo form_dropdown('category_id',$categories) ."</p>";

echo "<p><label for='pname'>Name</label><br/>";
$data = array('name'=>'name','id'=>'pname','size'=>25);
echo form_input($data) ."</p>";

echo "<p><label for='short'>Short Description</label><br/>";
$data = array('name'=>'shortdesc','id'=>'short','size'=>40);
echo form_input($data) ."</p>";

echo "<p><label for='long'>Long Description</label><br/>";
$data = array('name'=>'longdesc','id'=>'long','rows'=>5, 'cols'=>'40');
echo form_textarea($data) ."</p>";
```

Don't forget to use `form_upload()` to designate file upload fields for image and thumbnail. Your back-end process is expecting files from these two fields.

```
echo "<p><label for='uimage'>Upload Image</label><br/>";
$data = array('name'=>'image','id'=>'uimage');
echo form_upload($data) ."</p>";

echo "<p><label for='uthumb'>Upload Thumbnail</label><br/>";
$data = array('name'=>'thumbnail','id'=>'uthumb');
echo form_upload($data) ."</p>";

echo "<p><label for='status'>Status</label><br/>";
$options = array('active' => 'active', 'inactive' => 'inactive');
echo form_dropdown('status',$options) ."</p>";
```

Finally, wrap up your form with any remaining fields and a `form_submit()` and `form_close()`.

```
echo "<p><label for='group'>Grouping</label><br/>";
$data = array('name'=>'grouping','id'=>'group','size'=>10);
echo form_input($data) ."</p>";

echo "<p><label for='price'>Price</label><br/>";
$data = array('name'=>'price','id'=>'price','size'=>10);
echo form_input($data) ."</p>";

echo "<p><label for='featured'>Featured?</label><br/>";
$options = array('true' => 'true', 'false' => 'false');
echo form_dropdown('featured',$options) ."</p>";

echo form_submit('submit','create product');
echo form_close();
?>
```

Your product creation form should look somewhat like Figure 6-10.

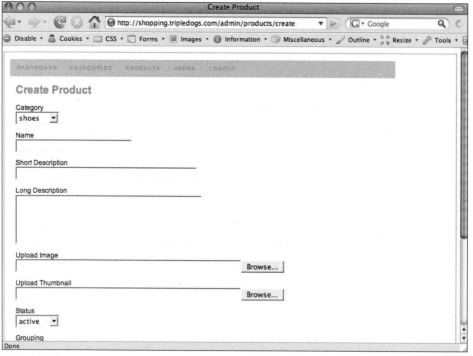

Figure 6-10

Creating the Product Edit Page

The edit() function of the admin/products controller is pretty much a clone of the create() process, except that you have to load in the existing product information. Without further ado, here's the edit() function itself:

```
function edit($id=0){
    if ($this->input->post('name')){
        $this->MProducts->updateProduct();
        $this->session->set_flashdata('message','Product updated');
        redirect('admin/products/index','refresh');
    }else{

        $data['title'] = "Edit Product";
        $data['main'] = 'admin_product_edit';
        $data['product'] = $this->MProducts->getProduct($id);
        $data['categories'] = $this->MCats->getCategoriesDropDown();
        $this->load->vars($data);
        $this->load->view('dashboard');
    }
}
```

In this case, you only have to create one new MProducts function, one called `updateProduct()`. It is very much like the `addProduct()` function except that it performs a SQL update instead of a SQL insert.

```php
function updateProduct(){
  $data = array(
    'name' => $_POST['name'],
    'shortdesc' => $_POST['shortdesc'],
    'longdesc' => $_POST['longdesc'],
    'status' => $_POST['status'],
    'grouping' => $_POST['grouping'],
    'category_id' => $_POST['category_id'],
    'featured' => $_POST['featured'],
    'price' => $_POST['price']

  );
  $config['upload_path'] = './images/';
  $config['allowed_types'] = 'gif|jpg|png';
  $config['max_size'] = '200';
  $config['remove_spaces'] = true;
  $config['overwrite'] = false;
  $config['max_width'] = '0';
  $config['max_height'] = '0';
  $this->load->library('upload', $config);

  if(!$this->upload->do_upload('image')){
    $this->upload->display_errors();
    exit();
  }
  $image = $this->upload->data();

  if ($image['file_name']){
    $data['image'] = "/images/".$image['file_name'];
  }

  if(!$this->upload->do_upload('thumbnail')){
    $this->upload->display_errors();
    exit();
  }
  $thumb = $this->upload->data();

  if ($thumb['file_name']){
    $data['thumbnail'] = "/images/".$thumb['file_name'];
  }
  $this->db->where('id', $_POST['id']);
  $this->db->update('products', $data);
}
```

Again, please make sure that the folder designated by upload_path is writable!

Finally, here's the admin_product_edit view, which in many regards is the same form as admin_product_create, except it posts to a different controller function (admin/products/edit), contains a hidden field with the product ID (needed by the `updateProduct()` function!), and loads values from the database for that particular product into the form fields.

```php
<h1><?php echo $title;?></h1>

<?php
echo form_open_multipart('admin/products/edit');

echo "<p><label for='parent'>Category</label><br/>";
echo form_dropdown('category_id',$categories,$product['category_id']) ."</p>";

echo "<p><label for='pname'>Name</label><br/>";
$data = array('name'=>'name','id'=>'pname','size'=>25, 'value' =>
            $product['name']);
echo form_input($data) ."</p>";

echo "<p><label for='short'>Short Description</label><br/>";
$data = array('name'=>'shortdesc','id'=>'short','size'=>40, 'value' =>
            $product['shortdesc']);
echo form_input($data) ."</p>";

echo "<p><label for='long'>Long Description</label><br/>";
$data = array('name'=>'longdesc','id'=>'long','rows'=>5, 'cols'=>'40', 'value' =>
            $product['longdesc']);
echo form_textarea($data) ."</p>";

echo "<p><label for='uimage'>Upload Image</label><br/>";
$data = array('name'=>'image','id'=>'uimage');
echo form_upload($data) ."<br/>Current image: ". $product['image']."</p>";

echo "<p><label for='uthumb'>Upload Thumbnail</label><br/>";
$data = array('name'=>'thumbnail','id'=>'uthumb');
echo form_upload($data) ."<br/>Current thumbnail: ". $product['thumbnail']."</p>";

echo "<p><label for='status'>Status</label><br/>";
$options = array('active' => 'active', 'inactive' => 'inactive');
echo form_dropdown('status',$options, $product['status']) ."</p>";

echo "<p><label for='group'>Grouping</label><br/>";
$data = array('name'=>'grouping','id'=>'group','size'=>10, 'value' =>
            $product['grouping']);
echo form_input($data) ."</p>";

echo "<p><label for='price'>Price</label><br/>";
$data = array('name'=>'price','id'=>'price','size'=>10, 'value' =>
            $product['price']);
echo form_input($data) ."</p>";

echo "<p><label for='featured'>Featured?</label><br/>";
$options = array('true' => 'true', 'false' => 'false');
echo form_dropdown('featured',$options, $product['featured']) ."</p>";

echo form_hidden('id',$product['id']);
echo form_submit('submit','update product');
echo form_close();
?>
```

Your Edit form should look like Figure 6-11 when all is said and done.

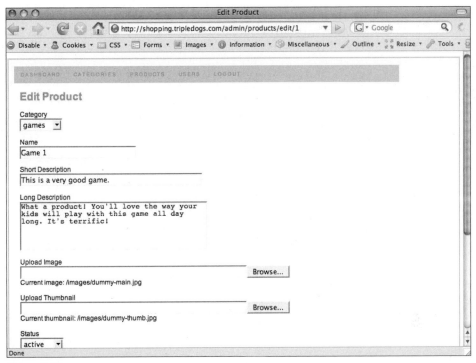

Figure 6-11

Creating the Product Delete Function

The product delete process will be as simple as the category delete function. Instead of actually deleting a product (which might disrupt any number of ongoing shopping cart orders), you'll opt to set a particular product's status to "inactive."

Just as with the category `delete()` function, the product `delete()` function will take the fourth URI segment as a product ID, pass that ID to a model function called `deleteProduct()`, and then redirect the user to the product home page.

```
function delete($id){

  $this->MProducts->deleteProduct($id);
  $this->session->set_flashdata('message','Product deleted');
  redirect('admin/products/index','refresh');
}
```

The `deleteProduct()` function looks suspiciously like the `deleteCategory()` function created in the previous section. And it should, too, as it was basically copied and the table name changed to *products*.

```
function deleteProduct($id){
    $data = array('status' => 'inactive');
    $this->db->where('id', $id);
    $this->db->update('products', $data);
}
```

Creating the User Management Tools

Creating the User management tools will take the very same paths you took in creating Product and Category management tools. In fact, you should be able to copy and paste your controllers, models, and views, and with judicious name changing, create a basic framework in just a few minutes.

In fact, you already know a lot of what you'll need in your model right now, so you might as well build it out before you get started. For example, you know that you'll need a way to retrieve one and all users. You also need a way to add, update, and delete/deactivate a user.

Here's the complete MAdmins model (remembering that you created the `verifyUser()` function previously in the chapter). At this stage of the game, nothing in this model should be a surprise to you, as the functions are all the standard ones for retrieving, adding, and updating database records.

```
<?php

class MAdmins extends Model{

    function MAdmins(){
        parent::Model();
    }

    function verifyUser($u,$pw){
        $this->db->select('id,username');
        $this->db->where('username',$u);
        $this->db->where('password', $pw);
        $this->db->where('status', 'active');
        $this->db->limit(1);
        $Q = $this->db->get('admins');
        if ($Q->num_rows() > 0){
            $row = $Q->row_array();
            $_SESSION['userid'] = $row['id'];
            $_SESSION['username'] = $row['username'];
        }else{
            $this->session->set_flashdata('error', 'Sorry, your username or password is
                incorrect!');
        }
    }

    function getUser($id){
        $data = array();
        $options = array('id' => $id);
```

```php
    $Q = $this->db->getwhere('admins',$options,1);
    if ($Q->num_rows() > 0){
      $data = $Q->row_array();
    }
    $Q->free_result();
    return $data;
  }

  function getAllUsers(){
    $data = array();
    $Q = $this->db->get('admins');
    if ($Q->num_rows() > 0){
    foreach ($Q->result_array() as $row){
      $data[] = $row;
    }
  }
  $Q->free_result();
  return $data;
  }


  function addUser(){
  $data = array('username' => $_POST['username'],
    'email' => $_POST['email'],
    'status' => $_POST['status'],
    'password' => $_POST['password']
  );
  $this->db->insert('admins',$data);
  }

  function updateUser(){
  $data = array('username' => $_POST['username'],
    'email' => $_POST['email'],
    'status' => $_POST['status'],
    'password' => $_POST['password']
  );
    $this->db->where('id',$_POST['id']);
    $this->db->update('admins',$data);
  }


  function deleteUser($id){
    $data = array('status' => 'inactive');
    $this->db->where('id', $id);
    $this->db->update('admins', $data);
  }
}
?>
```

Creating the User Home Page

The user home page is called with the `index()` function. Just as with the product and category home page, the function loads a view and provides a listing of all users (thanks to your MAdmins `getAllUsers()` function!) to that view.

```
function index(){
  $data['title'] = "Manage Users";
  $data['main'] = 'admin_admins_home';
  $data['admins'] = $this->MAdmins->getAllUsers();
  $this->load->vars($data);
  $this->load->view('dashboard');
}
```

The view itself, admin_admins_home, is pretty much a clone of the other home pages except that you'll be looping on the `$admins` array and using *username* instead of *name* while printing.

```
<h1><?php echo $title;?></h1>
<p><?php echo anchor("admin/admins/create", "Create new user");?>
<?php
if ($this->session->flashdata('message')){
  echo "<div class='message'>".$this->session->flashdata('message')."</div>";
}

if (count($admins)){
  echo "<table border='1' cellspacing='0' cellpadding='3' width='400'>\n";
  echo "<tr valign='top'>\n";
  echo "<th>ID</th>\n<th>Username</th><th>Status</th><th>Actions</th>\n";
  echo "</tr>\n";
  foreach ($admins as $key => $list){
    echo "<tr valign='top'>\n";
    echo "<td>".$list['id']."</td>\n";
    echo "<td>".$list['username']."</td>\n";
    echo "<td align='center'>".$list['status']."</td>\n";
    echo "<td align='center'>";
    echo anchor('admin/admins/edit/'.$list['id'],'edit');
    echo " | ";
    echo anchor('admin/admins/delete/'.$list['id'],'delete');
    echo "</td>\n";
    echo "</tr>\n";
  }
  echo "</table>";
}
?>
```

At the end of the process, your admin home page should look like Figure 6-12.

Figure 6-12

Creating the User Create Page

Here's the `create()` function for the admin/admins controller:

```
function create(){
  if ($this->input->post('username')){
    $this->MAdmins->addUser();
    $this->session->set_flashdata('message','User created');
    redirect('admin/admins/index','refresh');
  }else{
    $data['title'] = "Create User";
    $data['main'] = 'admin_admins_create';
    $this->load->vars($data);
    $this->load->view('dashboard');
  }
}
```

There's nothing new or fancy here. Check for POST data. If you see any, use the `addUser()` function to add the user. If not, show the admin_admins_create view. Here's that view — a simple form:

```
<h1><?php echo $title;?></h1>

<?php
echo form_open('admin/admins/edit');
```

```
echo "<p><label for='uname'>Username</label><br/>";
$data = array('name'=>'username','id'=>'uname','size'=>25,
        'value'=>$admin['username']);
echo form_input($data) ."</p>";

echo "<p><label for='email'>Email</label><br/>";
$data = array('name'=>'email','id'=>'email','size'=>50, 'value'=>$admin['email']);
echo form_input($data) ."</p>";

echo "<p><label for='pw'>Password</label><br/>";
$data = array('name'=>'password','id'=>'pw','size'=>25,
        'value'=>$admin['password']);
echo form_password($data) ."</p>";

echo "<p><label for='status'>Status</label><br/>";
$options = array('active' => 'active', 'inactive' => 'inactive');
echo form_dropdown('status',$options, $admin['status']) ."</p>";

echo form_hidden('id',$admin['id']);
echo form_submit('submit','update admin');
echo form_close();
?>
```

This form should look like Figure 6-13 when you're done.

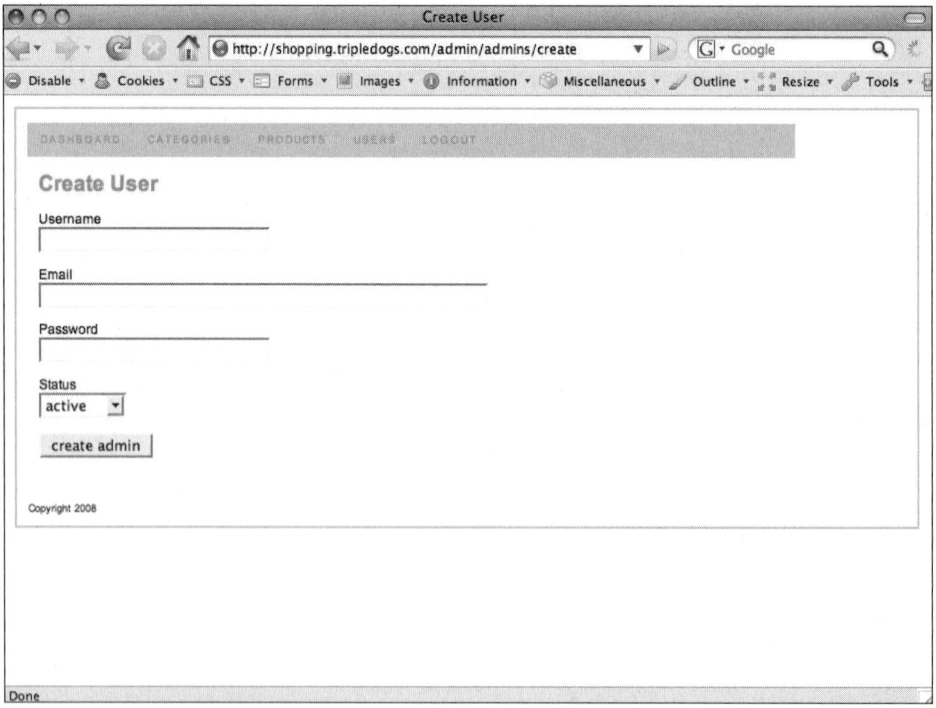

Figure 6-13

Creating the User Edit Page

Without belaboring the obvious, here's the `edit()` function in the admin/admins controller:

```
function edit($id=0){
  if ($this->input->post('username')){
    $this->MAdmins->updateUser();
    $this->session->set_flashdata('message','User updated');
    redirect('admin/admins/index','refresh');
  }else{
$data['title'] = "Edit User";
    $data['main'] = 'admin_admins_edit';
    $data['admin'] = $this->MAdmins->getUser($id);
    $this->load->vars($data);
    $this->load->view('dashboard');
  }
}
```

Very much the same thing is being done as in the other edit functions. Check for POST data. If you see any, run `updateUser()`, and redirect the user back to the admins home page. If you don't see any POST data, load the admin_admins_edit view.

The admin_admins_edit view is a simple form. The same rules apply for this Edit form as with all the rest.

```
<h1><?php echo $title;?></h1>

<?php
echo form_open('admin/admins/edit');
echo "<p><label for='uname'>Username</label><br/>";
$data = array('name'=>'username','id'=>'uname','size'=>25,
            'value'=>$admin['username']);
echo form_input($data) ."</p>";

echo "<p><label for='email'>Email</label><br/>";
$data = array('name'=>'email','id'=>'email','size'=>50, 'value'=>$admin['email']);
echo form_input($data) ."</p>";

echo "<p><label for='pw'>Password</label><br/>";
$data = array('name'=>'password','id'=>'pw','size'=>25,
            'value'=>$admin['password']);
echo form_password($data) ."</p>";

echo "<p><label for='status'>Status</label><br/>";
$options = array('active' => 'active', 'inactive' => 'inactive');
echo form_dropdown('status',$options, $admin['status']) ."</p>";

echo form_hidden('id',$admin['id']);
echo form_submit('submit','update admin');
echo form_close();
?>
```

When you're done working on the edit function, you should end up with something that looks like Figure 6-14.

Figure 6-14

Creating the Admin Delete Function

Finally, here's the `delete()` function in the admin/admins controller. Just as with products and categories, you've decided to set an admin user's status to inactive instead of deleting him.

```
function delete($id){

    $this->MAdmins->deleteUser($id);
    $this->session->set_flashdata('message','User deleted');
    redirect('admin/admins/index','refresh');
}
```

Securing Passwords

Security is one of those things that shouldn't wait for a refactoring iteration somewhere down the line. Why not? Because the call may come tomorrow to ship your code "stat," and if the application is working, it will likely ship with whatever gaping security holes you've left in it.

At this point, one of the biggest gaping security holes is the fact that the application deals with plaintext passwords. It stores plaintext passwords in the database, and it compares plaintext passwords provided by the user to whatever is stored in the database. Anyone who is able to break into the database will have a list of available user passwords that he can fool around with to his heart's content.

You're going to remedy that situation very quickly while you're working inside the user admin area. In fact, it's likely that you're already logged in, so none of this will impede your work in progress. If you're not already logged in, do so now. That way, none of the following work "locks you out" of the system.

The first thing you're going to do is add `dohash()` to your `addUser()` and `updateUser()` functions in the MAdmins model. The `dohash()` function uses SHA1 to encrypt a string (really, it's a hash, but the end result is a scrambled string) and is therefore ideal for obfuscating passwords in database storage.

In Chapter 3, you set a 32-character string as your encryption key in config.php. CodeIgniter will use this key as the salt for `dohash()`. *If you haven't set that key before this point, do so now.*

```
function addUser(){
  $data = array('username' => $_POST['username'],
                'email' => $_POST['email'],
                'status' => $_POST['status'],
                'password' => substr(dohash($_POST['password']),0,16)
  );
  $this->db->insert('admins',$data);
}

function updateUser(){
  $data = array('username' => $_POST['username'],
                'email' => $_POST['email'],
                'status' => $_POST['status'],
                'password' => substr(dohash($_POST['password']),0,16)
  );
  $this->db->where('id',id_clean($_POST['id']));
  $this->db->update('admins',$data);
}
```

Now that you have that change in your code, immediately edit the admin user and type **kids** into the password field, and click Submit. If you were to view the database record for that user in the database, you'd see that the password field contained a nonsense string of random characters.

Before leaving this topic, you have to do one more thing. You have to add the `dohash()` function to `verifyUser()`. The basic idea is very simple: Take the submitted password from the user and run `dohash()` on it. Then compare that value with the value stored in the database. If they match up, you have a legitimate password!

```
function verifyUser($u,$pw){
  $this->db->select('id,username');
  $this->db->where('username',$u);
  $this->db->where('password', substr(dohash($pw),0,16));
  $this->db->where('status', 'active');
  $this->db->limit(1);
  $Q = $this->db->get('admins');

  if ($Q->num_rows() > 0){
    $row = $Q->row_array();
    $_SESSION['userid'] = $row['id'];
```

```
        $_SESSION['username'] = $row['username'];
    }else{
        $this->session->set_flashdata('error', 'Sorry, your username or password is
            incorrect!');
    }
}
```

It's that simple to secure an application. Please note that in this particular application, you want to use `substr()` to cut your encrypted string down to a maximum of 16 characters, as that is the size of the password field you're using. The SHA1 hash process converts most strings to 32- or 64-length strings, and you want to compare the right things.

Revisiting the Sprint Backlog

You know there are still a few things left on your to-do list, but honestly you've completed a heck of a lot of work in a very short period of time. It's time to review the backlog to see how far you've come.

1. Create a series of admin controllers (in their own folder). **DONE.**

2. Secure those controllers and build a login form on the public side. **DONE.**

3. Create a new model for admin users. **DONE.**

4. Create controllers and views to administer those users. **DONE.**

5. Expand, as needed, the models for orders, products, and categories. **DONE.**

6. Create a dashboard view. **DONE.**

7. Create CRUD (create, review, update, delete) screens for products and categories. **DONE.**

8. Create import and export functions for products and categories.

9. Add an easy way to assign products to categories and groups in batch mode.

Conclusion

In this chapter, you built a series of basic administrative tools that allow Claudia the ability to manage her eCommerce site. In the next chapter, you will complete the two items left on the backlog and gather feedback from the client, who no doubt will have additional upgrades for you.

As you continue working with CodeIgniter, keep the following points in mind:

❑   It is entirely appropriate to organize controllers and views into folders.

❑   Creating forms that allow you to create or edit data is fairly simple, and once you create the first step, it's easy to create similar tools for other tables.

❑   It's always OK to work incrementally. Just because you don't have the perfect set of fields for a form, or you haven't applied security or validation, that shouldn't stop you dead in the water. The idea is to move quickly and provide the customer with working code.

❑   It's also quite all right to break your work up into logical patterns. Once you get the hang of building models, views, and controllers, you may find yourself building your controllers out of whole cloth, and then filling in what you need in your models and views to support those controllers. Other times, you may decide to build out your model in its entirety before creating controllers and views.

7

Improving the Dashboard

In Chapter 6, you built a rudimentary administrative dashboard that allows the client to manage categories, products, and other details on the site. In this chapter, you're add some more advanced functionality to the dashboard and also address some issues that have been lingering in the project. For example, what happens when you delete a category or product? What do you do about colors and sizes?

By the end of the chapter, you should have a fully functioning admin panel, with every item from the current sprint backlog addressed.

Batch Mode Operations

One of the more prominent items on the sprint backlog is allowing Claudia to assign categories and groupings to her products in batch mode. Access to such a tool would save her a lot of time, as the only way she can update these settings is by editing one product at a time.

The easiest way to add a batch mode process to the products home view is to make it into a form. You want to end up with one checkbox per product listing (using the product ID as the value of each checkbox), a dropdown list for category selection, and a text field that accepts a grouping string.

Once you have all that in the view, you'll create a specialized function in the products controller and a corresponding model function that will handle the updates for you. Then, all you have to do is post the form to that specialized controller function, and you have a batch mode operator!

In the following code, the form elements have been placed inside admin_products_home view. The bold lines represent new code.

```php
<h1><?php echo $title;?></h1>
<p><?php echo anchor("admin/products/create", "Create new product");?>
<?php
if ($this->session->flashdata('message')){
  echo "<div class='message'>".$this->session->flashdata('message')."</div>";
}

if (count($products)){
  echo form_open("admin/products/batchmode");
  echo "<p>Category: ". form_dropdown('category_id',$categories);
  echo " ";
  $data = array('name'=>'grouping','size'=>'10');
  echo "Grouping: ". form_input($data);
  echo form_submit("submit","batch update");
  echo "</p>";
  echo "<table border='1' cellspacing='0' cellpadding='3' width='500'>\n";
  echo "<tr valign='top'>\n";
  echo "<th> </th><th>ID</th>\n
        <th>Name</th>\n
        <th>Status</th>\n
        <th>Actions</th>\n";
  echo "</tr>\n";
  foreach ($products as $key => $list){
    echo "<tr valign='top'>\n";
    echo "<td align='center'>".form_checkbox('p_id[]',$list['id'],FALSE)."</td>";
    echo "<td>".$list['id']."</td>\n";
    echo "<td>".$list['name']."</td>\n";
    echo "<td align='center'>".$list['status']."</td>\n";
    echo "<td align='center'>";
    echo anchor('admin/products/edit/'.$list['id'],'edit');
    echo " | ";
    echo anchor('admin/products/delete/'.$list['id'],'delete');
    echo "</td>\n";
    echo "</tr>\n";
  }
  echo "</table>";
  echo form_close();
}
?>
```

Essentially, the form at the top of the view will post to a new controller function called `batchmode()`. The form will pass in an array of product IDs (captured from the `p_id` checkbox array), a category ID (from the category dropdown), and a grouping label (from the text field).

The important thing here is that each product ID embedded in a checkbox matches the product ID you're dealing with. This is easily handled by simply adding the checkbox as you loop through the `$products` array.

The grouping field is very simple — just give the user a little bit of space to type in a text string. You'll use that text string (along with a selected `category_id`) to update the products database.

To make the category dropdown work, you will need to update the `index()` function of the admin/ products controller. All you have to do is add one line, passing in a list of subcategory IDs and names. In fact, all you have to do is copy a similar line from the `edit()` function:

```
function index(){
  $data['title'] = "Manage Products";
  $data['main'] = 'admin_product_home';
  $data['products'] = $this->MProducts->getAllProducts();
  $data['categories'] = $this->MCats->getCategoriesDropDown();
  $this->load->vars($data);
  $this->load->view('dashboard');
}
```

The result should look a lot like Figure 7-1.

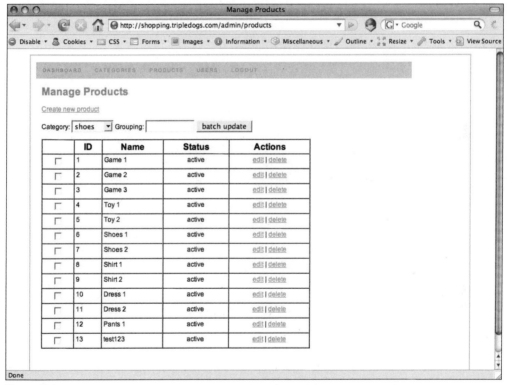

Figure 7-1

Now it's time to work on the `batchmode()` function. As you're dealing with several important pieces of data when you receive the form post, it might be a good idea to simply echo out what you receive. After you parse out the data array, you can write a better function.

Here's a simple `batchmode()` function that uses `print_r()` to reveal the structure and content of the incoming POST data:

```
function batchmode(){
    echo "<pre>";
    print_r($_POST);
    echo "</pre>";
}
```

If you go back to the form, enter some test data, check a few boxes, and click the Submit button, you might see the following array on the screen:

```
Array
(
    [category_id] => 1
    [grouping] => testing
    [submit] => batch update
    [p_id] => Array
        (
            [0] => 1
            [1] => 2
            [2] => 3
        )
)
```

In other words, when you eventually pass along this array to the MProducts model, you're going to give it a distinct category ID, a grouping, and an array of product IDs.

Keeping all of that in mind, rewrite the `batchmode()` function like so:

```
function batchmode(){
    $this->MProducts->batchUpdate();
    redirect('admin/products/index','refresh');
}
```

All you have to do now is create the `batchUpdate()` function in the MProducts model. The first thing this function must do is make sure that there are actually products to update. You can do that easily enough by using `count()` against the incoming `p_id` array.

If your count comes up 0, then use `flashdata()` to set an appropriate message, but don't actually perform any database updates.

```
function batchUpdate(){
    if (count($this->input->post('p_id'))){

    }else{
        $this->session->set_flashdata('message', 'Nothing to update!');
    }
}
```

If there are incoming product IDs to work with, you want to create a `$data` array that will hold the `category_id` and grouping data from the form. Then you want to extract the values of the `p_id` array with `array_values()` and `implode()` (using the comma as a glue) and feed that list to the `$this->db->where()` method.

Here's the whole `batchUpdate()` function:

```
function batchUpdate(){
    if (count($this->input->post('p_id'))){
        $data = array('category_id' => $this->input->post('category_id'),
                      'grouping' => $this->input->post('grouping')
        );
        $idlist = implode(",",array_values($this->input->post('p_id')));
        $where = "id in ($idlist)";
        $this->db->where($where);
        $this->db->update('products',$data);
        $this->session->set_flashdata('message', 'Products updated');
    }else{
        $this->session->set_flashdata('message', 'Nothing to update!');
    }
}
```

At this point, feel free to test out your new functionality. Notice that this batch update entirely replaces the `category_id` and grouping fields for the selected products. In other words, if certain products already have settings, this batch mode process will overwrite what's there.

When you submit your form results, you should see something similar to Figure 7-2.

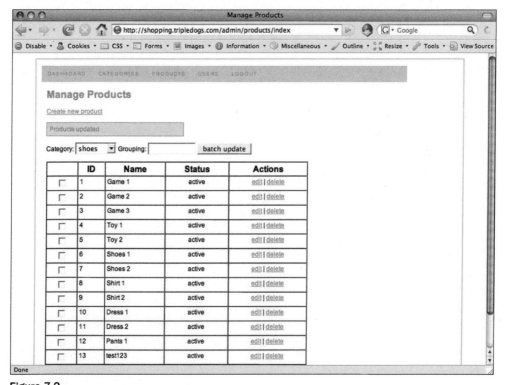

Figure 7-2

If you edit any of the products you processed, you'll see that the category and grouping fields were updated. In short order, you've addressed an important issue and made life for Claudia and her staffers a lot easier. It's time to move on to the import/export features.

Importing and Exporting

Importing and exporting data are crucial to any application's success. They give the customer more power and flexibility than you can provide with just a web application alone. Why? Because many business applications are intimately tied to spreadsheets, and being able to accept data (and output data) in CSV (comma-separated values) or TSV (tab-separated values) format can make life better for the user along various dimensions. For example, if Claudia had to upload 100 products into her product inventory one at a time, that would be very time-consuming. On the other hand, if she could export a CSV file from Excel and then import that file, she might be able to get all 100 products into the system with one pass, thus saving her a great deal of time and effort.

In this section, you first build an export function for Categories and then take what you've learned and do the same thing for Products. Once all that is done, you will do the slightly harder work of importing data from a spreadsheet into the Products table.

Creating an Export Function for Categories

In this example, you're going to start with the model. Why? Because in CodeIgniter 1.6 and higher, you have access to a very neat tool called dbutil. Its formal name is the Database Utility Class.

What does it do? It's a class that helps you manage your database. The methods found in the class help you list databases, optimize and repair tables, back up your database, and export in both CSV and XML formats. It's the ability to export in CSV format that you care about the most at the moment.

To invoke this class, simply call it:

```
$this->load->dbutil();
```

Once the class is loaded, you can then call the methods like this:

```
$this->dbutil->csv_from_result();
```

Now it's time to create the exporter for categories. Open the MCats model and create an exportCsv() function. The first thing you need to do in this function is load the Database Utility Class:

```
function exportCsv(){
   $this->load->dbutil();
}
```

Once you have it loaded, create a simple query that selects all data from the categories table. Why not just reuse one of the handy functions built in previous chapters (like getAllCategories())? Well, you really don't need that much horsepower in this case — particularly as those other functions create neat arrays that are ready for further processing.

All you need in this instance is a result set object, which you hand off to the `csv_from_result()` method. That's the first argument. The second argument is the field delimiter (the default is tab, but you'll want to set a comma). You want to set a comma because it's the comma that makes it a comma-separated file, as opposed to a tab-separated file. The third argument is the record delimiter (a good suggestion is "\n"). You want to set a new line ("\n") as this is pretty much the universally agreed notation for "new record." It's much easier to process each line of data that way with PHP when you import the file.

Here's the completed `exportCsv()` function:

```
function exportCsv(){
  $this->load->dbutil();
  $Q = $this->db->query("select * from categories");
  return $this->dbutil->csv_from_result($Q,",","\n");
}
```

Please note that `csv_from_result()` doesn't actually create a file, just a CSV string of text. To create a downloadable file, you'll need to do some work in the appropriate controller.

Speaking of which, let's turn our attention to the admin/categories controller. Again, you'll need to build a new function, one called `export()`.This function is also pretty simple, but it has two very important jobs. First, it must call the new model function, capturing the CSV string in a variable. Then it must invoke the `force_download()` feature of the Download helper to create a file that is downloaded to the user's desktop or laptop.

The `force_download()` function is described in Chapter 3. It's basically a very useful CodeIgniter helper function that writes the headers in such a way that the data you create get captured in a file. Of course, along the way you need to also provide the function with a filename (in this case, *category_export .csv*).

Here's the `export()` function in all its six-line glory. If you have written export functions in the past, please note that all of this was accomplished with 11 lines of code (five in the model, six in the controller).

```
function export(){
  $this->load->helper('download');
  $csv = $this->MCats->exportCsv();
  $name = "category_export.csv";
  force_download($name,$csv);

}
```

What's left to do? You need to add a link to the admin_categories_home view that will invoke the controller function. A good place for it is next to the Create link. That part of the view is presented below.

```
<h1><?php echo $title;?></h1>
<p><?php echo anchor("admin/categories/create", "Create new category");?> | <?php
echo anchor("admin/categories/export","Export");?></p>
```

When you run the test by clicking the Export link, you should see a download dialog appear, as depicted in Figure 7-3.

Figure 7-3

If you have a spreadsheet tool (like Numbers on the Mac or the more ubiquitous Excel), you should be able to open the CSV file and see results similar to Figure 7-4.

	A	B	C	D	E	F	G
1	id	name	shortdesc	longdesc	status	parentid	
2		1 shoes	Shoes for boys and girls.		active	7	
3		2 shirts	Shirts and blouses.		active	7	
4		3 pants	Stylish, durable pants for	active		7	
5		4 dresses	Pretty dresses for the appl	active		7	
6		5 toys	Toys that are fun and men	active		8	
7		6 games	Fun for the whole family.		active	8	
8		7 clothes	Clothes for school and pla	active		0	
9		8 fun	It's time to unwind!		active	0	
10		9 test	testing	Testing!!!!	inactive	0	
11							
12							
13							
14							

Figure 7-4

Notice that you could go back and refine this export by sorting by certain fields, but at the end of the day you have to ask yourself, "Why bother?" After all, you're exporting the data in a spreadsheet-friendly way, so any further sorting and filtering can be done in the spreadsheet.

Creating an Export Function for Products

Creating the export function for Products is going to follow pretty much the same path you took with Categories. In fact, it's very much exactly the same, except that your URLs will differ slightly, as will your SQL query. As there aren't that many differences, there's no point belaboring the obvious.

Here's the `exportCsv()` function that gets added to the MProducts model:

```
function exportCsv(){
  $this->load->dbutil();
  $Q = $this->db->query("select * from products");
  return $this->dbutil->csv_from_result($Q,",","\n");
}
```

Please note that the SQL query is now pulling from the Products table.

Here's the controller function `export()` in admin/products:

```
function export(){
  $this->load->helper('download');
  $csv = $this->MProducts->exportCsv();
  $name = "product_export.csv";
  force_download($name,$csv);
}
```

Again, all you're doing is calling the model function and then piping that data into `force_download()`.

Finally, here's the link inserted into the admin_products_home view:

```
<p><?php echo anchor("admin/products/create", "Create new product");?> | <?php echo
anchor("admin/products/export","Export");?></p>
```

Go ahead and give the Export link a test. You should see a download dialog box appear, and it should feature "product_export.csv" as the filename, as shown in Figure 7-5.

Figure 7-5

Importing a CSV Import Library for Products

As hinted at above, building an import function takes a lot more work than just exporting. Why is that? Well, the short answer is that you are accepting data from a user, and users can make mistakes. They might not line up their data columns right. Or they might not give you the kind of data you're expecting — for example, you may be expecting a `category_id` field, but they give you the name of a category.

There's enough complexity in this kind of application that you may be sorely tempted to find a third-party CSV import tool and add it to your libraries and helpers. In point of fact, a class called CSVReader can be found in the CodeIgniter wiki area, and you're going to use the basic functionality provided by this class to facilitate your efforts. CSVReader was authored by Pierre Jean Turpeau and is available at the following URL: www.codeigniter.com/wiki/CSVReader. Essentially, this library allows you to parse either CSV text or CSV in a file (which naturally needs to be uploaded first or already be on the file system) and return an array of data that can be uploaded into a database table. When you download it, add it to the /system/application/libraries folder, which will keep the libraries for this particular CodeIgniter application separate from the core libraries.

Before continuing, though, it might be helpful to cover some of the ground rules of using custom libraries:

- ❏ The filename you use must be capitalized. (The library you're using is CSVReader.php.)
- ❏ Class declarations must also be capitalized (e.g., class CSVReader()).
- ❏ Class names and filenames must match.
- ❏ Custom libraries should be stored in /system/application/libraries to keep them separate from the core CodeIgniter libraries.

Once you've installed a library, you can load it in the familiar way:

```
$this->load->library('CSVReader');
```

Any methods can be called using arrow notation and the lowercase library name:

```
$this->csvreader->parseFile($path);
```

Please note that you will probably want to change the default separator from ";" to "," in this particular library. If you don't change it, the CSVReader library will try to split your data on the ";" character. Since you're exporting comma-separated data, that wouldn't work very well for you.

Now that you've installed a third-party library, it's time to get to work. The best way to approach this problem is to start with the admin_products_home view first. You're going to add a very simple form to the top of that view that will allow an administrator to upload a CSV file.

```php
<h1><?php echo $title;?></h1>
<p><?php echo anchor("admin/products/create", "Create new product");?>
        | <?php echo anchor("admin/products/export","Export");?></p>

<?php
echo form_open_multipart("admin/products/import");
$data = array('name' => 'csvfile', 'size'=>15);
echo form_upload($data);
echo form_hidden('csvinit',true);
echo form_submit('submit','IMPORT');
echo form_close();
?>
```

The form should look something like Figure 7-6.

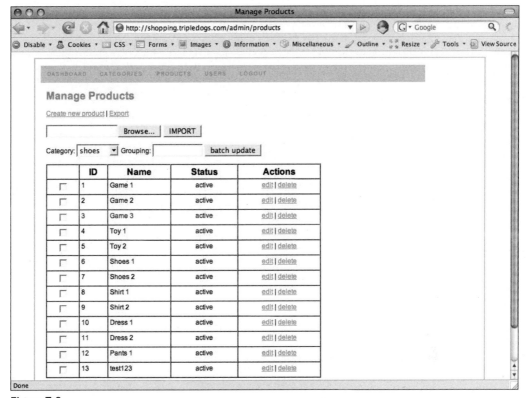

Figure 7-6

The next part is where you start using the CSVReader library. You're going to add an importCsv() function to the MProducts model. In this function, you're going to load two libraries: upload and CSVReader. You're going to upload the CSV files into the /tmp directory and use the parseFile() method to parse the document and return an array of data.

```
function importCsv(){
  $config['upload_path'] = '/tmp/';
  $config['allowed_types'] = 'csv';
  $config['max_size'] = '2000';
  $config['remove_spaces'] = true;
  $config['overwrite'] = true;
  $this->load->library('upload', $config);
  $this->load->library('CSVreader');

  if(!$this->upload->do_upload('csvfile')){
  $this->upload->display_errors();
  exit();
  }
  $csv = $this->upload->data();
  $path = $csv['full_path'];

  return $this->csvreader->parseFile($path);
}
```

Now it's time to work inside the admin/products controller. There you're going to create an `import()` function, which will test for the existence of a `csvinit` POST field. If it finds it, it will call the MProducts model, run the `importCsv()` function, and then pass that data over to a view. This constitutes a preview function so that users can be sure that they're uploading the proper data.

```php
function import(){
  if ($this->input->post('csvinit')){
    $data['csv'] = $this->MProducts->importCsv();
    $data['title'] = "Preview Import Data";
    $data['main'] = 'admin_product_csv';
    $this->load->vars($data);
    $this->load->view('dashboard');

  }elseif($this->input->post('csvgo')){

  }

}
```

Another small check here: If a different POST field is detected, one called `csvgo`, the system will commit the CSV data to the Products database table. You'll see more on that shortly. First, you need to build the admin_product_csv view.

The admin_product_csv view doesn't need to be complicated. All that's needed is to take the data from the parsed CSV lines and drop them all into a table, making sure that each table cell has an accompanying hidden field with the relevant data from the CSV file. At the end of the form, you add a hidden field that is named csvgo, and then you submit the entire thing back to the `import()` function.

What follows is the admin_product_csv view. The view opens with a simple check to make sure that the incoming $csv array has lines in it and then opens with a form post to admin/products/import. Notice that the form has a Cancel and a Submit button.

```php
<?php
if (count($csv)){
  echo form_open('admin/products/import');
  echo form_submit('cancel','<< start over');
  echo form_submit('submit','finalize import >>');
  ?>
```

After the preliminaries are finished, build the table header by looping through the first line of the $csv array. Trim out any white space, and ignore any thumbnail or image data. (The administrative users like Claudia or one of her employees can go back and upload images one at a time once they're done importing the CSV data.)

```php
<table border='1' cellspacing='0' cellpadding='5'>
<tr valign='top'>
<?php
$headers = array_keys($csv[0]);
  foreach ($headers as $v){
    $hdr = trim(str_replace('"','',$v));
    if ($hdr != '' && !eregi("thumbnail",$hdr) && !eregi("image",$hdr)){
```

```
        echo "<th>".$hdr."</th>\n";
      }
    }
  ?>
  </tr>
```

Next, loop through the entire $csv array, and print out any data you may find. Remember to trim for white space and create hidden form fields as you go. Also note that each hidden form field is an array whose key corresponds to the line number you're processing in the $csv array. This may sound confusing, but it will keep all your data neatly packaged when it comes time to process it. You want to end up with an array of elements, with line numbers for keys and the corresponding data for each line as the values. That way you can easily unpack what you need on the other side and have it match the incoming CSV data.

```php
<?php
foreach ($csv as $key => $line){
  echo "<tr valign='top'>\n";
  foreach ($line as $f => $d){
    $FIELD = trim(str_replace('"','',$f));
    $FDATA = trim(str_replace('"','',$d));
    if ($FIELD != '' && !eregi("thumbnail",$FDATA) && !eregi("image",$FDATA)){
      echo "<td>";
      echo $FDATA . "\n";
      echo form_hidden("line_$key"."[".$FIELD."]",$FDATA);
      echo "</td>\n";
    }
  }
  echo "</tr>\n";
}
?>
</table>
```

Don't forget to add the important csvgo hidden field. That way the import() function will know how to process the incoming request.

```php
<?php
  echo form_hidden('csvgo',true);
  echo form_close();
```

Finally, print out an error message if the incoming $csv array is empty.

```php
  }else{
    echo "<h1>We detected a problem...</h1>";
    echo "<p>No records to import! Please try again.</p>";
  }
?>
```

The result of all your efforts should look like Figure 7-7.

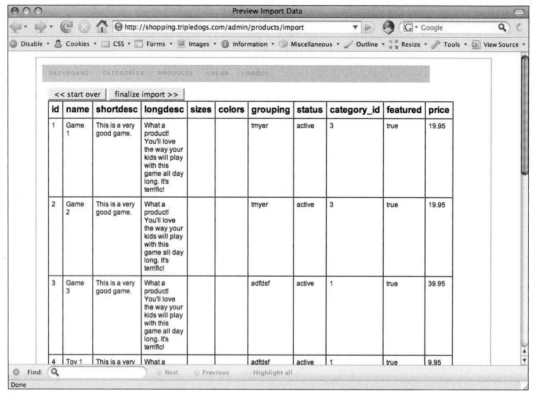

Figure 7-7

Now turn your attention to the data array that you end up with at the end of the process. Here's what a short snippet will look like, with each line number processed neatly into its fields:

```
Array
(
    [submit] => finalize import >>
    [line_0] => Array
    (
        [id] => 1
        [name] => Game 1
        [shortdesc] => This is a very good game.
        [longdesc] => What a product! You'll love the way your kids will play with
                this game all day long. It's terrific!
        [sizes] =>
        [colors] =>
        [grouping] => tmyer
        [status] => active
        [category_id] => 3
        [featured] => true
        [price] => 19.95
    )
)
```

```
[line_1] => Array
(
    [id] => 2
    [name] => Game 2
    [shortdesc] => This is a very good game.
    [longdesc] => What a product! You'll love the way your kids will play with
            this game all day long. It's terrific!
    [sizes] =>
    [colors] =>
    [grouping] => tmyer
    [status] => active
    [category_id] => 3
    [featured] => true
    [price] => 19.95
)
)...
```

It doesn't take too much of a leap to figure out how to send this data array to a special model function. Before you do that, of course, you have to know whether you're supposed to send the data on or the user has clicked "Start over."

Therefore, go back to your import() function and add another branch inside the elseif branch of the logic. Inside that branch, you'll check for the string "finalize" in the Submit button. If you find it, run a function called csv2db() (which you'll be building shortly) and use flash data to set a status update. If not, set a different message. At the end of the process, redirect the user to the admin/products/index page.

```
function import(){
    if ($this->input->post('csvinit')){
        $data['csv'] = $this->MProducts->importCsv();
        $data['title'] = "Preview Import Data";
        $data['main'] = 'admin_product_csv';
        $this->load->vars($data);
        $this->load->view('dashboard');

    }elseif($this->input->post('csvgo')){
        if (eregi("finalize", $this->input->post('submit'))){
            $this->MProducts->csv2db();
            $this->session->set_flashdata('message','CSV data imported');
        }else{
            $this->session->set_flashdata('message','CSV data import cancelled');
        }
        redirect('admin/products/index','refresh');
    }
}
```

The final part of the import feature is the MProducts function called csv2db(). This is an extremely simple function that loops through the data array and performs either an insert or update function, depending on whether it finds an ID field.

No further processing is necessary at that point, because the keys serve as database field names. As long as they match what's in the database, the data import will work. Remember to remove the submit and csvgo fields from the data stream!

```
function csv2db(){
  unset($_POST['submit']);
  unset($_POST['csvgo']);

  foreach ($_POST as $line => $data){
    if (isset($data['id'])){
      $this->db->where('id',$data['id']);
      unset($data['id']);
      $this->db->update('products',$data);
    }else{
      $this->db->insert('products',$data);
    }
  }
}
```

At the moment, you haven't added any checks in this process to protect the database from badly composed headers or field names that don't exist. All of these issues will be addressed in the security chapter.

As usual, the most complicated part of the entire process seems to be the view. The model and controller functions were very easy to put together. This is just another example of CodeIgniter providing power and flexibility without extreme complexity.

It's time for another client review.

The Client Review

When you walk Claudia through the new work you've done, she's ecstatic. She admits that the import and export features are rudimentary, but that they provide her with more than enough functionality to get started.

As pleased as you are with her reaction, you still need answers to various important questions.

"Claudia, I have some questions for you. These questions seem simple, but they're important to answer now before the site goes live."

"Go ahead," Claudia says, shrugging her shoulders.

So far, you've been able to handle just about everything that's come up, so you've built up a lot of good will and trust.

"The first question has to do with deleted categories," you say. "The system isn't really deleting categories, of course, just setting their status to 'inactive.' However, any top-level category that is inactive won't show any subcategories, even if they are live. And any products assigned to an inactive subcategory are also not going to show up on the site."

"I think it makes sense to keep live subcategories hidden if a top-level category is made inactive," Claudia says. "That way I can choose to hide an entire section of the site if there are problems, or if we're working on a bunch of price changes."

She thinks while you take notes. She's pondering the second issue, what to do with products of an inactive category.

"In the second case, would it be possible to tell the administrator if there are any products that are about to be orphaned, and then give them the opportunity to reassign those products?"

"Of course," you answer. "I can set it up such that all products can be reassigned to a single category, or, if you like, I can build a form that allows you to pick and choose where individual products go."

In the back of your mind, you start working out the solution for building a form to reassign individual products to different categories. Instead of giving the user a single choice for category reassignment, you'd provide a dropdown after each product, and key that dropdown to the product ID.

She thinks a little bit more and finally answers: "Ninety-nine percent of the time, we're going to be happy with reassigning all products from one category to another category, so I'm not too worried about picking and choosing. The user can always go back to the products home page and run a batch category assignment on those products."

You nod, knowing that the simplest approach almost always solves the problem. "That sounds great," you say, writing down notes. "Next on the agenda: What do we do with deleted products? Again, we're just deactivating them, but what happens if those products are in someone's Shopping Cart?"

"I don't think it would be smart at all to remove a product from somebody's order," Claudia says. "If it's in the order, let's allow them to keep it and check out."

"That's easy enough," you answer, taking notes. "If you change your mind later on, all I have to do is run a small query at checkout to make sure that all the product IDs in the Shopping Cart are still active. If we find anything amiss, we can warn the site visitor."

"Sounds good," Claudia says. "I really appreciate how easy you're making all of this, by the way."

"No problem. OK, the next question has to do with colors and sizes. I'm not sure what to do with these fields. We put them in at the beginning, but so far we're not storing data in them or using the data in any way."

"Well, it would be great if we could just assign colors and sizes to our products. Maybe with some checkboxes?"

"And would you like the ability to maintain what colors and sizes are available?"

Claudia nods. "That would be great. We wouldn't have to bug you for any updates then."

You laugh. "Yes, that would be good. One last question: This is in regard to user privileges in the dashboard. Are there certain users who might have access to just a few functions?"

Claudia thinks for a few seconds and finally shakes her head. "At this point, I trust my employees to do just about anything in the retail store, so it would be silly to restrict them on the online portion of the store. I'll be on it just about every day, so if I see anything strange, I can fix it."

"OK," you answer, "Time for me to get back to work!"

Of course, if Claudia had wanted to limit her employees' accessibility, you would handle the user privileges differently. The best way to handle user privileges is to create and administer user groups. Each group would have different modules assigned to it. That way you could easily assign different users to each group and provide yourself with a lot of flexibility. In other words, if Group A had access to modules 1, 2, and 3, and if User Y were assigned to Group A, he or she would have the right access. If you wanted to remove access to a particular group, you could shift the user to a different group, or drop a module from the group. In your database, your Groups table would have a primary key and a name. You would need a mapping table (to designate which modules could be accessed by which group), and you would need to add a group_id designator to a user (and then add a groups dropdown to the view on the appropriate admin screens).

Reassigning Products from Deleted Categories

Now that you've met with Claudia, you know how she wants to handle potentially orphaned products. Orphaned products come about as a natural result of deleting a "container" like a category. If the category goes away, what do you do with all the items that it is "holding"? Now that you know what Claudia's expectations are, it's an easy matter of adding a bit of processing to the end of the admin/ categories/delete function.

Here's a quick look at that function to refresh your memory:

```
function delete($id){
    $this->MCats->deleteCategory($id);
    $this->session->set_flashdata('message','Category deleted');
    redirect('admin/categories/index','refresh');
}
```

What you're going to need when you rewrite this function is some way to check for orphaned products. The best way to do that is to create a checkOrphans() function in the MCats model. This function accepts a category ID as its only argument and then returns an array of products that match that category_id.

```
function checkOrphans($id){
    $data = array();
    $this->db->select('id,name');
    $this->db->where('category_id',$id);
    $Q = $this->db->get('products');
        if ($Q->num_rows() > 0){
            foreach ($Q->result_array() as $row){
                $data[$row['id']] = $row['name'];
            }
        }
    $Q->free_result();
    return $data;
}
```

Now that you have this function in place, you can rewrite the `delete()` controller function.

```
function delete($id){
  $this->MCats->deleteCategory($id);
  $orphans = $this->MCats->checkOrphans($id);
  if (count($orphans)){
    $this->session->set_userdata('orphans',$orphans);
    redirect('admin/categories/reassign/'.$id,'refresh');
  }else{
    $this->session->set_flashdata('message','Category deleted');
    redirect('admin/categories/index','refresh');
  }
}
```

In other words, go ahead and run `deleteCategory()`, but then run a check on how many orphans were left behind. If none are detected, send the user back to the index page of categories as before. If you find orphans, store the information in a session variable and redirect to admin/categories/refresh.

Just as simple is the `reassign()` controller function. First, check to see if there are any POST data. If there are POST data, it means that the user has visited the admin_cat_reassign page and assigned the products to a new category. Run the `reassignProducts()` model function (you'll add it to the MProducts model shortly), and redirect the user to the category index with the appropriate message.

Otherwise, build the admin_cat_reassign view.

```
function reassign($id=0){
  if ($_POST){
    $this->MProducts->reassignProducts();
    $this->session->set_flashdata('message','Category deleted and products
        reassigned');
    redirect('admin/categories/index','refresh');
  }else{
    $data['category'] = $this->MCats->getCategory($id);
    $data['title'] = "Reassign Products";
    $data['main'] = 'admin_cat_reassign';
    $data['categories'] = $this->MCats->getCategoriesDropDown();
    $this->load->vars($data);
    $this->load->view('dashboard');
  }
}
```

The admin_cat_reassign view should simply list all the products that are about to be orphaned, and then provide the user with a simple dropdown box, so they can choose a new category. Remember to remove the ID of the category that is being deleted, of course — no sense in having that in the dropdown!

```
<h1><?php echo $title;?></h1>
<p>The following products are about to be orphaned. They used to belong to the
    <b><?php echo $category['name'];?></b> category, but now they need to be
    reassigned.</p>
```

207

```
<ul>
<?php
foreach ($this->session->userdata('orphans') as $id => $name){
  echo "<li>$name</li>\n";
}
?>
</ul>

<?php
echo form_open('admin/categories/reassign');
unset($categories[$category['id']]);
echo form_dropdown('categories',$categories);
echo form_submit('submit','reassign');
echo form_close();
?>
```

If you load all these changes into the system and then delete a category that contains orphaned products, you should see something like Figure 7-8.

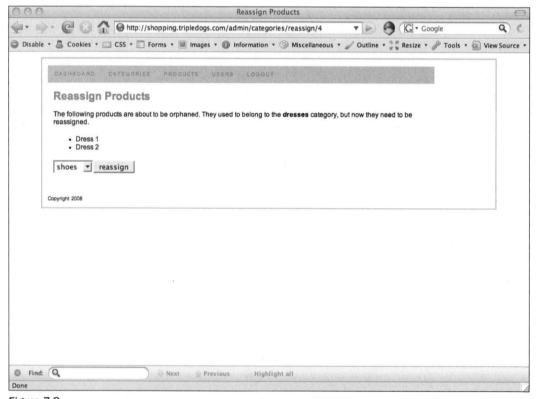

Figure 7-8

You're not done yet, though. You still need to create the MProducts function `reassignProducts()`. This function pulls the `category_id` from the incoming form POST data and converts the orphans session array into a comma-delimited list. From that you can create a WHERE...IN clause and update the Products table.

```
function reassignProducts(){
    $data = array('category_id' => $this->input->post('categories'));
    $idlist = implode(",",array_keys($this->session->userdata('orphans')));
    $where = "id in ($idlist)";
    $this->db->where($where);
    $this->db->update('products',$data);
}
```

Notice that this `reassignProducts()` function goes in the MProducts model. Even though you've been working with MCats for a while, don't be fooled. Keep related functions together — in this case, the relationship is with the database table products.

When you test this new workflow, you should see a message on the categories index that confirms the actions taken — in this case, the category was deleted, and its products were reassigned. The screen should look something like Figure 7-9.

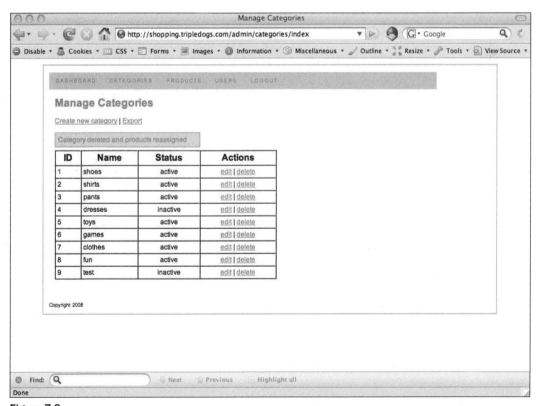

Figure 7-9

Reworking Colors and Sizes for Products

Reworking the way you're handling colors and sizes takes quite a bit of work. Ideally, you want to avoid these kinds of changes, but sometimes it is inevitable. This change has been left in here on purpose to show you how to handle this kind of situation in real life.

As you'll see, there's no need to panic, because CodeIgniter is flexible enough to let you rework just about any change, no matter how complex. Before you jump in, though, it's definitely worth the time to write out a list of all the changes that need to be made.

You will need to:

1. Create two new database tables, one for colors and the other for sizes. A good suggestion is to keep them simple, with ID, name, and status fields. You will also need mapping tables to store individual settings for each product.

2. Delete any references to the old product color/size fields. (Don't forget the MProducts model!)

3. Create two new models for your new tables, with simple functions that allow you to retrieve, add, edit, and deactivate colors and sizes.

4. Create the administrative functions for both colors and sizes.

5. Add color and size checkboxes to the product create/edit views.

6. Use the information in the mapping tables to display color and size data on the public side of the Shopping Cart.

Let's get to work.

Creating New Database Tables

You need to create four tables: colors, sizes, products_colors, and products_sizes. The first table, colors, has three fields: ID, name, and status.

```
CREATE TABLE 'colors' (
'id' INT NOT NULL AUTO_INCREMENT ,
'name' VARCHAR ( 32 ) NOT NULL ,
'status' ENUM( 'active', 'inactive' ) NOT NULL ,
PRIMARY KEY ( 'id' )
);
```

The sizes table is almost identical, except it has a different name:

```
CREATE TABLE 'sizes' (
'id' INT NOT NULL AUTO_INCREMENT ,
'name' VARCHAR ( 32 ) NOT NULL ,
'status' ENUM( 'active', 'inactive' ) NOT NULL ,
PRIMARY KEY ( 'id' )
);
```

The products_colors and products_sizes tables keep track of which selections have been made for any product. Remember, any given product can have multiple colors and sizes associated with it. Each of these tables needs to have one field that points back to products and another field that points back to either colors or sizes.

Here is the products_colors table. Notice that both the `product_id` and `color_id` fields are primary keys.

```
CREATE TABLE 'products_colors' (
'product_id' INT NOT NULL ,
'color_id' INT NOT NULL ,
PRIMARY KEY ( 'product_id' , 'color_id' )
);
```

And here is the products_sizes table:

```
CREATE TABLE 'products_sizes' (
'product_id' INT NOT NULL ,
'size_id' INT NOT NULL ,
PRIMARY KEY ( 'product_id' , 'size_id' )
);
```

Deleting References to Legacy Colors and Sizes

Now that you have your new tables, drop the colors and sizes fields from the Products table, and remove any references to these defunct fields in your MProducts model, particularly the `addProduct()` and `updateProduct()` functions.

```
ALTER TABLE 'products'
  DROP 'sizes',
  DROP 'colors';
```

Creating New Models

Right now, you're going to create two basic models without any functions in them just so you'll have them. Then you're going to add your two new models to the autoload list.

Here's the MColors model (/system/application/models/mcolors.php):

```php
<?php
class MColors extends Model{

  function MColors(){
    parent::Model();
  }
}//end class
?>
```

Here's the MSizes model (/system/application/models/msizes.php):

```php
<?php
class MSizes extends Model{

  function MSizes(){
    parent::Model();
  }
}//end class
?>
```

Finally, here's the updated `$autoload['model']` line from /system/application/config/autoload.php:

```php
$autoload['model'] = array('MCats', 'MProducts', 'MOrders', 'MAdmins',
'MSizes', 'MColors');
```

Creating Admin Screens for Colors

You're going to create a new Colors controller in the /system/application/controllers/admin folder. In almost every respect, it's going to be as simple as the admin/admins controller, so you might as well use the admin/admins controller as your guide.

First is the initial setup and check for security credentials:

```php
<?php

class Colors extends Controller {
  function Colors(){
    parent::Controller();
    session_start();

    if ($_SESSION['userid'] < 1){
      redirect('welcome/verify','refresh');
    }
  }
```

The `index()` function is extremely simple. All you want to do is show all the colors that are available in the colors database table.

```php
function index(){
  $data['title'] = "Manage Colors";
  $data['main'] = 'admin_colors_home';
  $data['colors'] = $this->MColors->getAllColors();
  $this->load->vars($data);
  $this->load->view('dashboard');
}
```

The `create()` function checks for POST data. If it finds POST data, it runs `createColor()`. Otherwise, it displays the admin_colors_create view. (To save time, you'll create all the model functions after you're done with the controller.)

```
function create(){
  if ($this->input->post('name')){
    $this->MColors->createColor();
    $this->session->set_flashdata('message','Color created');
    redirect('admin/colors/index','refresh');
  }else{
    $data['title'] = "Create Color";
    $data['main'] = 'admin_colors_create';
    $this->load->vars($data);
    $this->load->view('dashboard');
  }
}
```

Very similar things are in the `edit()` function. Notice the use of the `$id` argument to pull out the appropriate color from the colors database.

```
function edit($id=0){
  if ($this->input->post('name')){
    $this->MColors->updateColor();
    $this->session->set_flashdata('message','Color updated');
    redirect('admin/colors/index','refresh');
  }else{
    $data['title'] = "Edit Color";
    $data['main'] = 'admin_colors_edit';
    $data['color'] = $this->MColors->getColor($id);
    $this->load->vars($data);
    $this->load->view('dashboard');
  }
}
```

Finally, here's the `delete()` function. It also uses `$id` argument to act on the appropriate color ID.

```
function delete($id){
  $this->MColors->deleteColor($id);
  $this->session->set_flashdata('message','Color deleted');
  redirect('admin/colors/index','refresh');
}

}//end class
?>
```

Now it's time to create your MColors model functions. You're going to need `getColor()`, `getAllColors()`, `createColor()`, `updateColor()`, and `deleteColor()`. Because you've built similar functions in all of your models so far, they're shown on the next page without extraneous context.

For a good refresher on how such functions are built, see the section on "Creating the Category Management Tools" in Chapter 6.

```
function getColor($id){
  $data = array();
  $options = array('id' => $id);
  $Q = $this->db->getwhere('colors',$options,1);
  if ($Q->num_rows() > 0){
    $data = $Q->row_array();
  }

  $Q->free_result();
  return $data;
}

function getAllColors(){
  $data = array();
  $Q = $this->db->get('colors');
  if ($Q->num_rows() > 0){
    foreach ($Q->result_array() as $row){
      $data[] = $row;
    }
  }
  $Q->free_result();
  return $data;
}

function createColor(){
  $data = array(
 'name' => $_POST['name'],
    'status' => $_POST['status']
  );

  $this->db->insert('colors', $data);
}

function updateColor(){
  $data = array(
 'name' => $_POST['name'],
    'status' => $_POST['status']
  );

  $this->db->where('id', $_POST['id']);
  $this->db->update('colors', $data);
}

function deleteColor($id){
  $data = array('status' => 'inactive');
  $this->db->where('id', $id);
  $this->db->update('colors', $data);
}
```

While you're at it, create a `getActiveColors()` function as well. You need it shortly:

```
function getActiveColors(){
  $data = array();
  $this->db->select('id,name');
  $this->db->where('status','active');
  $Q = $this->db->get('colors');
  if ($Q->num_rows() > 0){
    foreach ($Q->result_array() as $row){
      $data[$row['id']] = $row['name'];
    }
  }
  $Q->free_result();
  return $data;
}
```

It's time to start creating views. The first is admin_colors_home. It's almost exactly the same as the admin_admins_home view, so just duplicate that one and make the necessary tweaks to point to colors-based views, controller functions, and data arrays.

```
<h1><?php echo $title;?></h1>
<p><?php echo anchor("admin/colors/create", "Create new color");?>
<?php
if ($this->session->flashdata('message')){
  echo "<div class='message'>".$this->session->flashdata('message')."</div>";
}

if (count($colors)){
  echo "<table border='1' cellspacing='0' cellpadding='3' width='400'>\n";
  echo "<tr valign='top'>\n";
  echo "<th>ID</th>\n<th>Name</th><th>Status</th><th>Actions</th>\n";
  echo "</tr>\n";
  foreach ($colors as $key => $list){
    echo "<tr valign='top'>\n";
    echo "<td>".$list['id']."</td>\n";
    echo "<td>".$list['name']."</td>\n";
    echo "<td align='center'>".$list['status']."</td>\n";
    echo "<td align='center'>";
    echo anchor('admin/colors/edit/'.$list['id'],'edit');
    echo " | ";
    echo anchor('admin/colors/delete/'.$list['id'],'delete');
    echo "</td>\n";
    echo "</tr>\n";
  }
  echo "</table>";
}
?>
```

If you were to load the admin/colors/index controller in your browser, you would see something similar to Figure 7-10.

Figure 7-10

There aren't any records in the table, but that's OK. You'll shortly be creating a view that will allow you to create colors, and then you'll use the form to populate the table.

The admin_colors_create view is about as simple as it gets. It is just a short form that prompts the user for a color name and status:

```php
<h1><?php echo $title;?></h1>

<?php
echo form_open('admin/colors/create');
echo "<p><label for='name'>Name</label><br/>";
$data = array('name'=>'name','id'=>'name','size'=>25);
echo form_input($data) ."</p>";

echo "<p><label for='status'>Status</label><br/>";
$options = array('active' => 'active', 'inactive' => 'inactive');
```

```
echo form_dropdown('status',$options) ."</p>";

echo form_submit('submit','create color');
echo form_close();
?>
```

If you click the "create color" link from the colors index, you should see a form similar to Figure 7-11.

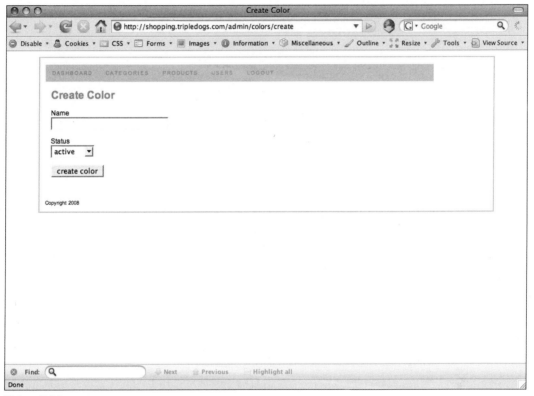

Figure 7-11

Now that you have a Create form, go ahead and create four basic colors: red, green, yellow, and blue. By the time you're done, you should have a colors index that looks like Figure 7-12.

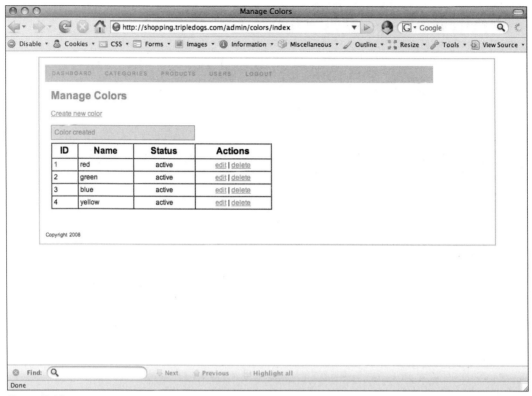

Figure 7-12

The admin_colors_edit view is jus as simple as the admin_colors_create view. Don't forget to pull in the data from `$color` and to embed a hidden color ID field.

```php
<h1><?php echo $title;?></h1>

<?php
echo form_open('admin/colors/edit');
echo "<p><label for='name'>Name</label><br/>";
$data = array('name'=>'name','id'=>'name','size'=>25, 'value'=>$color['name']);
echo form_input($data) ."</p>";

echo "<p><label for='status'>Status</label><br/>";
$options = array('active' => 'active', 'inactive' => 'inactive');
echo form_dropdown('status',$options, $color['status']) ."</p>";

echo form_hidden('id',$color['id']);
echo form_submit('submit','update color');
echo form_close();
?>
```

There's no need to show a screenshot of the Edit screen, as you've got the idea by now.

Don't forget to add links to Colors in the global navigation view (admin_header)! While you're at it, add a link in there for sizes, as that's next on the to-do list.

```
<div id='globalnav'>
<ul>
<li><?php echo anchor("admin/dashboard/index","dashboard");?></li>
<li><?php echo anchor("admin/categories/","categories");?></li>
<li><?php echo anchor("admin/products/", "products");?></li>
<li><?php echo anchor("admin/colors/", "colors");?></li>
<li><?php echo anchor("admin/sizes/", "sizes");?></li>
<li><?php echo anchor("admin/admins/", "users");?></li>
<li><?php echo anchor("admin/dashboard/logout/", "logout");?></li>
</ul>
</div>
```

One last bit of busywork: Add colors and sizes to the main dashboard view (admin_home):

```
<ul>
<li><b><?php echo anchor("admin/categories/","Manage Categories");?>.</b>
<br/>
Create, edit, delete and manage product categories on your online store.
</li>
<br/>
<li><b><?php echo anchor("admin/products/","Manage Products");?>.</b>
<br/>
Create, edit, delete and manage products on your online store.
</li>
<br/>

<li><b><?php echo anchor("admin/colors/","Manage Colors");?>.</b>
<br/>
Create, edit, delete and manage colors available to products.
</li>
<br/>

<li><b><?php echo anchor("admin/sizes/","Manage Sizes");?>.</b>
<br/>
Create, edit, delete and manage sizes available to products.
</li>
<br/>

<li><b><?php echo anchor("admin/admins/","Manage Users");?>.</b>
<br/>
Create, edit, delete and manage users who can access this dashboard.
</li>
<br/>

<li><b><?php echo anchor("admin/dashboard/logout/","Logout");?>.</b>
<br/>
Exit this dashboard when you're done.
</li>
<br/>
</ul>
```

When you're all done, your dashboard home page should look like Figure 7-13. Note the changes in the global navigation along the top, too.

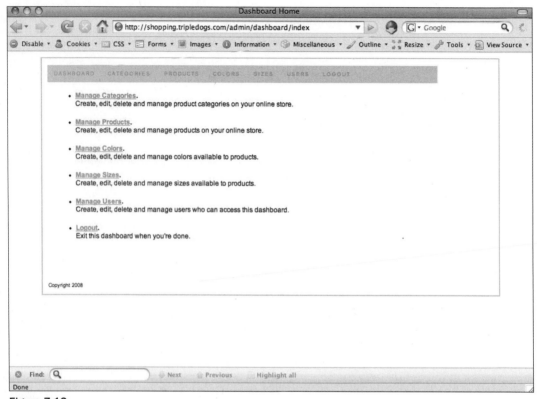

Figure 7-13

Creating Admin Screens for Sizes

Because the Sizes table is practically identical to the Colors table, you're going to be able to save a great deal of time in this section. All you have to do is copy the controller, model, and three view files you used for colors and repurpose them for sizes. Practically all you have to do is change out sizes for colors within the code, and you've got another working admin section.

For example, here is the admin/sizes controller. Please note that it is precisely identical in structure to the admin/colors controller, except it uses the sizes nomenclature for redirects, labeling, and model functions:

```php
<?php

class Sizes extends Controller {
  function Sizes(){
    parent::Controller();
```

```
    if ($this->session->userdata('userid') < 1){
      redirect('welcome/verify','refresh');
    }
  }


function index(){
  $data['title'] = "Manage Sizes";
  $data['main'] = 'admin_sizes_home';
  $data['sizes'] = $this->MSizes->getAllSizes();
  $this->load->vars($data);
  $this->load->view('dashboard');
}

function create(){
  if ($this->input->post('name')){
    $this->MSizes->createSize();
    $this->session->set_flashdata('message','Size created');
    redirect('admin/sizes/index','refresh');
  }else{
    $data['title'] = "Create Size";
    $data['main'] = 'admin_sizes_create';
    $this->load->vars($data);
    $this->load->view('dashboard');
  }
}

function edit($id=0){
  if ($this->input->post('name')){
    $this->MSizes->updateSize();
    $this->session->set_flashdata('message','Size updated');
    redirect('admin/sizes/index','refresh');
  }else{
    $data['title'] = "Edit Size";
    $data['main'] = 'admin_sizes_edit';
    $data['size'] = $this->MSizes->getSize($id);
    $this->load->vars($data);
    $this->load->view('dashboard');
  }
}

function delete($id){
  $this->MSizes->deleteSize($id);
  $this->session->set_flashdata('message','Size deleted');
  redirect('admin/sizes/index','refresh');
}
}//end class
?>
```

Without belaboring the obvious, here are all the MSizes model functions you will need. Again, nothing should strike you as out of the ordinary here.

```
function getSize($id){
  $data = array();
  $options = array('id' => $id);
  $Q = $this->db->getwhere('sizes',$options,1);
  if ($Q->num_rows() > 0){
    $data = $Q->row_array();
  }

  $Q->free_result();
  return $data;
}

function getAllSizes(){
  $data = array();
  $Q = $this->db->get('sizes');
  if ($Q->num_rows() > 0){
    foreach ($Q->result_array() as $row){
      $data[] = $row;
    }
  }
  $Q->free_result();
  return $data;
}

function getActiveSizes(){
  $data = array();
  $this->db->select('id,name');
  $this->db->where('status','active');
  $Q = $this->db->get('sizes');
  if ($Q->num_rows() > 0){
    foreach ($Q->result_array() as $row){
      $data[$row['id']] = $row['name'];
    }
  }
  $Q->free_result();
  return $data;
}

function createSize(){
  $data = array(
    'name' => $_POST['name'],
    'status' => $_POST['status']
  );

  $this->db->insert('sizes', $data);
}
```

```
function updateSize(){
  $data = array(
    'name' => $_POST['name'],
    'status' => $_POST['status']
  );

  $this->db->where('id', $_POST['id']);
  $this->db->update('sizes', $data);

}

function deleteSize($id){
  $data = array('status' => 'inactive');
  $this->db->where('id', $id);
  $this->db->update('sizes', $data);

}
```

Here's the admin_sizes_home view, precisely like colors except it uses the sizes nomenclature for data arrays and links:

```
<h1><?php echo $title;?></h1>
<p><?php echo anchor("admin/sizes/create", "Create new size");?>
<?php
if ($this->session->flashdata('message')){
    echo "<div class='message'>".$this->session->flashdata('message')."</div>";
}

if (count($sizes)){
    echo "<table border='1' cellspacing='0' cellpadding='3' width='400'>\n";
    echo "<tr valign='top'>\n";
    echo "<th>ID</th>\n<th>Name</th><th>Status</th><th>Actions</th>\n";
    echo "</tr>\n";
    foreach ($sizes as $key => $list){
      echo "<tr valign='top'>\n";
      echo "<td>".$list['id']."</td>\n";
      echo "<td>".$list['name']."</td>\n";
      echo "<td align='center'>".$list['status']."</td>\n";
      echo "<td align='center'>";
      echo anchor('admin/sizes/edit/'.$list['id'],'edit');
      echo " | ";
      echo anchor('admin/sizes/delete/'.$list['id'],'delete');
      echo "</td>\n";
      echo "</tr>\n";
    }
    echo "</table>";
}
?>
```

Here is the admin_sizes_create view:

```php
<h1><?php echo $title;?></h1>

<?php
echo form_open('admin/sizes/create');
echo "<p><label for='name'>Name</label><br/>";
$data = array('name'=>'name','id'=>'name','size'=>25);
echo form_input($data) ."</p>";

echo "<p><label for='status'>Status</label><br/>";
$options = array('active' => 'active', 'inactive' => 'inactive');
echo form_dropdown('status',$options) ."</p>";

echo form_submit('submit','create size');
echo form_close();
?>
```

And the admin_sizes_edit view:

```php
<h1><?php echo $title;?></h1>

<?php
echo form_open('admin/sizes/edit');
echo "<p><label for='name'>Name</label><br/>";
$data = array('name'=>'name','id'=>'name','size'=>25, 'value'=>$size['name']);
echo form_input($data) ."</p>";

echo "<p><label for='status'>Status</label><br/>";
$options = array('active' => 'active', 'inactive' => 'inactive');
echo form_dropdown('status',$options, $size['status']) ."</p>";

echo form_hidden('id',$size['id']);
echo form_submit('submit','update size');
echo form_close();
?>
```

Once you have all the views in place, add a few sizes into the system. When you're done, you should end up with a sizes index that looks somewhat like Figure 7-14.

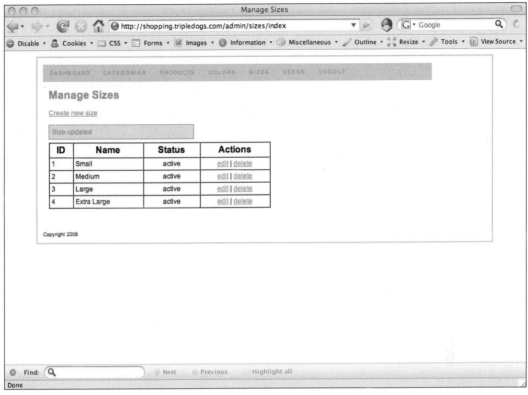

Figure 7-14

Adding Color and Size Checkboxes to Products

Now that the administrative screens for colors and sizes are all in, let's add a set of simple interface elements to the admin_product_create and admin_product_edit views. As soon as those two changes are made, you will then need to update the backend processes to keep the products_sizes and products_colors tables in sync.

First, open the admin/products controller and add two simple calls to the create() function. You want to call getActiveColors() and getActiveSizes() from their respective models. You can then use the data from those two calls to create checkboxes for colors and sizes inside the Create form.

```
function create(){
  if ($this->input->post('name')){
    $this->MProducts->addProduct();
    $this->session->set_flashdata('message','Product created');
    redirect('admin/products/index','refresh');
  }else{
    $data['title'] = "Create Product";
    $data['main'] = 'admin_product_create';
    $data['categories'] = $this->MCats->getCategoriesDropDown();
```

```
        $data['colors'] = $this->MColors->getActiveColors();
        $data['sizes'] = $this->MSizes->getActiveSizes();
        $this->load->vars($data);
        $this->load->view('dashboard');
    }
}
```

In the admin_product_create view, you're going to process the $colors and $sizes data arrays inside two separate fieldsets. The fieldsets will keep the checkboxes visually separate from the rest of the form. Place the two fieldsets just above the Submit button.

```
echo form_fieldset('Colors');
foreach ($colors as $key => $value){
  echo form_checkbox('colors[]', $key, FALSE). $value;
}
echo form_fieldset_close();

echo form_fieldset('Sizes');
foreach ($sizes as $key => $value){
  echo form_checkbox('sizes[]', $key, FALSE). $value;
}
echo form_fieldset_close();
```

What you end up with is something akin to Figure 7-15.

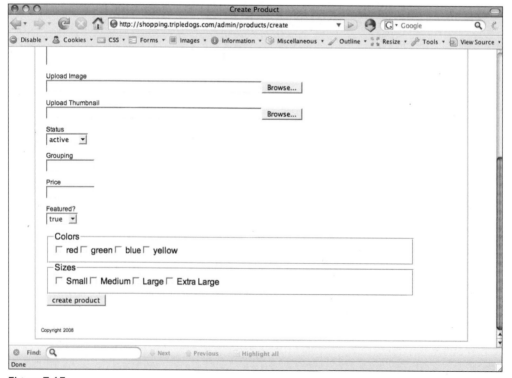

Figure 7-15

226

Notice that color selections are saved in a `colors[]` array, and size selections are saved in a `sizes[]` array. This means that you will need to do an extra bit of processing to update the products_sizes and products_colors databases.

Open the MProducts model in your editor and find the `createProduct()` function. What you want to do right after the insert command (regular text, not bold, below) is to use CodeIgniter to figure out what the newly created product's ID is. You will need this information in order to properly populate the mapping tables (products_colors and products_sizes). You can get this ID by using the `$this->db->insert_id()` function.

Once you have that product ID, you can loop through the colors and sizes and create records in the products_sizes and products_colors mapping tables.

```
$this->db->insert('products', $data);

$new_product_id = $this->db->insert_id();

if (count($_POST['colors'])){
  foreach ($_POST['colors'] as $value){
    $data = array('product_id' => $new_product_id,
            'color_id' => $value);
    $this->db->insert('products_colors',$data);
  }
}

if (count($_POST['sizes'])){
  foreach ($_POST['sizes'] as $value){
    $data = array('product_id' => $new_product_id,
            'size_id' => $value);
    $this->db->insert('products_sizes',$data);
  }
}
```

You're going to want to do all of this in the edit view, with two additions. First, you will need to add two functions to the MProducts model to extract colors and sizes already assigned to a given product. These functions should return a list of color and size IDs. You can then check these lists to see if any checkboxes should be checked.

Here are the functions for the MProducts model. Predictably, they are called `getAssignedColors()` and `getAssignedSizes()`.

```
function getAssignedColors($id){
  $data = array();
  $this->db->select('color_id');
  $this->db->where('product_id',$id);
  $Q = $this->db->get('products_colors');
  if ($Q->num_rows() > 0){
    foreach ($Q->result_array() as $row){
      $data[] = $row['color_id'];
    }
  }
}
```

```
     $Q->free_result();
     return $data;
  }

  function getAssignedSizes($id){
     $data = array();
     $this->db->select('size_id');
     $this->db->where('product_id',$id);
     $Q = $this->db->get('products_sizes');
     if ($Q->num_rows() > 0){
       foreach ($Q->result_array() as $row){
         $data[] = $row['size_id'];
       }
     }
     $Q->free_result();
     return $data;
  }
```

Next, update the edit() function of the admin/products controller. Don't forget to grab all the available colors and sizes as well as the assigned ones. Remember that you will need both sets of data, as the first will give you the available checkboxes, and the second set will tell you which checkboxes are actually checked.

```
  function edit($id=0){
     if ($this->input->post('name')){
       $this->MProducts->updateProduct();
       $this->session->set_flashdata('message','Product updated');
       redirect('admin/products/index','refresh');
     }else{
       $data['title'] = "Edit Product";
       $data['main'] = 'admin_product_edit';
       $data['product'] = $this->MProducts->getProduct($id);
       $data['categories'] = $this->MCats->getCategoriesDropDown();
       $data['assigned_colors'] = $this->MProducts->getAssignedColors($id);
       $data['assigned_sizes'] = $this->MProducts->getAssignedSizes($id);
       $data['colors'] = $this->MColors->getActiveColors();
       $data['sizes'] = $this->MSizes->getActiveSizes();
       $this->load->vars($data);
       $this->load->view('dashboard');
     }
  }
```

Next, open the admin_product_edit view and add your fieldsets and checkboxes, just as you did on the admin_product_create view. This time, however, you're going to check for the presence of a color or size ID in the assigned arrays you've built.

```
  echo form_fieldset('Colors');
  foreach ($colors as $key => $value){
     if (in_array($key,$assigned_colors)){
       $checked = TRUE;
     }else{
       $checked = FALSE;
     }
```

```
      echo form_checkbox('colors[]', $key, $checked). $value;
    }
    echo form_fieldset_close();

    echo form_fieldset('Sizes');
    foreach ($sizes as $key => $value){
      if (in_array($key,$assigned_sizes)){
        $checked = TRUE;
      }else{
        $checked = FALSE;
      }
      echo form_checkbox('sizes[]', $key, $checked). $value;
    }
    echo form_fieldset_close();
```

Once you have these changes loaded, you should be able to edit a product that has color and size settings associated with it and see checked choices on the interface, as shown in Figure 7-16.

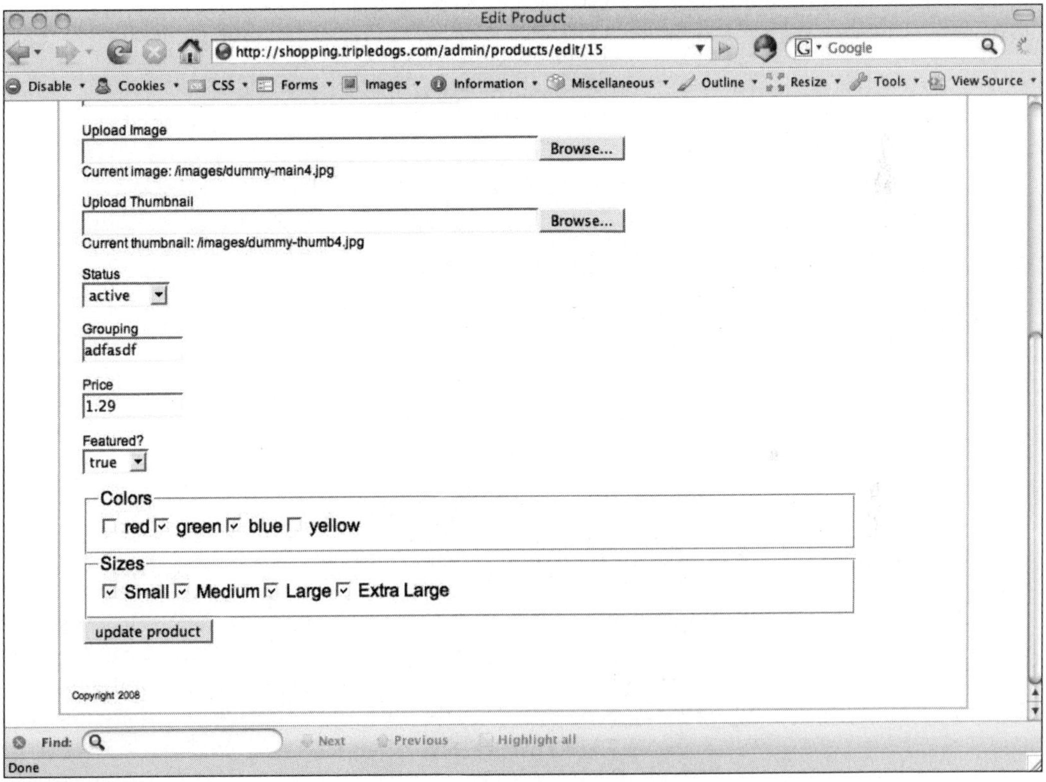

Figure 7-16

The next thing you need to do is to delete any color and size mappings already in the products_colors and products_sizes tables for a given product and then repopulate those data from the newly checked color and size choices.

Why do it that way? Because it's so much easier (not to mention more efficient) to clean the slate and add new values than to keep track of every item, doing updates as needed or deleting extraneous items that don't match the previous state.

You can delete a given set of color and size settings with the following commands:

```
$this->db->where('product_id', $_POST['id']);
$this->db->delete('products_colors');
$this->db->where('product_id', $_POST['id']);
$this->db->delete('products_sizes');
```

Now that you've deleted all the existing settings, repopulate from the incoming checkboxes. Please note that if there are no checkboxes for color or size, you're OK! Since you've deleted all the previous entries made, it is theoretically possible to have a product without color or size attributes.

```
if (count($_POST['colors'])){
  foreach ($_POST['colors']  as $value){
    $data = array('product_id' => $_POST['id'],
            'color_id' => $value);
    $this->db->insert('products_colors',$data);
  }
}

if (count($_POST['sizes'])){
  foreach ($_POST['sizes']  as $value){
    $data = array('product_id' => $_POST['id'],
            'size_id' => $value);
    $this->db->insert('products_sizes',$data);
  }
}
```

Your work on the admin side is now complete. All that's left to do is to add color and size assignments to the public pages.

Displaying Color and Size Information on Public Pages

To display color and size information on the public pages, all you have to do is open the welcome controller in an editor and make some small changes to the product() function. These changes are pretty much the same lines you added to the edit() function of the admin/products controller.

```
function product($productid){
  $product = $this->MProducts->getProduct($productid);
  if (!count($product)){
    redirect('welcome/index','refresh');
  }
  $data['grouplist'] = $this->MProducts->getProductsByGroup(3,$product['grouping'],
          $productid);
  $data['product'] = $product;
```

```
    $data['title'] = "Claudia's Kids | ". $product['name'];
    $data['main'] = 'product';
    $data['navlist'] = $this->MCats->getCategoriesNav();
    $data['assigned_colors'] = $this->MProducts->getAssignedColors($productid);
    $data['assigned_sizes'] = $this->MProducts->getAssignedSizes($productid);
    $data['colors'] = $this->MColors->getActiveColors();
    $data['sizes'] = $this->MSizes->getActiveSizes();
    $this->load->vars($data);
    $this->load->view('template');
}
```

In other words, you're going to reuse the model functions and resulting data arrays on the public side. To make these lists appear, simply loop through $assigned_colors and $assigned_sizes and then look up the names in $colors and $sizes on the product view.

Here's the entire view again, to refresh your memory, with the specific code in bold:

```
<div id='pleft'>

<?php
if ($this->session->flashdata('conf_msg')){ //change!
  echo "<div class='message'>";
  echo $this->session->flashdata('conf_msg');
  echo "</div>";
}
?>
<?php
  echo "<img src='".$product['image']."' border='0' align='left'/>\n";
  echo "<h2>".$product['name']."</h2>\n";
  echo "<p>".$product['longdesc'] . "<br/>\n";
  echo "Colors: ";
  foreach ($assigned_colors as $value){
  echo $colors[$value] . " ";
  }
  echo "<br/>";
  echo "Sizes: ";
  foreach ($assigned_sizes as $value){
    echo $sizes[$value] . " ";
  }
  echo "<br/>";
  echo anchor('welcome/cart/'.$product['id'],'add to cart') . "</p>\n";
?>
</div>

<div id='pright'>
<?php
  foreach ($grouplist as $key => $list){
    echo "<div class='productlisting'><img src='".$list['thumbnail']."'
          border='0' class='thumbnail'/>\n";
    echo "<h4>".$list['name']."</h4>\n";
```

```
        echo anchor('welcome/product/'.$list['id'],'see details') . "<br/>\n";
        echo anchor('welcome/cart/'.$list['id'],'add to cart') . "\n</div>";
    }
?>
</div>
```

Your product view should look something like Figure 7-17 when you're done.

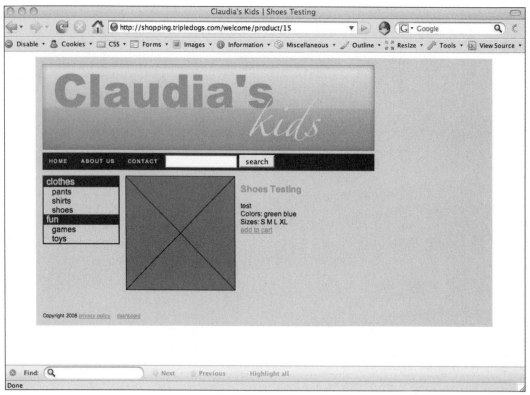

Figure 7-17

Revisiting the Sprint Backlog

When you review the sprint backlog, you're pleased to see that all items have been completed, not to mention an extensive rewrite of how product colors and sizes feature in the application.

1. Create a series of admin controllers (in their own folder). **DONE.**

2. Secure those controllers and build a login form on the public side. **DONE.**

3. Create a new model for admin users. **DONE.**

4. Create controllers and views to administer those users. **DONE.**

5. Expand, as needed, the models for orders, products, and categories. **DONE.**

6. Create a dashboard view. **DONE.**

7. Create CRUD (create, review, update, delete) screens for products and categories. **DONE.**

8. Create import and export functions for products and categories. **DONE.**

9. Add an easy way to assign products to categories and groups in batch mode. **DONE.**

Conclusion

In this chapter, you learned how to extend a basic set of administrative screens and add much needed functionality, like batch operations and import/export features. You even made a fairly wide-ranging series of changes involving colors and sizes.

In the next chapter, you'll add even more features to the site, including a Newsletter tool and a simple page manager.

Remember to keep these thoughts in mind as you continue working with CodeIgniter:

❏ If you find yourself in a situation in which you have to rework a big part of your application, don't panic. Make a list of all the changes that need to be made, and then systematically address those issues in your models, database tables, controllers, and views.

❏ Learn the power of such functions as $this->db->insert_id(), which allows you to track newly inserted IDs for any table.

❏ Never hesitate to reuse functionality. If you've written model functions for an admin dashboard, feel free to reuse those same functions on the public side.

Last-Minute Upgrades

8

In Chapter 7, you added quite a bit of functionality to the admin dashboard. Claudia and her staff can now import and export data, they can run certain operations in batch mode, and they can manage colors and sizes assigned to products. Along the way, you learned how to use an external library and put it to good use.

In this chapter, you meet with the client and make sure that you've covered all your bases with regard the interface. There are still a few things that need to be covered (such as being able to manage pages), and you're sure that she will want some way to communicate with her customers via e-mail. In this chapter, you are working outside the confines of a formal sprint. Although this can be a risky proposition in most cases, with some discipline and the aid of CodeIgniter, you should do fine.

> *In this chapter, you are working outside the confines of a "formal" sprint and "formal" sprint backlog. This sometimes happens, but there's no need to feel discomfort in these situations. The key to success with a less structured Agile approach is to set good boundaries and have realistic expectations about what can and can't be accomplished given the time (and other) constraints involved.*

With all that in mind, you meet with Claudia.

Meeting with the Client

When you show Claudia all the work you've done since the last time you met, she's positively thrilled.

"I love that I can manage colors and sizes so easily," she says. "Was that a difficult change to make?"

"No," you answer, "Once I had the administrative framework figured out, adding new screens wasn't hard at all."

"Good, because I need to ask you for a few more things," she says, and you both laugh. Isn't this how it always goes with clients? Of course!

"I need to be able to manage a handful of pages," Claudia says. "I don't need a full-fledged content management system, but I want to make changes to just a few pages without having to call you in all the time."

"I assume you're talking about the About Us, Privacy Policy, and Contact pages?"

"Yes, that's right. Just those three or four pages would do it."

"Not a problem. I've already been kicking around a few ideas for how something like that would work."

"Excellent. The other thing I need is a bit more complicated," Claudia admits. "I need a way to communicate with my customers over e-mail."

"Can you get more specific?"

"Of course," she says, pulling out some notes. "As you can see, I've given this some thought. I'd like it if visitors to my web site could subscribe to a newsletter. I'd like to have their e-mail addresses stored somewhere on the site. Then I'd like to be able to put together e-mail messages that go out to those folks."

"Sounds simple enough," you say. "Do you want to be able to store the messages and maybe reuse them in the future?"

"No, that's not necessary, as we can just blind-copy ourselves for now," she nods. "But it would be great to send out HTML e-mails to my subscribers."

"Do you need anything else, like being able to manage Unsubscribe requests?"

"It would be better for me if the customer could manage their own Unsubscribe requests, but yes, that is very necessary."

You look down at your notes and then smile. "Sounds like I've got some work cut out for me. How about if we visit again tomorrow to look at what I've come up with?"

"Sure thing," she says. "It feels like we're almost done … this is very exciting!"

With the client meeting now complete, it's time to review your notes and get to work on the upgrades.

Creating a Page Manager

Now that you understand Claudia's need for some simple page management (and to be clear, all she needs is a simple way to create and edit just a handful of pages), you can get started on the work. When creating a page manager, you need to keep several things in mind before you even start working.

1. You're not trying to build a full-on content management system. There's no need to get wrapped up in issues like workflow, privileges, and other advanced criteria.

2. You want to have an easy way to allow for WYSIWYG creation of HTML content. You'll likely be integrating some kind of online editor like TinyMCE or Xinha.

3. Don't forget that at some point you also need to integrate with the Welcome controller and the public pages.

You will need to take this in stages. First comes the database table (which will hold all the data involved with individual pages), then the model, then the controller, then the admin pages (the views that users actually interact with), then integrating the WYSIWYG editor, and finally, making it work with the Welcome controller.

Creating the Database Table

First things first, and that means creating the database table. In true Agile form, take the most straightforward path and create a table called *Pages*. The Pages table should have a primary field called id (which is de rigueur), and fields for a page name/title, keywords, description, status, the page content, and a short path.

Of all of these fields, the path is the least transparent at this point, but its value will become clear to you as you go. Basically, what you want is to be able to extract a page that matches a certain path. You'll be using the path as a "unique identifier" on the Welcome controller that will allow you to pull out the right data. For example, if you want to pull out the About page, you want to match that path.

To get you started, here is a quick CREATE TABLE SQL statement.

```
CREATE TABLE IF NOT EXISTS 'pages' (
  'id' int(11) NOT NULL auto_increment,
  'name' varchar(255) NOT NULL default '',
  'keywords' varchar(255) NOT NULL default '',
  'description' varchar(255) NOT NULL default '',
  'path' varchar(255) NOT NULL default '',
  'content' text NOT NULL,
  'status' enum('active','inactive') NOT NULL default 'active',
  PRIMARY KEY  ('id')
) ENGINE=MyISAM;
```

Creating the Model

The model for the Pages table should be kept to a bare minimum at this point. All you need are functions for retrieving one or all pages, for deleting a page, and for adding and updating a page.

As usual, start the model in the classic way. Note that following the earlier pattern, you'll call this model *MPages*:

```php
<?php

class MPages extends Model{

    function MPages(){
        parent::Model();
    }
```

The getPage() function pulls out one page from the Pages table, based on ID.

```php
    function getPage($id){
        $data = array();
        $this->db->where('id',$id);
        $this->db->limit(1);
        $Q = $this->db->get('pages');
        if ($Q->num_rows() > 0){
            $data = $Q->row_array();
        }
        $Q->free_result();
        return $data;
    }
```

The getPagePath() function does the same thing as getPage(), except you pass in a path as an argument. You'll be using this function on the Welcome controller to extract one page for a given address.

```php
    function getPagePath($path){
        $data = array();
        $this->db->where('path',$path);
        $this->db->where('status', 'active');
        $this->db->limit(1);
        $Q = $this->db->get('pages');
        if ($Q->num_rows() > 0){
            $data = $Q->row_array();
        }
        $Q->free_result();
        return $data;
    }
```

The `getAllPages()` function extracts all pages from the Pages database table.

```
function getAllPages(){
  $data = array();
  $Q = $this->db->get('pages');
  if ($Q->num_rows() > 0){
    foreach ($Q->result_array() as $row){
      $data[] = $row;
    }
  }
  $Q->free_result();
  return $data;
}
```

The `addPage()` function allows you to add a record to the Pages database table.

```
function addPage(){
  $data = array(
    'name' => $_POST['name'],
    'keywords' => $_POST['keywords'],
    'description' => $_POST['description'],
    'status' => $_POST['status'],
    'path' => $_POST['path'],
    'content' => $_POST['content']
  );

  $this->db->insert('pages', $data);
}
```

Please note that in this instance, as in any CodeIgniter situation dealing with POST data, you can use `$this->input->post()` *instead of* `$_POST`. *The main difference? The CodeIgniter function will return FALSE (Boolean) if the item does not exist or contains no data.*

The `updatePage()` function lets you update a record in the Pages database table.

```
function updatePage(){
  $data = array(
    'name' => $_POST['name'],
    'keywords' => $_POST['keywords'],
    'description' => $_POST['description'],
    'status' => $_POST['status'],
    'path' => $_POST['path'],
    'content' => $_POST['content']

  );

  $this->db->where('id', $_POST['id']);
  $this->db->update('pages', $data);

}
```

Finally, the `deletePage()` function lets you deactivate a record in the Pages database table. Just like with products, it's probably not such a good idea to actually delete records. Instead, just setting their status indicators to "inactive" is enough.

```
function deletePage($id){
    $data = array('status' => 'inactive');
    $this->db->where('id', $id);
    $this->db->update('pages', $data);
}
}//end class
?>
```

One last thing before moving on to the controller: Don't forget to add MPages to the autoloaded models list in your autoload.php.

```
$autoload['model'] = array('MCats', 'MProducts', 'MOrders', 'MAdmins', 'MSizes',
'MColors', 'MPages');
```

Creating the Admin/Pages Controller

The admin/pages controller is also extremely simple and is based on all the other controllers you've created so far in the administrative component. In fact, at this point you could copy and paste any of the other controllers you've already built and make serious headway here.

In this Pages controller, you need the standard set of functions: `index()`, `create()`, `edit()`, and `delete()`. When you start the Pages controller, don't forget to check for the presence of the session variable userID. If it hasn't been set, send the user back to the Welcome controller, so he or she can log in.

```
<?php

class Pages extends Controller {
  function Pages(){
    parent::Controller();
    session_start();

    if ($_SESSION['userid'] < 1){
      redirect('welcome/verify','refresh');
    }
  }
}
```

The `index()` function is very straightforward. Simply load all the pages from the database with `getAllPages()` from the MPages model, and load a view called admin_pages_home.

```
function index(){
  $data['title'] = "Manage Pages";
  $data['main'] = 'admin_pages_home';
  $data['pages'] = $this->MPages->getAllPages();
  $this->load->vars($data);
  $this->load->view('dashboard');
}
```

The create() function checks for POST data. If there is a page name in the POST data, then add the page using your model function addPage(). If there aren't any POST data, show the admin_pages_create view.

```php
function create(){
  if ($this->input->post('name')){
    $this->MPages->addPage();
    $this->session->set_flashdata('message','Page created');
    redirect('admin/pages/index','refresh');
  }else{
    $data['title'] = "Create Page";
    $data['main'] = 'admin_pages_create';
    $this->load->vars($data);
    $this->load->view('dashboard');
  }
}
```

The same thing goes for the edit() function. If you detect POST data, use updatePage() to update the record in the database. If not, load the admin_pages_edit function and retrieve the appropriate pages record using the passed-in argument $id.

```php
function edit($id=0){
  if ($this->input->post('name')){
    $this->MPages->updatePage();
    $this->session->set_flashdata('message','Page updated');
    redirect('admin/pages/index','refresh');
  }else{
    $data['title'] = "Edit Page";
    $data['main'] = 'admin_pages_edit';
    $data['page'] = $this->MPages->getPage($id);
    $this->load->vars($data);
    $this->load->view('dashboard');
  }
}
```

Finally, the delete() function takes whatever you pass in as an argument ($id) and passes that value to deletePage().

```php
function delete($id){
  $this->MPages->deletePage($id);
  $this->session->set_flashdata('message','Page deleted');
  redirect('admin/pages/index','refresh');
}

}//end class
?>
```

Creating the Administrative Views

For the page manager, you'll need three views:

- ❏ A home page, where you list all the pages available in the Pages table
- ❏ A Create page, where you allow a new page to be added to the Pages table
- ❏ An Edit page, where you allow an existing page to be updated

In other words, the views for this tool are pretty much the same as the views for all the other tools that you've built so far.

Before you jump into all those changes, it's best if you update the admin_home and admin_header views. The admin_header view contains all the navigation for the admin tools:

```php
<div id='globalnav'>
<ul>
<li><?php echo anchor("admin/dashboard/index","dashboard");?></li>
<li><?php echo anchor("admin/categories/","categories");?></li>
<li><?php echo anchor("admin/pages/", "pages");?></li>
<li><?php echo anchor("admin/products/", "products");?></li>
<li><?php echo anchor("admin/colors/", "colors");?></li>
<li><?php echo anchor("admin/sizes/", "sizes");?></li>
<li><?php echo anchor("admin/admins/", "users");?>
</li><li><?php echo anchor("admin/dashboard/logout/", "logout");?></li>
</ul>
</div>
```

The admin_home view contains basic information about each module.

```php
<ul>
<li><b><?php echo anchor("admin/categories/","Manage Categories");?>.</b>
<br/>
Create, edit, delete and manage product categories on your online store.
</li>
<br/>
<li><b><?php echo anchor("admin/products/","Manage Products");?>.</b>
<br/>
Create, edit, delete and manage products on your online store.
</li>
<br/>
<li><b><?php echo anchor("admin/pages/","Manage Pages");?>.</b>
<br/>
Create, edit, delete and manage pages on your online store.
</li>
<br/>
<li><b><?php echo anchor("admin/colors/","Manage Colors");?>.</b>
<br/>
```

```
Create, edit, delete and manage colors available to products.
</li>
<br/>

<li><b><?php echo anchor("admin/sizes/","Manage Sizes");?>.</b>
<br/>
Create, edit, delete and manage sizes available to products.
</li>
<br/>

<li><b><?php echo anchor("admin/admins/","Manage Users");?>.</b>
<br/>
Create, edit, delete and manage users who can access this dashboard.
</li>
<br/>

<li><b><?php echo anchor("admin/dashboard/logout/","Logout");?>.</b>
<br/>
Exit this dashboard when you're done.
</li>
<br/>
</ul>
```

Creating the Home Page View

The admin_pages_home view is very simple. It consists of a link that allows the user to create a new page, followed by a table that lists every single page in the database. In other words, the table renders the results of the getAllPages() model function invoked in the controller.

```php
<h1><?php echo $title;?></h1>
<p><?php echo anchor("admin/pages/create", "Create new page");?></p>
<?php
if ($this->session->flashdata('message')){
  echo "<div class='message'>".$this->session->flashdata('message')."</div>";
}

if (count($pages)){
  echo "<table border='1' cellspacing='0' cellpadding='3' width='400'>\n";
  echo "<tr valign='top'>\n";
  echo "<th>ID</th>\n<th>Name</th><th>Status</th><th>Actions</th>\n";
  echo "</tr>\n";
  foreach ($pages as $key => $list){
    echo "<tr valign='top'>\n";
    echo "<td>".$list['id']."</td>\n";
    echo "<td>".$list['name']."</td>\n";
    echo "<td align='center'>".$list['status']."</td>\n";
    echo "<td align='center'>";
    echo anchor('admin/pages/edit/'.$list['id'],'edit');
    echo " | ";
    echo anchor('admin/pages/delete/'.$list['id'],'delete');
    echo "</td>\n";
    echo "</tr>\n";
  }
  echo "</table>";
}
?>
```

Also, please note that as in the other home page views you've created, you're also allowing the use of a flash data message to pass on relevant status information to the user.

Once you're done, you should see something similar to Figure 8-1 in your web browser.

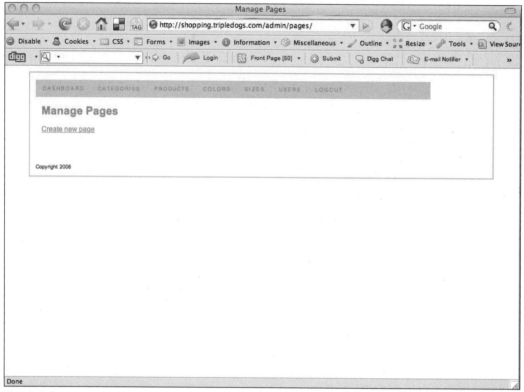

Figure 8-1

Creating the Create Page View

The admin_pages_create view is just like every other create view you've built so far. It is a simple form with fields for name, keywords, description, path, status, and content.

```php
<h1><?php echo $title;?></h1>

<?php
echo form_open('admin/pages/create');
echo "<p><label for='pname'>Name</label><br/>";
$data = array('name'=>'name','id'=>'pname','size'=>25);
echo form_input($data) ."</p>";

echo "<p><label for='short'>Keywords</label><br/>";
$data = array('name'=>'keywords','id'=>'short','size'=>40);
echo form_input($data) ."</p>";

echo "<p><label for='desc'>Description</label><br/>";
$data = array('name'=>'description','id'=>'desc','size'=>40);
echo form_input($data) ."</p>";

echo "<p><label for='fpath'>Path/FURL</label><br/>";
$data = array('name'=>'path','id'=>'fpath','size'=>50);
echo form_input($data) ."</p>";

echo "<p><label for='long'>Content</label><br/>";
$data = array('name'=>'content','id'=>'long','rows'=>5, 'cols'=>'40');
echo form_textarea($data) ."</p>";

echo "<p><label for='status'>Status</label><br/>";
$options = array('active' => 'active', 'inactive' => 'inactive');
echo form_dropdown('status',$options) ."</p>";

echo form_submit('submit','create page');
echo form_close();
?>
```

Please note the use of FURL in this context. It's shorthand for "friendly URL." A friendly URL means different things to different people, but at the end of the day, what you want is something that is easy to remember and type (hence "friendly"). For example, www.example.com /about is much friendlier than www.example.com/page/3 or www.example.com/page.php?id=3 (the last example isn't typical of CodeIgniter, by the way).

Your admin_pages_create view should look like Figure 8-2 when you're done.

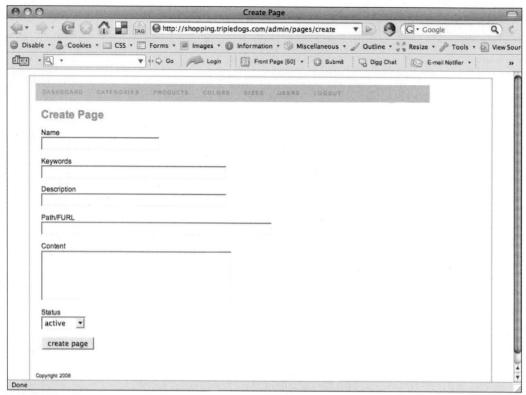

Figure 8-2

Creating the Edit Page View

The admin_pages_edit view is identical to the admin_pages_create view except for three tiny differences. First, it is posting to admin/pages/edit instead of admin/pages/create. Second, it contains a hidden ID field that you'll use to update the right record in the Pages table. Third, you're pulling in the existing record from the database to populate the form fields.

```
<h1><?php echo $title;?></h1>

<?php
echo form_open('admin/pages/edit');
echo "<p><label for='pname'>Name</label><br/>";
$data = array('name'=>'name','id'=>'pname','size'=>25, 'value' => $page['name']);
echo form_input($data) ."</p>";

echo "<p><label for='short'>Keywords</label><br/>";
$data = array('name'=>'keywords','id'=>'short', 'size'=>40, 'value' =>
        $page['keywords']);
echo form_input($data) ."</p>";

echo "<p><label for='desc'>Description</label><br/>";
```

```
$data = array('name'=>'description','id'=>'desc', 'size'=>40, 'value' =>
        $page['description']);
echo form_input($data) ."</p>";

echo "<p><label for='fpath'>Path/FURL</label><br/>";
$data = array('name'=>'path','id'=>'fpath', 'size'=>50, 'value' => $page['path']);
echo form_input($data) ."</p>";

echo "<p><label for='long'>Content</label><br/>";
$data = array('name'=>'content','id'=>'long', 'rows'=>5, 'cols'=>'40', 'value' =>
        $page['content']);
echo form_textarea($data) ."</p>";

echo "<p><label for='status'>Status</label><br/>";
$options = array('active' => 'active', 'inactive' => 'inactive');
echo form_dropdown('status',$options,$page['status']) ."</p>";

echo form_hidden('id',$page['id']);
echo form_submit('submit','update page');
echo form_close();
?>
```

When you're done, your admin_pages_edit view should look like Figure 8-3.

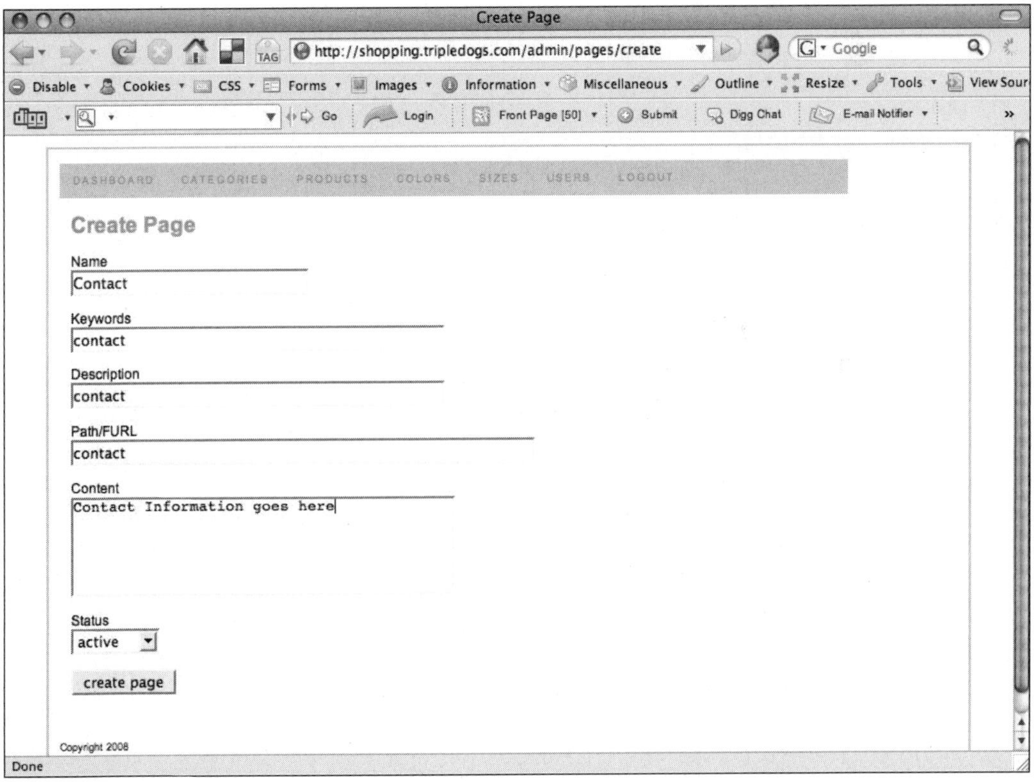

Figure 8-3

Choosing and Integrating a WYSIWYG Editor

There are dozens of great WYSIWYG editors out there. Many of them are free or low-cost, and almost all of them give the user a reasonable amount of control over HTML layouts, fonts, headers, and miscellaneous markup.

There was a time when a lot of folks on the Web knew HTML markup, but that hasn't been true for a long time. More and more people are coming to the Web from a diversity of backgrounds, and nobody has an interest (it seems) in learning the basics of good markup. This is why you want to provide them with an easy-to-use tool.

The tool you're going to integrate in this example is TinyMCE, available at `http://tinymce .moxiecode.com`. If you have another favorite tool, feel free to use it.

Once you download the TinyMCE code, pull out the tiny_mce folder (and its contents) and FTP it up to the already established /js/ folder. Once all those files have been placed on the server, open the admin_ pages_create and admin_pages_edit views, and make a small change before the <h1> line:

```
<?php echo $this->tinyMce;?>
<h1><?php echo $title;?></h1>
```

This is just a placeholder for now! To set the value for `$this->tinyMce`, open your Pages controller, and add the following code to the constructor:

```
function Pages(){
  parent::Controller();

  if ($this->session->userdata('userid') < 1){
    redirect('welcome/verify','refresh');
  }

  $this->tinyMce = '
    <!-- TinyMCE -->
    <script type="text/javascript" src="'.
      base_url().'js/tiny_mce/tiny_mce.js"></script>
    <script type="text/javascript">
      tinyMCE.init({
        // General option
        smode : "textareas",
        theme : "simple"
      });
    </script>
    <!-- /TinyMCE -->
    ';
}
```

This loads TinyMCE with the "simple" theme. If you were to load the admin_pages_create view in your browser, you would see something very similar to Figure 8-4.

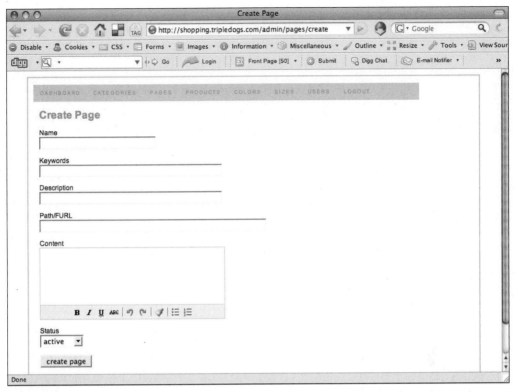

Figure 8-4

Updating the Welcome Controller

Now that you've built the administrative tools to manage pages, tie this into the Welcome controller so that you can display pertinent information on select pages — such as the About Us page, the Privacy page, and the Contact page.

Open the Welcome controller in a text editor, and scroll down to the end, where you should see three stub functions for about_us(), contact(), and privacy(). You're going to delete those three and replace them with a single function called pages(). Why? Because it makes no sense to give Claudia unlimited capability to create new pages, but no way to add those pages except through hard-coded controller functions.

Here's what the pages() function will look like when you're done:

```
function pages($path){
   $page = $this->MPages->getPagePath($path);
   $data['main'] = 'page';
   $data['title'] = $page['name'];
   $data['page'] = $page;
   $data['navlist'] = $this->MCats->getCategoriesNav();
   $this->load->vars($data);
   $this->load->view('template');
}
```

Now that you have this in place, you have another interesting problem. On some of your other public-facing views, you may have links in place to "welcome/verify" or "welcome/about_us," but with your new controller function, the path will be more like "welcome/pages/verify."

Simply make those edits as needed, primarily in your footer and header files. Now Claudia is free to create as many pages as she likes and link to them within her pages. All you have to do is tell her what the URL is going to be, and she'll be able to create those links successfully.

When you're done, your Privacy page ought to be pulling in whatever is in the database record for that page, as pictured in Figure 8-5.

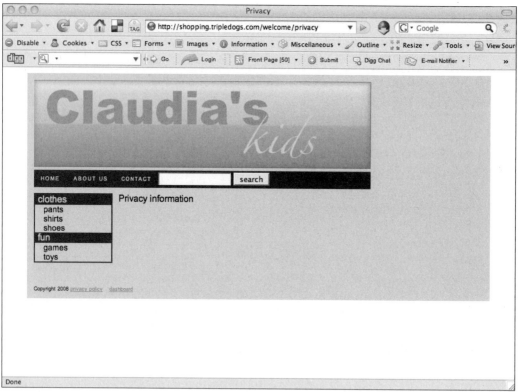

Figure 8-5

Creating a Newsletter Tool

If you're getting nervous at the thought of creating an e-mail Newsletter tool, don't be. Like any other task in CodeIgniter, you have to think it through in stages and then plan your work accordingly. This reduces the complexity of the task to more manageable parts.

Here are the pieces you'll need to make this work:

- ❏ Some kind of simple form that site visitors can fill out
- ❏ A controller function that accepts the form entry
- ❏ A database table in which to store the information from the form
- ❏ A model that facilitates the use of the form
- ❏ An administrative set of screens that let you manage subscribers and e-mails

As usual, you're going to work from the back forward; that is, you're going to establish the database table and the model first and then work out the controller functions and, eventually, the look and feel of the form itself and where to place it.

Creating the Database Table and Model

The database table for this part of the project should be kept to a minimal number of fields to keep the task of updating it as simple as possible. Although some might argue that you need many different kinds of fields to track subscribers, all you really need is name and email. Your database table will then have three fields: a primary field (id), a name field, and an e-mail field. Nothing more is required to get started.

```
CREATE TABLE 'subscribers' (
  'id' int(11) NOT NULL auto_increment,
  'name' varchar(255) NOT NULL,
  'email' varchar(255) NOT NULL,
  PRIMARY KEY  ('id')
) ENGINE=MyISAM;
```

Creating a model based on this simple table should also be old hat to you by now. For right now, you just need three functions in your model: to subscribe, unsubscribe, and show all subscribers. You're going to call this model *MSubscribers*.

```php
<?php

class MSubscribers extends Model{

  function MSubscribers(){
    parent::Model();
  }

  function createSubscriber(){
    $data = array(
      'name' => $_POST['name'],
      'email' => $_POST['email']
    );

    $this->db->insert('subscribers', $data);
  }
```

```
function removeSubcriber($id){
  $this->db->where('id', $id);
  $this->db->delete('subscribers');
}

function getAllSubscribers(){
  $data = array();
  $Q = $this->db->get('subscribers');
  if ($Q->num_rows() > 0){
    foreach ($Q->result_array() as $row){
      $data[] = $row;
    }
  }
  $Q->free_result();
  return $data;
}

}//end class
?>
```

Don't forget to autoload it:

```
$autoload['model'] = array('MCats', 'MProducts', 'MOrders','MAdmins','MSizes',
'MColors', 'MPages', 'MSubscribers');
```

Adding a `subscribe()` *Function*

As you might imagine, you're going to create a form that will post data to welcome/subscribe. Before creating that form, it may be helpful to build out that controller function first.

Basically, the idea behind this function is to take the incoming POST data and post that data to the Subscribers table. First you want to make sure that the e-mail in question is valid (with a little help from the e-mail helper provided by CodeIgniter). If the e-mail is invalid or if the form doesn't have a name filled in, then redirect the user to the home page with an error message. Otherwise, run `createSubscriber()`, and display a confirmation message.

Here is the `subscribe()` function in its entirety:

```
function subscribe(){
  if ($this->input->post('email')){
    $this->load->helper('email');
    if (!valid_email($this->input->post('email'))){
      $this->session->set_flashdata('subscribe_msg', 'Invalid email. Please try
          again!');
      redirect('welcome/index','refresh');
    }
```

```
    $this->MSubscribers->createSubscriber();
    $this->session->set_flashdata('subscribe_msg', 'Thanks for subscribing!');
    redirect('welcome/index','refresh');
  }else{
    $this->session->set_flashdata('subscribe_msg', "You didn't fill out the
        form!");
    redirect('welcome/index','refresh');
  }
}
```

Creating the Form

Finally, you can work on the form. You need to allow for two form fields — a name and an email. You also know that you need to post to welcome/subscribe. That's all you really need in order to create the form. In the example below, fieldsets and labels are used, but other approaches are equally valid.

One important note: The Subscription form has been added to the home view. As you can see, it is a simple form that prompts the user to fill in his name and e-mail address. In this particular case, the example uses a fieldset to delineate the form, but you could use any visual design convention to separate it from other parts of the page.

```
<div id='pleft'>
<?php
  echo "<img src='".$mainf['image']."' border='0' align='left'/>\n";
  echo "<h2>".$mainf['name']."</h2>\n";
  echo "<p>".$mainf['shortdesc'] . "<br/>\n";
  echo anchor('welcome/product/'.$mainf['id'],'see details') . "<br/>\n";
  echo anchor('welcome/cart/'.$mainf['id'],'add to cart') . "</p>\n";
?>

<br style='clear:both'><br/>
<?php
if ($this->session->flashdata('subscribe_msg')){
  echo "<div class='message'>";
  echo $this->session->flashdata('subscribe_msg');
  echo "</div>";
}
echo form_open("welcome/subscribe");
echo form_fieldset('Subscribe To Our Newsletter');
$data = array('name'=>'name', 'id' => 'name','size'=>'25');
echo "<p><label for='name'>Name</label><br/>";
echo form_input($data) . "</p>";
$data = array('name'=>'email', 'id' => 'email', 'size'=>'25');
echo "<p><label for='email'>Email</label><br/>";
echo form_input($data) . "</p>";
echo form_submit("submit","subscribe");
echo form_fieldset_close();
echo form_close();
?>
</div>

<div id='pright'>
<?php
```

```
    foreach ($sidef as $key => $list){
      echo "<div class='productlisting'><img src='".$list['thumbnail']."' border='0'
          class='thumbnail'/>\n";
      echo "<h4>".$list['name']."</h4>\n";
      echo anchor('welcome/product/'.$list['id'],'see details') . "<br/>\n";
      echo anchor('welcome/cart/'.$list['id'],'add to cart') . "\n</div>";
    }
  ?>
  </div>
```

Once you're done, your home page should look something like Figure 8-6.

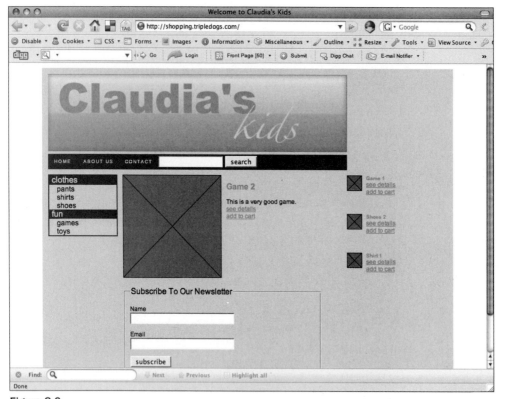

Figure 8-6

Creating Administrative Screens

The administrative screens for the subscribers' area will be fairly similar to all the rest, except for a few key differences:

❏   There will be a home page to show off key data about subscribers, but there won't be any way to create or update those subscribers.

❑   There will be a way to unsubscribe people from the list, both via e-mail and on the admin screen.

❑   There will be a way to create a new message, reusing the WYSIWYG editor you installed for the page manager.

Creating a Simple Controller

To start off with, all you need is a bare-bones controller with `index()`, `delete()`, and `sendemail()` functions. For now, you can leave the `sendemail()` function as spare as possible, as you can fill in the details later:

```php
<?php

class Subscribers extends Controller {
  function Subscribers(){
    parent::Controller();

    if ($this->session->userdata('userid') < 1){
      redirect('welcome/verify','refresh');
    }
  }

  function index(){
    $data['title'] = "Manage Subscribers";
    $data['main'] = 'admin_subs_home';
    $data['subscribers'] = $this->MSubscribers->getAllSubscribers();
    $this->load->vars($data);
    $this->load->view('dashboard');
  }


  function delete($id){
    $this->MSubscribers->removeSubscriber($id);
    $this->session->set_flashdata('message','Subscriber deleted');
    redirect('admin/subscribers/index','refresh');
  }

  function sendemail(){
    //fill in the rest later
    $data['title'] = "Send Email";
    $data['main'] = 'admin_subs_mail';
    $this->load->vars($data);
    $this->load->view('dashboard');
  }
}//end class
?>
```

Creating the Subscriber Home Page View

The next step is to create the admin_subs_home view. This view is exactly like all the rest you've built in the admin section so far, except it doesn't allow the user to edit existing (or create new) subscribers. Also, it offers a link to `sendemail()`.

```php
<h1><?php echo $title;?></h1>
<p><?php echo anchor("admin/subscribers/sendemail", "Create new email");?></p>
<?php
if ($this->session->flashdata('message')){
  echo "<div class='message'>".$this->session->flashdata('message')."</div>";
}

if (count($subscribers)){
  echo "<table border='1' cellspacing='0' cellpadding='3' width='400'>\n";
  echo "<tr valign='top'>\n";
  echo "<th>ID</th>\n<th>Name</th><th>Email</th><th>Actions</th>\n";
  echo "</tr>\n";
  foreach ($subscribers as $key => $list){
    echo "<tr valign='top'>\n";
    echo "<td>".$list['id']."</td>\n";
    echo "<td>".$list['name']."</td>\n";
    echo "<td>".$list['email']."</td>\n";
    echo "<td align='center'>";
    echo anchor('admin/pages/delete/'.$list['id'],'unsubscribe');
    echo "</td>\n";
    echo "</tr>\n";
  }
  echo "</table>";
}
?>
```

Updating Navigation in Views

Before you return to the controller function called `sendmail()`, it's worth your time to update the admin_home and admin_header views to include links to your new controller.

Here's the update in admin_home (in bold):

```php
<ul>
. . .

<br/>
<li><b><?php echo anchor("admin/subscribers/","Manage Subscribers");?>.</b>
<br/>
Manage subscribers and send out emails.
</li>

<li><b><?php echo anchor("admin/admins/","Manage Users");?>.</b>
<br/>
Create, edit, delete and manage users who can access this dashboard.
</li>
<br/>

<li><b><?php echo anchor("admin/dashboard/logout/","Logout");?>.</b>
<br/>
Exit this dashboard when you're done.
</li>
<br/>
</ul>
```

And here's the update in admin_header (in bold):

```
<div id='globalnav'>
<ul>
<li><?php echo anchor("admin/dashboard/index","dashboard");?></li>
<li><?php echo anchor("admin/categories/","categories");?></li>
<li><?php echo anchor("admin/pages/", "pages");?></li>
<li><?php echo anchor("admin/products/", "products");?></li>
<li><?php echo anchor("admin/colors/", "colors");?></li>
<li><?php echo anchor("admin/sizes/", "sizes");?></li>
<li><?php echo anchor("admin/subscribers/", "subscribers");?></li>
<li><?php echo anchor("admin/admins/", "users");?></li>
<li><?php echo anchor("admin/dashboard/logout/", "logout");?></li>
</ul>
</div>
```

When all is said and done, the home page for the subscribers area should look like Figure 8-7.

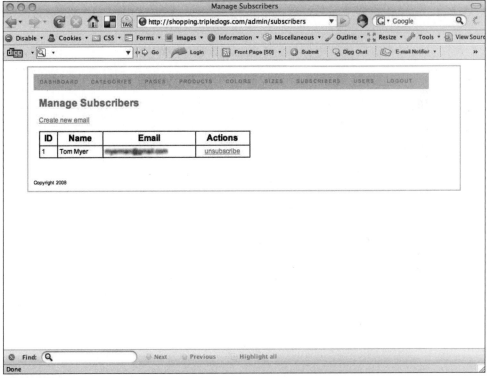

Figure 8-7

Creating the admin_subs_mail View

There is one last thing to do before revisiting the sendemail() function in the admin/subscribers controller: Create the form that will allow the user to send out an e-mail to everyone on the subscriber list. The form itself will be very simple, with a subject line, a text area for content, and a Submit button. It's also a good idea to include a checkbox for sending a test e-mail only.

Here's the markup for the admin_subs_mail view:

```php
<?php
echo form_open('admin/subscribers/sendemail');

echo "<p><label for='subject'>Subject</label><br/>";
$data = array('name' => 'subject', 'id' => 'subject', 'size' => 50);
echo form_input($data);
echo "</p>";

echo "<p><label for='message'>Message</label><br/>";
$data = array('name' => 'message', 'id' => 'message', 'rows' => 20, 'cols' => 50);
echo form_textarea($data);
echo "</p>";

echo "<p>".form_checkbox('test', 'true', TRUE) . " <b>This is a test!</b></p>";
echo form_submit('submit','send email');
echo form_close();
?>
```

Your form should look somewhat like Figure 8-8 at this point.

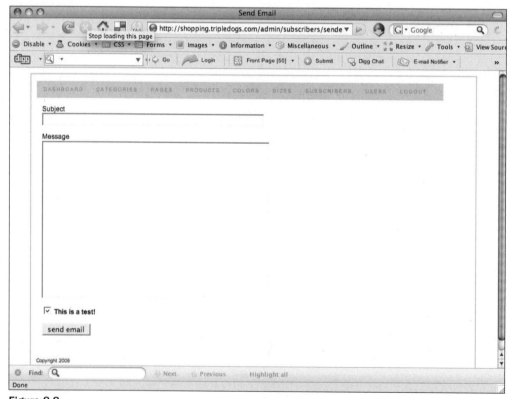

Figure 8-8

Integrating the TinyMCE Editor

If you've been paying attention, you'll notice that the text area isn't WYSIWYG. That's because you haven't added the necessary code to make that happen! Remember what you did before, in the pages area? You added a small bit of code to the controller's constructor, then echoed the appropriate piece on the view.

Therefore, in your Subscribers controller, add this bit to the constructor function:

```
function Subscribers(){
  parent::Controller();

  if ($this->session->userdata('userid') < 1){
    redirect('welcome/verify','refresh');
  }

  $this->tinyMce = '
    <!-- TinyMCE -->
    <script type="text/javascript" src="'.  base_url()
      .'js/tiny_mce/tiny_mce.js"></script>
    <script type="text/javascript">
      tinyMCE.init({
      // General options
      mode : "textareas",
      theme : "simple"
      });
    </script>
    <!-- /TinyMCE -->
  ';
}
```

Next, add the following line to the top of the admin_subs_email view:

```
echo $this->tinyMce;
```

The result should look something like Figure 8-9.

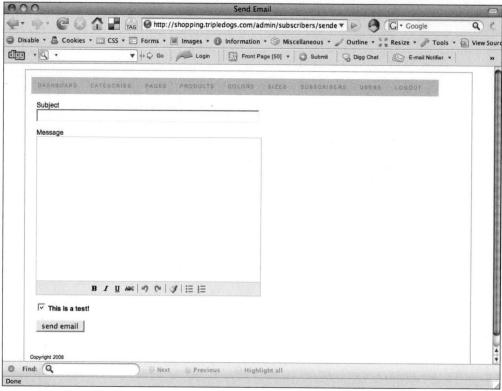

Figure 8-9

Rewriting the `sendemail()` *Function*

Now it's time to rewrite the `sendemail()` function you wrote above. You have three possible outcomes, in order of simplicity:

❑ **There are no POST data** — If so, simply send the user to the admin_subs_mail view, so she can compose a message.

❑ **There are POST data, and the test flag is TRUE** — In this case, simply send the composed message to the test recipient (in your case, Claudia).

❑ **There are POST data, and the test flag is FALSE** — In this case, extract the subscribers from the database using the `getAllSubscribers()` function of MSubscribers, and then send the message to those subscribers.

The way this three-part logic tree manifests itself is as an if-else condition, with the first if branch (POST data exist) having its own if-else branch (is this a test message?) embedded in it.

It's almost as complicated talking about it as seeing it in action, so without further ado, here's the code.

```
function sendemail(){
  if ($this->input->post('subject')){
    $test = $this->input->post('test');
    $subject = $this->input->post('subject');
    $msg = $this->input->post('message');
    if ($test){
      $this->email->clear();
      $this->email->from('claudia@example.com', 'ClaudiasKids.net');
      $this->email->to('claudia@example.com');
      $this->email->subject($subject);
      $this->email->message($msg);
      $this->email->send();
      $this->session->set_flashdata('message', "Test email sent");
    }else{
      $subs = $this->MSubscribers->getAllSubscribers();
      foreach ($subs as $key => $list){
        $unsub = "<p><a href='". base_url()."welcome/unsubscribe/"
               .$list['id']. "'>Unsubscribe</a></p>";
        $this->email->clear();
        $this->email->from('claudia@example.com', 'ClaudiasKids.net');
        $this->email->to($list['email']);
        $this->email->bcc('claudia@example.com');
        $this->email->subject($subject);
        $this->email->message($msg . $unsub);
        $this->email->send();
      }
      $this->session->set_flashdata('message', count($subs) . " emails sent");
    }
    redirect('admin/subscribers/index','refresh');
  }else{
    $data['title'] = "Send Email";
    $data['main'] = 'admin_subs_mail';
    $this->load->vars($data);
    $this->load->view('dashboard');
  }
}
```

The E-mail class is very simple: it allows you to quickly and easily send e-mails without too much fuss. Since you're autoloading the class, there's no need to invoke it specifically.

First you run $this->email->clear() to clear out any settings or variables. You set the "from" address with $this->email->from(), the "to" address with $this->email->to(), and so on. Once you've set the subject and message parameters, you can send with $this->email->send().

The only thing you're doing differently is checking for a test message. If the user has indicated a test message, then send to a single test address. Otherwise, loop through all the subscribers pulled from the database table, adding an unsubscribe method to the end of the message.

Unsubscribing from within an E-mail

Notice that the last thing you're appending to the e-mail is a line of HTML:

```
$unsub = "<p><a href='". base_url()."welcome/unsubscribe/"
       .$list['id']. "'>Unsubscribe</a></p>";
```

Essentially, at the bottom of each e-mail will be a small Unsubscribe link that, when clicked, will drive traffic back to the welcome/unsubscribe function and pass in that subscriber's ID. That ID needs to be passed to the `removeSubscriber()` function of the MSubcribers model in order to delete the subscriber from the subscribers list.

What this means is that you need to add one more function to the Welcome controller. You'll call it `unsubscribe()`, and it will very much mimic the actions taken in the admin/subscribers/delete controller function, except it won't require a login.

Here's the new function for the Welcome controller:

```
function unsubscribe($id){
  $this->MSubscribers->removeSubscriber($id);
  $this->session->set_flashdata('subscribe_msg','You have been unsubscribed!');
  redirect('welcome/index','refresh');
}
```

Making Some Last-Minute Upgrades

You now have a working e-mail Newsletter tool, but it could stand a bit of polish. For example, if you send a test e-mail, you have no choice but to create the e-mail anew before you can send it out again for real. It would be nice if the system remembered your subject line and HTML content, so you could send it out to the subscribers.

This is an easy fix. All you have to do is send the user right back to the form if she has sent out a test and prompt her to send the message again for real if she is ready to go. There are any number of ways to store the subject line and message, like session, cookie, or database. You have to remember, though, that using a cookie or session means that you might lose some data (you'll run into size limitations), so the safest route is to store this information in a database table or log file.

Because you now know how to work with database tables, it might be a good idea to look at how to use the File helper. The File helper contains a handful of functions that help you read, write, and manipulate files on the server.

You're going to write the subject and message from the POST data to a log file in the /tmp directory. To simplify things later on, you'll use some kind of unique delimiter, such as three pipes (| | |) or two colons (::) to separate the two. If you're dealing with a test situation, you're going to bounce the user back to the form and fill in the form fields with whatever is stored in the log file.

In the following code snippet, the File helper is loaded at the very top. If there is a test situation, write the subject and message from the POST data to the log file in /tmp and redirect to admin/subscribers/sendmail. Finally, if you are on the `sendmail()` function, if the value of the message flash data variable is set to "Test email sent," do a read of the log file to pass that data into the view.

```
function sendemail(){
  $this->load->helper('file');
  if ($this->input->post('subject')){
    $test = $this->input->post('test');
    $subject = $this->input->post('subject');
    $msg = $this->input->post('message');
    if ($test){
      $this->email->clear();
```

```php
        $this->email->from('claudia@example.com', 'ClaudiasKids.net');
        $this->email->to('myerman@gmail.com');
        $this->email->subject($subject);
        $this->email->message($msg);
        $this->email->send();
        $this->session->set_flashdata('message', "Test email sent");
        write_file('/tmp/email.log', $subject ."|||".$msg);
        redirect('admin/subscribers/sendemail','refresh');
      }else{
        $subs = $this->MSubscribers->getAllSubscribers();
        foreach ($subs as $key => $list){
          $unsub = "<p><a href='". base_url()."welcome/unsubscribe/"
              .$list['id']. "'>Unsubscribe</a></p>";
          $this->email->clear();
          $this->email->from('claudia@example.com', 'ClaudiasKids.net');
          $this->email->to($list['email']);
          $this->email->bcc('claudia@example.com');
          $this->email->subject($subject);
          $this->email->message($msg . $unsub);
          $this->email->send();
        }
        $this->session->set_flashdata('message', count($subs) . " emails sent");
      }
      redirect('admin/subscribers/index','refresh');
    }else{
      if ($this->session->flashdata('message') == "Test email sent"){
        $lastemail = read_file('/tmp/email.log');
        list($subj,$msg) = explode("|||",$lastemail);
        $data['subject'] = $subj;
        $data['msg'] = $msg;
      }else{
        $data['subject'] = '';
        $data['msg'] = '';
      }
      $data['title'] = "Send Email";
      $data['main'] = 'admin_subs_mail';
      $this->load->vars($data);
      $this->load->view('dashboard');
    }
  }
}
```

Finally, it's time to update the view. You need to set it such that the values for the subject and message fields accept the values from the controller. That's easily remedied by adding a value index for each form field's array.

One last thing: It would be good to add a way to display the flash data message, so that users know if a test e-mail was sent:

```php
<?php
echo $this->tinyMce;
if ($this->session->flashdata('message')){
  echo "<div class='message'>".$this->session->flashdata('message')."</div>";
}
```

```
echo form_open('admin/subscribers/sendemail');

echo "<p><label for='subject'>Subject</label><br/>";
$data = array('name' => 'subject', 'id' => 'subject', 'size' => 50,
        'value'=>$subject);
echo form_input($data);
echo "</p>";

echo "<p><label for='message'>Message</label><br/>";
$data = array('name' => 'message', 'id' => 'message', 'rows' => 20, 'cols' => 50,
        'value'=>$msg);
echo form_textarea($data);
echo "</p>";

echo "<p>".form_checkbox('test', 'true', TRUE) . " This is a test!</p>";
echo form_submit('submit','send email');
echo form_close();
?>
```

When you're all done, your efforts should look like Figure 8-10 if you send a test e-mail.

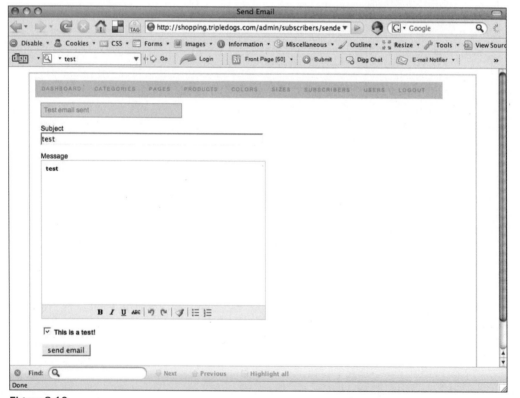

Figure 8-10

One last upgrade is needed before you can move on. Previously in this chapter, the idea was floated that removing duplicates from the e-mail addresses, before sending out a newsletter blast, might be a good idea. There are two ways of accomplishing this task, and either is good depending on where you're at in a project.

❑ A good way to remove duplicates is to do it when people subscribe. Run a quick check on subscribe and only enter them in the system if they're brand new.

❑ Another way to achieve the same goal is to run a quick check right before an e-mail blast goes out.

When you stop and think about it, though, what if someone has subscribed multiple times in the database (through no fault of their own or because of simply not remembering an earlier subscribe attempt). If they ever unsubscribe, they unsubscribe once, but may continue to get more mailings in the future. So the best way to handle this is to run a quick check before you subscribe someone.

The solution is simple: rewrite the `createSubscriber()` function in MSubscribers such that you run a quick `count_all_results()` query. If the count comes back as 0, then run your `insert()`. Otherwise, don't do anything.

```
function createSubscriber(){
  $this->db->where('email', $_POST['email']);
  $this->db->from('subscribers');
  $ct = $this->db->count_all_results();

  if ($ct == 0){
    $data = array(
      'name' => $_POST['name'],
      'email' => $_POST['email']
    );

    $this->db->insert('subscribers', $data);
  }
}
```

Meeting with the Client

After you're done with all the little tweaks, you take Claudia on a quick tour of the new functionality. She loves the fact that she can add new pages and create HTML e-mails. She knows she can now start adding real products and data to the web site.

"As you work with the site, you're going to notice a few things," you tell her. "For example, you may need more database fields to store information, or the WYSIWYG editor might need more options added to it. Just make a list and we'll talk in a few days."

"What are you going to be doing until then?" she asks.

"Well, I'm going to be doing a sweep tomorrow to secure the web site. Anywhere there might be a place for someone to cause mischief, I'm going to make it harder for them to do that. I'm also going to be running a few tests for performance and setting up caching so your site can handle lots of visitors."

"Sounds good! Then we can turn on the checkout features and go live!"

"We're just about there. It's exciting, isn't it?"

Conclusion

In this chapter, you added a simple page management feature to the site, as well as a rudimentary but effective Newsletter tool that Claudia can use to communicate with her customers. In the next chapter, you're going to apply some security features to your application and tweak the site for performance.

Remember to keep these thoughts in mind as you continue working with CodeIgniter:

❑　It's been said many times in this book, but it bears repeating: Just about any programming task can be handled in CodeIgniter if you break it into small enough pieces and/or phases.

❑　Learn how to use such tools as the E-mail and File helpers — they help you conquer mundane tasks like validating an e-mail address or writing log files.

❑　Don't be afraid to reuse or copy views, models, and controllers when you build new functionality.

❑　Sometimes upgrades and requests happen outside the regular notion of sprints. In this chapter, you saw a scenario in which two medium-sized additions were made to the functionality without the need for an extra sprint. Use your best judgment in these situations. They happen all the time, and it would be less practical to be 100 percent rigid about not undertaking them. However, if you don't feel comfortable making on-the-fly adjustments, then you can certainly create a process around them.

9

Security and Performance

In Chapter 8, you added two vital pieces to Claudia's web site: a simple page manager and a simple newsletter manager. In this chapter, you're going to tie up two loose ends: security and performance. You're going to do an audit of security issues, and in the process tighten up some issues on the administrative panels. In Chapter 3, you opted to protect against XSS (cross-site scripting) attacks, but that still doesn't cover everything. For example, you haven't addressed form validation. You're also going to do some basic performance benchmarking and then put caching in place.

Please note that in a real project, you'd probably undergo security and performance issues in a more immediate way, and, in fact, you have implemented various minimal safeguards as you've progressed. However, because this is a book, and because security is such an important topic, it's likely that readers might skip to this chapter, and thus the topic is presented here as a whole.

Security

Web-based security is a pretty broad field, but at the end of the day, as far as you're concerned, security is a question of threat level (or vulnerability) and opportunity. In all likelihood, an attack that is fairly common against a completely unprotected target will be tried long before an obscure attack on an unknown or hidden target. Your job is not to defend against every possible situation, but it is your job to make sure that your systems are secure enough to make the attacker try somewhere else. What this comes down to is a "defense-in-depth" attitude that will help you keep your applications secure from malicious users.

That being said, the number one rule of web application security is that user input cannot be trusted. In fact, any data that are received from any process can't be trusted. They should all be considered tainted and need to be filtered one way or another. For example, 99 percent of the time, the URI strings that are passed around will be OK, but someone will try to hack the URIs, trying to pass in a very long ID, for example, to your model. Your job is to make sure that doesn't happen.

CodeIgniter has some built-in security processes that will help you sleep better at night, including the following:

❑ The out-of-the-box configuration only allows certain characters in URI strings. You can add more allowable characters by editing the /system/application/config/config.php file, but doing so will create further openings for certain attacks. The allowable characters are:

   ❑ Alphanumeric text

   ❑ Tilde (~)

   ❑ Period (.)

   ❑ Colon (:)

   ❑ Underscore (_)

   ❑ Dash (-)

❑ The global GET array is unset by CodeIgniter's Input class and is therefore totally disallowed (you can turn this back on if you indicate use of query strings in the config.php file), but you will still need to process and escape any URI segments that you work with.

❑ The PHP globals POST and COOKIE are allowed, but all other globals are disallowed.

❑ The magic_quotes_runtime directive is turned off, which means that you don't have to remove slashes when you query data from the database.

Filtering User Input

The first step in securing your application has to do with filtering any and all user input — and, in fact, filtering any and all data coming from any process (such as POST, COOKIE, server systems, log files, whatever).

For the most part, this work of filtering user input will be done in the models. It is in the models that you take URI segments or POST data (for example) and do something useful with them (like insert data into a database or retrieve data from a table). In some cases, you'll need to fortify your controllers as well.

One way to attack the problem is to edit the models in alphabetical order, starting with MAdmins and proceeding through to MSubscribers.

Securing the MAdmins Model

First, it's helpful to imagine the MAdmins model stripped of all the security you've already put in. Imagine that there is no XSS filtering happening, and that there's no dohash() in operation for passwords. At the end of this section, you'll put the code back to where it was at the end of Chapter 6 and run through it again.

Why are you rewriting history, as it were? Because you need to understand how to secure an application, and this section introduces you to two approaches. The first is fairly manual, and the second involves extending the CodeIgniter Security helper.

With that in mind, let's delve into the MAdmins model.

The most important function to protect is the verifyUser() function. Specifically, you want to use $this->db->escape() to escape the incoming username and password strings.

```
function verifyUser($u,$pw){
  $this->db->select('id,username');
  $this->db->where('username',$this->db->escape($u));
  $this->db->where('password', $this->db->escape($pw));
  $this->db->where('status', 'active');
  $this->db->limit(1);
  $Q = $this->db->get('admins');
  if ($Q->num_rows() > 0){
    $row = $Q->row_array();
    $this->session->set_userdata('userid',$row['id']);
    $this->session->set_userdata('username',$row['username']);
  }else{
    $this->session->set_flashdata('error', 'Sorry, your username or password is
incorrect!');
  }
}
```

You can do the same with `getUser()` — simply escape the incoming `$id` variable.

```
function getUser($id){
  $data = array();
  $options = array('id' => $this->db->escape($id));
  $Q = $this->db->getwhere('admins',$options,1);
  if ($Q->num_rows() > 0){
    $data = $Q->row_array();
  }
  $Q->free_result();
  return $data;
}
```

For `addUser()` and `updateUser()`, you're going to deploy a new function, `xss_clean()`, which is part of the Security helper (which you autoloaded back in Chapter 3). The `xss_clean()` function converts malicious-looking JavaScript or other suspicious characters into entity references.

```
function addUser(){
  $data = array('username' => xss_clean($_POST['username']),
                'email' => xss_clean($_POST['email']),
                'status' => xss_clean($_POST['status']),
                'password' => xss_clean($_POST['password'])
  );

  $this->db->insert('admins',$data);
}

function updateUser(){
  $data = array('username' => xss_clean($_POST['username']),
                'email' => xss_clean($_POST['email']),
                'status' => xss_clean($_POST['status']),
                'password' => xss_clean($_POST['password'])
  );
  $this->db->where('id',$this->db->escape($_POST['id']));
  $this->db->update('admins',$data);
}
```

Did you notice that at the end of `updateUser()`, the `$_POST['id']` is escaped? You're going to do the same thing with the incoming `$id` on `deleteUser()`:

```
function deleteUser($id){
    $data = array('status' => 'inactive');
    $this->db->where('id', $this->db->escape($id));
    $this->db->update('admins', $data);
}
```

Why are you escaping the incoming ID? Well, it's coming from the URI, which can be manipulated by the user. It's very easy for a user to add other content to the URI (e.g., a series of SQL commands) and try to affect your application.

Is this all you could be doing with these functions? Of course not! You can increase security until you restrict activity down to a very small subset of activities. For example, it might be a good idea to limit all incoming IDs to a length of 11 characters and to being an integer. Similarly, it would be a good idea to restrict other fields down to their max size in the database. Why 11 characters? Well, this is an arbitrary limit, some might say, but it really isn't. It's keyed to the maximum length of the INT type key field in your database. Limiting it to integers keeps other nasty things from happening, such as trying to pass in alpha characters or floating point numbers, or worse, hexadecimal characters.

Because these kinds of operations become tedious if done over and over again, you're going to take advantage of a CodeIgniter 1.6 feature that allows you to create your own helper functions. All you need to do is create a file called *MY_security_helper.php* in /system/application/helpers. Any functions you declare there will be added (or replace existing) functions in the Security helper.

In your new helper, you're going to create two functions. The first, `id_clean()`, will determine whether a passed-in ID is actually numeric and chop it down to a determined size. The second, `db_clean()`, will run `xss_clean()` on a string and also chop it down to a determined size.

These two functions are both extremely simple functions, but they allow you to do a lot of heavy lifting:

```
<?php
function id_clean($id,$size=11){
    return intval(substr($id,0,$size));
}

function db_clean($string,$size=255){
    return xss_clean(substr($string,0,$size));
}?>
```

The beauty of the `intval()` function is that it will render any non-zero-length string it encounters into an integer. For example, it converts the hexadecimal number 0x1A into the integer 26, and the floating point number 1.3333928920 into the integer 1. By further chopping it down to size with `substr()`, you reduce the chances of a buffer overflow attack or other similar malicious mischief.

With these two functions in place, you can transform and simplify your MAdmins model thus:

```
  function verifyUser($u,$pw){
    $this->db->select('id,username');
    $this->db->where('username',db_clean($u,16));
    $this->db->where('password', db_clean($pw,16));
    $this->db->where('status', 'active');
    $this->db->limit(1);
    $Q = $this->db->get('admins');
    if ($Q->num_rows() > 0){
      $row = $Q->row_array();
      $this->session->set_userdata('userid',$row['id']);
      $this->session->set_userdata('username',$row['username']);
    }else{
      $this->session->set_flashdata('error', 'Sorry, your
username or password is incorrect!');
    }
  }

  function getUser($id){
    $data = array();
    $options = array('id' => id_clean($id));
    $Q = $this->db->getwhere('admins',$options,1);
    if ($Q->num_rows() > 0){
      $data = $Q->row_array();
    }
    $Q->free_result();
    return $data;
  }

  function getAllUsers(){
    $data = array();
    $Q = $this->db->get('admins');
    if ($Q->num_rows() > 0){
      foreach ($Q->result_array() as $row){
        $data[] = $row;
      }
    }
    $Q->free_result();
    return $data;
  }


  function addUser(){
    $data = array('username' => db_clean($_POST['username'],16),
                  'email' => db_clean($_POST['email'],255),
                  'status' => db_clean($_POST['status'],8),
                  'password' => db_clean($_POST['password'],16)
      );

  $this->db->insert('admins',$data);
  }

  function updateUser(){
    $data = array('username' => db_clean($_POST['username'],16),
                  'email' => db_clean($_POST['email'],255),
```

```
                    'status' => db_clean($_POST['status'],8),
                    'password' => db_clean($_POST['password'],16)
    );
    $this->db->where('id',id_clean($_POST['id']));
    $this->db->update('admins',$data);
}


function deleteUser($id){
    $data = array('status' => 'inactive');
    $this->db->where('id', id_clean($id));
    $this->db->update('admins', $data);
}
```

Incorporating Previous Security Measures

Before moving on, it's important to revisit the addUser(), updateUser(), and verifyUser()
functions. At the end of Chapter 6, you used dohash() to secure passwords being saved to the database.
At that point, your code looked like this:

```
function addUser(){
    $data = array('username' => $_POST['username'],
                  'email' => $_POST['email'],
                  'status' => $_POST['status'],
                  'password' => substr(dohash($_POST['password']),0,16)
    );
    $this->db->insert('admins',$data);
}

function updateUser(){
    $data = array('username' => $_POST['username'],
                  'email' => $_POST['email'],
                  'status' => $_POST['status'],
                  'password' => substr(dohash($_POST['password']),0,16)
    );
    $this->db->where('id',id_clean($_POST['id']));
    $this->db->update('admins',$data);
}
function verifyUser($u,$pw){
    $this->db->select('id,username');
    $this->db->where('username',$u);
    $this->db->where('password', substr(dohash($pw),0,16);
    $this->db->where('status', 'active');
    $this->db->limit(1);
    $Q = $this->db->get('admins');

    if ($Q->num_rows() > 0){
        $row = $Q->row_array();
        $_SESSION['userid'] = $row['id'];
        $_SESSION['username'] = $row['username'];
    }else{
        $this->session->set_flashdata('error', 'Sorry, your username or password is
                incorrect!');
    }
}
```

Now that you've written the db_clean() function, which incorporates the substr() function, you want to change these three functions to look like the following code. Notice that it is important that you run dohash() on the password and then pass it to db_clean. Doing it in this order will ensure that you get the right 16 characters stored in the table.

If you want to avoid trouble, simply change your password field length to 32 characters and then use 32 as your size limiter on the db_clean() function.

```
function addUser(){
  $data = array('username' => db_clean($_POST['username'],16),
               'email' => db_clean($_POST['email'],255),
               'status' => db_clean($_POST['status'],8),
               'password' => db_clean(dohash($_POST['password']),16)
  );
  $this->db->insert('admins',$data);
}

function updateUser(){
  $data = array('username' => db_clean($_POST['username'],16),
               'email' => db_clean($_POST['email'],255),
               'status' => db_clean($_POST['status'],8),
               'password' => db_clean(dohash($_POST['password']),16)
  );
  $this->db->where('id',id_clean($_POST['id']));
  $this->db->update('admins',$data);
}

function verifyUser($u,$pw){
  $this->db->select('id,username');
  $this->db->where('username',db_clean($u,16));
  $this->db->where('password', db_clean(dohash($pw),16));
  $this->db->where('status', 'active');
  $this->db->limit(1);
  $Q = $this->db->get('admins');
  if ($Q->num_rows() > 0){
    $row = $Q->row_array();
    $_SESSION['userid'] = $row['id'];
    $_SESSION['username'] = $row['username'];
  }else{
    $this->session->set_flashdata('error', 'Sorry, your username or password is
        incorrect!');
  }
}
```

Securing the MCats Model

Once you've got the helper functions id_clean() and db_clean() in place, thanks to your work in the "Securing the MAdmins Model" section, you can make short work of the rest of the models. The MCats model, for example, only needs id_clean() in getCategory(), getSubCategories(), addCategory(), updateCategory(), and deleteCategory(). The addCategory() and updateCategory() functions also need the db_clean() function in any place you're adding information to the database.

Without belaboring the obvious, here are a few of those modified functions:

```
function getCategory($id){
  $data = array();
  $options = array('id' =>id_clean($id));
  $Q = $this->db->getwhere('categories',$options,1);
  if ($Q->num_rows() > 0){
    $data = $Q->row_array();
  }
  $Q->free_result();
  return $data;
}
function addCategory(){
  $data = array(
    'name' => db_clean($_POST['name']),
    'shortdesc' => db_clean($_POST['shortdesc']),
    'longdesc' => db_clean($_POST['longdesc'],5000),
    'status' => db_clean($_POST['status'],8),
    'parentid' => id_clean($_POST['parentid'])

  );

  $this->db->insert('categories', $data);
}

function updateCategory(){
  $data = array(
    'name' => db_clean($_POST['name']),
    'shortdesc' => db_clean($_POST['shortdesc']),
    'longdesc' => db_clean($_POST['longdesc'],5000),
    'status' => db_clean($_POST['status'],8),
    'parentid' => id_clean($_POST['parentid'])
  );

  $this->db->where('id', id_clean($_POST['id']));
  $this->db->update('categories', $data);

}

function deleteCategory($id){
  $data = array('status' => 'inactive');
  $this->db->where('id', id_clean($id));
  $this->db->update('categories', $data);
}
```

Securing the MColors Model

MColors is a very simple model. The only changes you'll need to make are to the `getColor()` function and the functions associated with adding, updating, and deleting content, which are:

- ❏ addColor()
- ❏ updateColor()
- ❏ deleteColor()
- ❏ getColor()

Here is the code:

```
function getColor($id){
  $data = array();
  $options = array('id' => id_clean($id));
  $Q = $this->db->getwhere('colors',$options,1);
  if ($Q-num_rows() > 0){
    $data = $Q->row_array();
  }
  $Q->free_result();
  return $data;
}

function createColor(){
  $data = array(
    'name' => db_clean($_POST['name'],32),
    'status' => db_clean($_POST['status'],8)
  );
  $this->db->insert('colors', $data);
}

function updateColor(){
  $data = array(
    'name' => db_clean($_POST['name'],32),
    'status' => db_clean($_POST['status'],8)

  );

  $this->db->where('id', id_clean($_POST['id']));
  $this->db->update('colors', $data);

}

function deleteColor($id){
  $data = array('status' => 'inactive');
  $this->db->where('id', id_clean($id));
  $this->db->update('colors', $data);
}
```

Securing the MOrders Model

Although the MOrders model never touches a database, that doesn't mean you can just ignore it. You have incoming data (a productid, in most cases) that need to be untainted before you should trust them.

In the case of the updateCart() function, simply add a line near the top of the function that runs the incoming $productid variable through id_clean():

```
function updateCart($productid,$fullproduct){
  //pull in existing cart first!
  $cart = $this->session->userdata('cart');
  $productid = id_clean($productid);
  $totalprice = 0;
  //function continues. . .
}
```

Do the same thing with the removeLineItem() function:

```
function removeLineItem($id){
  $id = id_clean($id);
  $totalprice = 0;
  $cart = $this->session->userdata('cart');
  //function continues...
}
```

The final function, updateCartAjax(), is a bit more complicated, but the principle remains the same. You're passing a list of IDs to the function, which gets pulled apart by explode() and then looped through like any array. Eventually, a second layer is pulled open by explode() (this time by splitting on the colon character). At this point, run id_clean on $fields[0] to clean up the ID and make it safe for handling.

```
function updateCartAjax($idlist){
  $cart = $this->session->userdata('cart');
  //split idlist on comma first
  $records = explode(',',$idlist);
  $updated = 0;
  $totalprice = $this->session->userdata('totalprice');
  if (count($records)){
    foreach ($records as $record){
      if (strlen($record)){
        //split each record on colon
        $fields = explode(":",$record);
        $id = id_clean($fields[0]);
        $ct = $fields[1];
    //rest of function . . .
}
```

Securing the MPages Model

MPages is just like all the rest. You need to protect the `getPage()` function, `getPagePath()`, and any function that inserts, updates, or deletes records. For example, here is the `addPage()` function:

```
function addPage(){
  $data = array(
  'name' => db_clean($_POST['name']),
  'keywords' => db_clean($_POST['keywords']),
    'description' => db_clean($_POST['description']),
    'status' => db_clean($_POST['status'],8),
  'path' => db_clean($_POST['path']),
  'content' => $_POST['content']
  );

  $this->db->insert('pages', $data);
}
```

Notice that in this case, the content field of the pages table should contain HTML content, so you're not going to add any restrictions to it.

The complete list of functions that must be secured in this model includes:

- ❑ `addPage()`
- ❑ `updatePage()`
- ❑ `deletePage()`
- ❑ `getPage()`
- ❑ `getPagePath()`

Securing the MProducts Model

The MProducts model is by far the largest in this application — and for good reason! Just about everything of consequence that happens in this application happens because of (or to) a product. Site visitors view products, navigate to products, and see related products. Colors and sizes that have been assigned to a product need to be displayed along with that product.

Some of the security cleanup will be very easy, such as with the `getProduct()` function:

```
function getProduct($id){
  $data = array();
  $options = array('id' => id_clean($id));
  $Q = $this->db->getwhere('products',$options,1);
  if ($Q->num_rows() > 0){
    $data = $Q->row_array();
  }
  $Q->free_result();
  return $data;
}
```

In other places, like the `batchUpdate()` function, you'll need to remember that you're passing in category_id and grouping strings that need to be escaped, well before they are processed by your final query:

```
function batchUpdate(){
  if (count($this->input->post('p_id'))){
    $data = array('category_id' => id_clean($_POST['category_id']),
                  'grouping' => db_clean($_POST['grouping'])
    );
    $idlist = implode(",",array_values($this->input->post('p_id')));
    $where = "id in ($idlist)";
    $this->db->where($where);
    $this->db->update('products',$data);
    $this->session->set_flashdata('message', 'Products updated');
  }else{
    $this->session->set_flashdata('message', 'Nothing to update!');
  }
}
```

The complete list of functions that need securing includes:

- ❑ getProduct()
- ❑ getProductsByCategory()
- ❑ getProductsByGroup()
- ❑ getRandomProducts()
- ❑ search()
- ❑ addProduct()
- ❑ updateProduct()
- ❑ deleteProduct()
- ❑ batchUpdate()

Securing the MSizes Model

Treat the MSizes model pretty much the same as you did MColors. The same rules apply in almost the identical places, give or take a function name change here or there.

```
function getSize($id){
  $data = array();
  $options = array('id' => id_clean($id));
  $Q = $this->db->getwhere('sizes',$options,1);
  if ($Q->num_rows() > 0){
    $data = $Q->row_array();
  }
  $Q->free_result();
  return $data;
}

function createSize(){
  $data = array(
```

```
        'name' => db_clean($_POST['name'],32),
        'status' => db_clean($_POST['status'],8)
    );

    $this->db->insert('sizes', $data);
}

function updateSize(){
  $data = array(
    'name' => db_clean($_POST['name'],32),
    'status' => db_clean($_POST['status'],8)

  );

    $this->db->where('id', id_clean($_POST['id']));
    $this->db->update('sizes', $data);
}

function deleteSize($id){
  $data = array('status' => 'inactive');
  $this->db->where('id', id_clean($id));
  $this->db->update('sizes', $data);
}
```

Securing the MSubscribers Model

The MSubscribers model is just as simple as MColors or MSizes. Here's how you would secure the updateSubscriber() function:

```
function updateSubscriber(){
  $data = array(
  'name' => db_clean($_POST['name']),
  'email' => db_clean($_POST['email'])
  );

    $this->db->where('id', id_clean($_POST['id']));
    $this->db->update('subscribers', $data);
}
```

The complete list of functions that need securing includes:

❑   getSubscriber()

❑   updateSubscriber()

❑   removeSubscriber()

❑   getSubscriber()

Securing the CSV Import Functions

At the moment, the CSV import functions in the MProducts model aren't very secure, in that they accept any header provided in the spreadsheet as a valid column name. There is also no escaping being performed on the data fields themselves.

Just as a quick reminder, here's the `importCsv()` function again:

```
function importCsv(){
  $config['upload_path'] = './csv/';
  $config['allowed_types'] = 'csv';
  $config['max_size'] = '2000';
  $config['remove_spaces'] = true;
  $config['overwrite'] = true;
  $this->load->library('upload', $config);
  $this->load->library('CSVReader');

  if(!$this->upload->do_upload('csvfile')){
    $this->upload->display_errors();
    exit();
  }
  $csv = $this->upload->data();
  $path = $csv['full_path'];
  return $this->csvreader->parseFile($path);
}
```

To ensure that the CSV headers are all correct, you might add your security to the `parseFile()` function of the CSVReader library. However, don't forget that at this point in the code, all you've done is upload a CSV file and prepare an intermediate view. This view is basically an HTML table with hidden fields that contain the data you're about to store in the Products database table.

What this means is that you have to intercept bad headers and data before they show up on the admin_products_csv view. To do that, you will need to add a single line of code to the `import()` function of the admin/products controller:

```
function import(){
  if ($this->input->post('csvinit')){
    $data['dbheaders'] = $this->db->list_fields('products');
    $data['csv'] = $this->MProducts->importCsv();
    $data['title'] = "Preview Import Data";
    $data['main'] = 'admin_product_csv';
    $this->load->vars($data);
    $this->load->view('dashboard');
  }elseif($this->input->post('csvgo')){
    if (eregi("finalize", $this->input->post('submit'))){
      $this->MProducts->csv2db();
      $this->session->set_flashdata('message','CSV data imported');
    }else{
      $this->session->set_flashdata('message','CSV data import cancelled');
    }
    redirect('admin/products/index','refresh');
  }
}
```

The `list_fields()` function provides you with a list of all the field names in a particular database table. You will use this list of field names in your view as a final check. Since you probably don't want to delete any data from the view (because this might cause some confusion on the part of the user), the best thing to do is mark each bad passage with a warning note, and then refuse to include the header's associated data in the final form. That way, any bad data will never be uploaded.

Here's how you would run the check on the headers. Notice that the incoming `$dbheaders` listing is checked using `in_array()`. The `$dbheaders` listing will be a zero-indexed array like the following:

```
(0 => 'id', 1 => 'name', 2 => 'something_else'. . . )
```

etc., And so on, depending on the names of the fields. A simple `in_array()` check will quickly detect if the `$hdr` variable you are processing does exist in the table. If it does exist, set `$error[$k]` to FALSE; otherwise, set `$error[$k]` to TRUE. If you have an error, then display an asterisk and "(error)" next to the header in the display.

```php
<?php
$error = array();
if (count($csv)){
  echo form_open('admin/products/import');
  echo form_submit('cancel','<< start over');
  echo form_submit('submit','finalize import >>');
?>
<table border='1' cellspacing='0' cellpadding='5'>
<tr valign='top'>
<?php
  $headers = array_keys($csv[0]);
  foreach ($headers as $k => $v){
    $hdr = trim(str_replace('"','',$v));
    if (in_array($hdr,$dbheaders)){
       $error[$hdr] = false;
    }else{
       $error[$hdr] = true;
    }
    if ($hdr != '' && !eregi("thumbnail",$hdr)
     && !eregi("image",$hdr)){
      echo "<th>".$hdr;
      if ($error[$hdr]){
      echo "* (error)\n";
      }
      echo "</th>\n";
    }
  }
}
?>
```

Now that you have a full list of which headers are in error, with the keys of the `$error` array matching the header names in the CSV file, you can quickly add a proviso in the second loop that only prints out a hidden field, if and only if, there are no errors for a given header.

```php
</tr>
<?php
  foreach ($csv as $key => $line){
    echo "<tr valign='top'>\n";
    foreach ($line as $f => $d){
      $FIELD = trim(str_replace('"','',$f));
      $FDATA = trim(str_replace('"','',$d));
      if ($FIELD != '' && !eregi("thumbnail",$FDATA)
          && !eregi("image",$FDATA)){
        echo "<td>";
```

```
        echo $FDATA . "\n";
        if ($error[$FIELD] == false){
          echo form_hidden("line_$key"."[".$FIELD."]",$FDATA);
        }else{
          echo " ";
        }
        echo "</td>\n";
      }
    }
    echo "</tr>\n";
  }
?>
</table>
<?php
  echo form_hidden('csvgo',true);
  echo form_close();
}else{
  echo "<h1>We detected a problem...</h1>";
  echo "<p>No records to import! Please try again.</p>";
}
?>
```

Handling Exceptions in Controller Functions

Once you have all of this work in place, you have a much more secure environment, at least when it comes to handling user input. However, you'll notice a few idiosyncrasies. For example, if you're visiting the site and try to visit a product page with a really large number, what do you think happens? Well, at this point, you're processing the getProduct() function with your new id_clean() function, so no harm can happen.

At this point, if you try to open up product/138939018830190938 or some other nonsensical number (or even /product/iamhackingyou), then you'll get sent back to the home page. Why? Because in your Welcome controller, you created the product() function in such a way as to send any visitors, who are trying to visit a non-live product, back to the home page:

```
function product($productid){
  $product = $this->MProducts->getProduct($productid);
  if (!count($product)){
    redirect('welcome/index','refresh');
  }
  //function continues. . .
}
```

In other words, you're using the passed-in argument to the getProduct() function to figure out which product to get from the database table. This model function automatically passes that ID argument through the custom id_clean() function added to the helper extension file.

If no record is retrieved from the database, then the $product array will be empty and will therefore not pass the count() test. (You're doing a similar test in the category() function.)

Some may argue that sending users back to the home page is a silly idea, that what you should be doing is sending them on to a custom 404 page, but the point is moot. Yes, you're doing a good thing by passing that URI segment argument through a filtering station. That way you make sure the ID is an integer, you escape any bad stuff that might be in it, and you chop it down to size (11 characters maximum). By passing it through that simple filter, you've greatly reduced the odds of something bad happening.

Furthermore, by doing another check after you've run the model, you ensure that you're sending the user to a legitimate page, and not some random page consisting of cryptic error messages that may or may not give the attacker insight into your system.

What you have to do now is add this kind of intelligence to the other controllers, specifically the edit() function of each admin controller. Why? Because you don't want to give someone the ability to edit a record that doesn't exist.

First, here is the edit() function in the admin/admins controller:

```
function edit($id=0){
  if ($this->input->post('username')){
    $this->MAdmins->updateUser();
    $this->session->set_flashdata('message','User updated');
    redirect('admin/admins/index','refresh');
  }else{
    $data['title'] = "Edit User";
    $data['main'] = 'admin_admins_edit';
    $data['admin'] = $this->MAdmins->getUser($id);
    if (!count($data['admin'])){
      redirect('admin/admins/index','refresh');
    }
    $this->load->vars($data);
    $this->load->view('dashboard');
  }
}
```

Next is the edit() function of the admin/categories controller:

```
function edit($id=0){
  if ($this->input->post('name')){
    $this->MCats->updateCategory();
    $this->session->set_flashdata('message','Category updated');
    redirect('admin/categories/index','refresh');
  }else{
    $data['title'] = "Edit Category";
    $data['main'] = 'admin_cat_edit';
    $data['category'] = $this->MCats->getCategory($id);
    $data['categories'] = $this->MCats->getTopCategories();
    if (!count($data['category'])){
      redirect('admin/categories/index','refresh');
    }
    $this->load->vars($data);
    $this->load->view('dashboard');
  }
}
```

Here is the edit() function of the admin/colors controller:

```
function edit($id=0){
  if ($this->input->post('name')){
    $this->MColors->updateColor();
    $this->session->set_flashdata('message','Color updated');
    redirect('admin/colors/index','refresh');
  }else{
    $data['title'] = "Edit Color";
    $data['main'] = 'admin_colors_edit';
    $data['color'] = $this->MColors->getColor($id);
    if (!count($data['color'])){
      redirect('admin/colors/index','refresh');
    }
    $this->load->vars($data);
    $this->load->view('dashboard');
  }
}
```

Here is the edit() function of the admin/pages controller:

```
function edit($id=0){
  if ($this->input->post('name')){
    $this->MPages->updatePage();
    $this->session->set_flashdata('message','Page updated');
    redirect('admin/pages/index','refresh');
  }else{
    $data['title'] = "Edit Page";
    $data['main'] = 'admin_pages_edit';
    $data['page'] = $this->MPages->getPage($id);
    if (!count($data['page'])){
      redirect('admin/pages/index','refresh');
    }
    $this->load->vars($data);
    $this->load->view('dashboard');
  }
}
```

Here is the edit() function of the admin/products controller:

```
function edit($id=0){
  if ($this->input->post('name')){
    $this->MProducts->updateProduct();
    $this->session->set_flashdata('message','Product updated');
    redirect('admin/products/index','refresh');
  }else{
    $data['title'] = "Edit Product";
    $data['main'] = 'admin_product_edit';
    $data['product'] = $this->MProducts->getProduct($id);
    $data['categories'] = $this->MCats->getCategoriesDropDown();
    $data['assigned_colors'] = $this->MProducts->getAssignedColors($id);
    $data['assigned_sizes'] = $this->MProducts->getAssignedSizes($id);
```

```
    $data['colors'] = $this->MColors->getActiveColors();
    $data['sizes'] = $this->MSizes->getActiveSizes();
    if (!count($data['product'])){
      redirect('admin/products/index','refresh');
    }
    $this->load->vars($data);
    $this->load->view('dashboard');
  }
}
```

Here is the edit() function of the admin/sizes controller:

```
function edit($id=0){
  if ($this->input->post('name')){
    $this->MSizes->updateSize();
    $this->session->set_flashdata('message','Size updated');
    redirect('admin/sizes/index','refresh');
  }else{
    $data['title'] = "Edit Size";
    $data['main'] = 'admin_sizes_edit';
    $data['size'] = $this->MSizes->getSize($id);
    if (!count($data['size'])){
      redirect('admin/sizes/index','refresh');
    }
    $this->load->vars($data);
    $this->load->view('dashboard');
  }
}
```

Finally, there is no edit() function in the admin/subscribers controller, so you're done!

Encrypting Sessions

So far, you've been using sessions without any encryption at all. This means that anyone who attempts to intercept the CodeIgniter session cookie will be able to read whatever is in it. You can remedy this situation easily enough by opening the config.php file (in the /system/application/config folder) and changing two settings.

The first is to set $config['sess_encrypt_cookie'] to TRUE:

```
$config['sess_encrypt_cookie'] = TRUE;
```

The second is to set a value for $config['encryption_key']. Choose a random string of 32 characters, using numbers and upper- and lowercase letters. Don't just use a word from a dictionary, and don't just type the same keys over and over again from your keyboard (i.e., **asdfhughugasdf**, etc.). Make it as random as you possibly can — one way to do that is to take a random bunch of letters and numbers and run it through the PHP sha1() function, which should return 32 characters.

Once you've done both of these things, place your config.php file on the server and click around. Then look inside your session cookie. Session data encrypted!

Additional Security Resources

Web application security is an enormous field, and there's no way to do it justice in such a short space. If you're interested in continuing your education, here are a few resources that will help you do that:

- ❏ *The Web Application Hacker's Handbook: Discovering and Exploiting Security Flaws*, by Dafydd Stuttard and Marcus Pinto — This book is a guide to identifying security flaws in web applications using real-world examples.

- ❏ *Essential PHP Security*, by Chris Shiflett — This book is short, but don't assume it's somehow deficient because of that. Just a single read-through will improve your security posture and educate you on just about everything you need to know.

- ❏ *PHP|architect's Guide to PHP Security*, by Ilia Alshanetsky — Ilia's book will educate you on some of the finer points of SQL injection, buffer overflow attacks, and other attacks.

- ❏ *Apache Security*, by Ivan Ristic — Ivan's book covers security principles (I especially like his take on security as a process, not an outcome) and delves deeply into different aspects of Apache security, like SSL, denial of service attacks, secure PHP installation, and more.

- ❏ PHP Security Consortium (`http://phpsec.org/`) — This web site contains various articles on security topics like input validation, spoofing, and XSS.

- ❏ Web Application Security–Web Application Component Toolkit (`www.phpwact.org/security/web_application_security`) — This page provides a list of common security vulnerabilities and concerns that are easy to fix at the application development level. Included in the list are additional resources as well as catalogs of well-known attacks (and their countermeasures).

- ❏ OWASP (`http://owasp.org`) — OWASP is a Wiki run by the Open Web Application Security Project.

Performance

Performance is usually the bane of any development effort. Things that you put together on a development server simply never seem to stand up to the pounding of real traffic. Once again, however, CodeIgniter comes to your aid with a set of profiling and benchmarking tools that allows you to see how your pages (and even sections of code) perform.

Profiling

If you're curious about performance of any page, you can turn on profiling and get a detailed report of what's happening. This is a useful thing to do before a site goes live.

To turn on profiling, open your Welcome controller in an editor, and make the following change to the constructor:

```
function Welcome(){
  parent::Controller();
  $this->output->enable_profiler(TRUE);
}
```

Now visit the home page and scroll down. You should see a table giving details on how your application performed. You'll see entries for controller load time, queries run, and other data. It should look something like Figure 9-1.

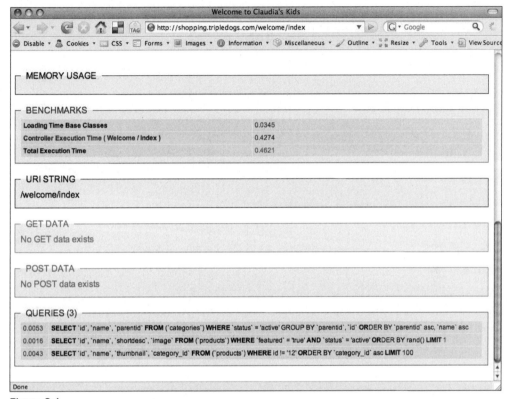

Figure 9-1

According to the example, the total execution time for the home page was about half a second. This is OK for a development server, but not acceptable for a real-life eCommerce site. It's time to start acting on this information to improve the situation.

Compressing Output

One obvious way to speed up your home page is to turn on output compression. Doing so enables Gzip output compression for faster page loads. All you have to do is set `$config['compress_output']` to TRUE in config.php, and CodeIgniter will test to see if the server its on supports Gzip compression. If so, then the server will use Gzip to speed things up.

There are two important things to keep in mind, however. Since not all browsers support Gzip compression, it will be ignored by those that can't handle it. Don't fret about this, though, because it is only the really old browsers that don't use HTTP/1.1 or understand the Accept-Encoding header. Here's a partial list of non-GZIP browsers:

- ❏ Netscape Navigator 3
- ❏ Netscape Communicator 4 (but only those before 4.06, and with errors after that version)
- ❏ Mozilla 0.9 (unless the user manually configures the browser to accept)
- ❏ Internet Explore 3.x and below
- ❏ Opera 3.5 and below
- ❏ Lynx 2.5 and below (some use separate Gzip command lines)

You might look at that list and think to yourself, "Isn't it time for people to upgrade?" You'd be amazed at how long people hang on to their favorite browser.

One more thing about compressing: If you have any white space at the end of your scripts, you'll start serving blank pages. Make sure that you keep the ends of your scripts tidy.

Please note that Gzip compression only affects how quickly a browser accepts and loads content, so it will not improve your server-side performance.

Caching

CodeIgniter's caching engine allows you to take dynamically created pages and save them in their fully rendered states on the server, then reuse those fully rendered pages for a specific amount of time. For example, the first time a user hits a query-intensive page, the page is cached for X amount of time, and all other visitors use the cached page until the cache expires.

Where are pages cached? Good question. They are written to the /system/cache folder that sits above your application.

With high-traffic web sites, caching can give you huge boosts in performance in a short amount of time. To put in caching, all you need to do is set a caching value for any controller function using the following command:

```
$this->output->cache(X);
```

where X is the number of minutes you want the cache to remain active before it is deleted and reset. That's it — there's nothing else to load or configure because caching is part of the Output class and is therefore ready to be used in your application.

For example, if you were to set a 30-minute cache in `welcome/index()`, you would do it like this:

```
function index(){
    $this->output->cache(30);
    $data['title'] = "Welcome to Claudia's Kids";
    $data['navlist'] = $this->MCats->getCategoriesNav();
    $data['mainf'] = $this->MProducts->getMainFeature();
    $skip = $data['mainf']['id'];
    $data['sidef'] = $this->MProducts->getRandomProducts(3,$skip);
    $data['main'] = 'home';
    $this->load->vars($data);
    $this->load->view('template');
}
```

If you were to reload the home page, you'd notice a few things right away. First off, it's likely that this first page load might take a bit longer. But there's no need to panic, as every subsequent visit will be speedier than the last. The other thing you'll notice is that all your profiling data have been removed. Again, there's no need to panic. Below, you'll learn how to use a more discreet way to display such data, using benchmarking.

If you were to look at your server's file system, you'd see that there are now files being written to the /system/cache folder, as shown in Figure 9-2.

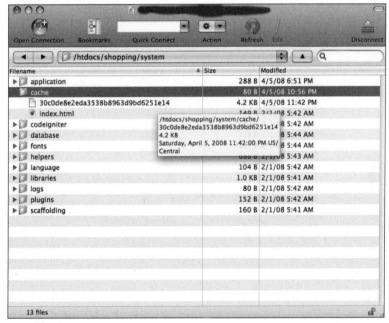

Figure 9-2

In this case, the file cryptically (no pun intended!) called *30c0de8e2eda3538b8963d9bd6251e14* is the home page that was being cached. You can confirm it by running the file through cat or another shell editor to see:

```
1207440748TS---><!DOCTYPE html PUBLIC "-//W3C//DTD XHTML 1.0 Strict//EN"
        "http://www.w3.org/TR/xhtml1/DTD/xhtml1-strict.dtd">
<html xmlns="http://www.w3.org/1999/xhtml" xml:lang="en" lang="en">
<head>
  <meta http-equiv="content-type" content="text/html; charset=utf-8" />
  <title>Welcome to Claudia's Kids</title>
<link href="http://shopping.tripledogs.com/css/default.css" rel="stylesheet"
  type="text/css" />
<script type="text/javascript">
//<![CDATA[
base_url = 'http://shopping.tripledogs.com/';
//]]>
</script>
<script type="text/javascript"
src="http://shopping.tripledogs.com/js/prototype.js"></script>
<script type="text/javascript"
src="http://shopping.tripledogs.com/js/scriptaculous.js" ></script>
<script type="text/javascript"
src="http://shopping.tripledogs.com/js/customtools.js" ></script>
</head>
<body>
<div id="wrapper">
  <div id="header">
  <a href="http://shopping.tripledogs.com/">
<img src="http://shopping.tripledogs.com/images/logo.jpg" border="0"/>
</a>

<div id='globalnav'>
<ul>
<li><a href=http://shopping.tripledogs.com/welcome/index
. . .
```

The first bit, the `1207440748TS--->`, is when this particular cached page expires, in UNIX time-stamp format.

Turning Off Profiling

It is time to turn off profiling, as you don't need it anymore. Simply erase the line from your controller, or set the profiler to FALSE.

```
function Welcome(){
  parent::Controller();
  $this->output->enable_profiler(FALSE);
}
```

Benchmarking

The Benchmark class can be used to mark start and end points in your code and to print out how much time (or how many resources) was used by that code. Benchmarking can be used in controllers, views, and models and are a great way to dig deeply into a performance-based problem.

To start off, open up your footer view (/system/application/views/footer.php), and add the following code to the file:

```
Copyright <?php echo date("Y"); ?>
<?php echo anchor("welcome/privacy","privacy policy");?>
   
<?php echo anchor("welcome/verify","dashboard");?>
   
<?php echo $this->benchmark->elapsed_time();?>
   
<?php echo $this->benchmark->memory_usage();?>
```

The `elapsed_time()` function will tell you how much time it took to render a page, from CodeIgniter framework initialization all the way through final output to the browser. The `memory_usage()` function will tell you how much memory was used.

Once you've loaded the view onto your site, visit one of the category pages. Remember, the home page is cached, so it's better to visit an uncached page. You should see something like Figure 9-3.

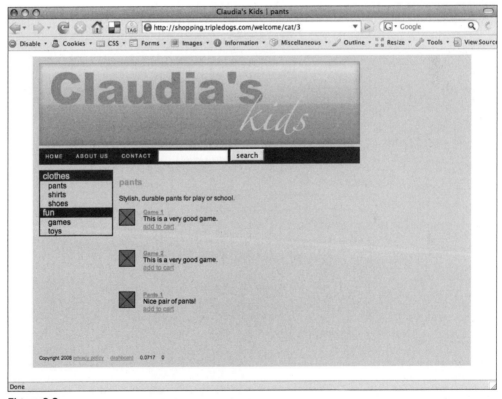

Figure 9-3

According to the benchmarking functions, it took 0.07 seconds (give or take) to render the page, and it used 0 memory. (It could also be showing zero because your copy of PHP didn't have --enable-memory-limit when it was compiled on the server. If that's the case, and you want to show this kind of data, you will need to recompile PHP with the --enable-memory-limit flag set. In other words, having to reinstall PHP may or may not be worth your time, depending on the kind of visibility you want on profiling.)

This kind of information is good, but what if you were trying to diagnose a more specific problem, like how long a specific query was taking? You could, for example, put the following markers down in your `welcome/cat()` function:

```
function cat($id){
    $this->benchmark->mark('query_start');
    $cat = $this->MCats->getCategory($id);
    $this->benchmark->mark('query_end');
    //function continues on. . .
}
```

Then, in your footer view, you could use `elapsed_time()` to print out the results:

```
   
Elapsed query time:
<?php echo $this->benchmark->elapsed_time('query_start','query_end');?>
```

Simply reload a category page to see something like Figure 9-4.

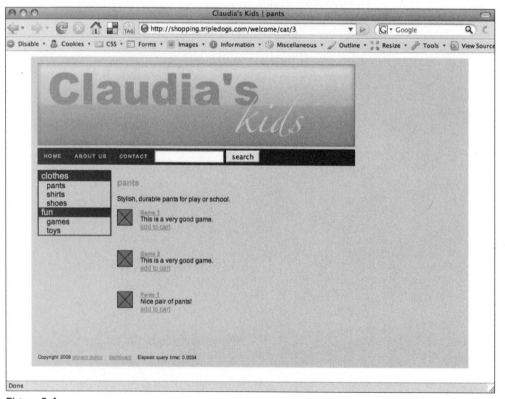

Figure 9-4

According to this example, the `getCategory()` model function is taking a total of 3/1,000-ths of a second to run. Not bad for government work!

Now you understand the basics about enhancing performance. Each site is different, and each one has different needs and resources. In each real-world project, you'll need to go through your application testing the different outcomes. With a combination of profiling, specific benchmarking, and caching, you should be able to scale your application to whatever audience needs may be out there.

Conclusion

In this chapter, you tackled security and performance issues. In the next chapter, you integrate the site with a checkout mechanism and tie up any remaining loose ends identified by Claudia.

Remember to keep these thoughts in mind as you continue working with CodeIgniter:

❑ You're free to use regular PHP measures like `strip_tags()` to control user input, but you can also use CodeIgniter's `xss_clean()`. You're also able to extend the Security helper with your own custom functions.

❑ Database queries are not automatically escaped by CodeIgniter's Active Record Class. If you use `insert()` and `update()`, you will need to take the extra steps to keep data secure.

❑ Your config file also contains protection against certain illegal characters in URI strings. Be careful that you don't introduce security vulnerabilities if you allow extra characters.

❑ Performance tools, like benchmarking and profiling, can help you identify problem areas in your code, whether that be sloppy controllers, bad queries, or slow-loading views. Use the tools at your disposal to find the problem before going live, then use caching to help scale the application to your audience needs.

10

Launch

In the past nine chapters, you've built a CodeIgniter application from the ground up. You've created a public-facing eCommerce site, added an administrative interface to it, and made various incremental upgrades throughout that kept the project manageable and on a sane track toward launch.

In this chapter, you put the finishing touches on the project and get it ready for launch. In order to do that, it's helpful to review the top remaining issues:

❏ Checkout hasn't been implemented. When users add items to their carts, they can't really check out yet. Most of this chapter is devoted to figuring this (and other checkout-related items) out.

❏ Speaking of checkout, there also needs to be some sanity checking done on prices and products in the user's Shopping Cart just prior to checkout. You're going to tackle this issue as well.

❏ Are there any remaining issues that Claudia and her staff are facing? For example, are file uploads and HTML issues all resolved?

❏ What about any compatibility issues? AJAX is being used on the public side of the house; do we need to make sure that users have JavaScript enabled?

One Last Sanity Check of Checkout

When you last worked on the shoppingcart view in Chapter 5, you created a simple table view with associated functionality that allowed the user to add or remove items from their PHP session-based cart.

As a quick reminder, here's the source code for the shoppingcart view:

```php
<h1>Shopping Cart</h1>
<div id='pleft'>

<?php echo form_open(); ?>
<table border='1' cellspacing='0' cellpadding='5'>
<?php
$TOTALPRICE = $_SESSION['totalprice'];

if (count($_SESSION['cart'])){
  foreach ($_SESSION['cart'] as $PID => $row){
    $data = array(
      'name' => "li_id[$PID]",
      'value'=>$row['count'],
      'id' => "li_id_$PID",
      'class' => 'process',
      'size' => 5
    );

  echo "<tr valign='top'>\n";
  echo "<td>". form_input($data) ."</td>\n";
  echo "<td id='li_name_".$PID."'>". $row['name']."</td>\n";
  echo "<td id='li_price_".$PID."'>". $row['price']."</td>\n";
  echo "<td id='li_total_".$PID."'>".$row['price'] * $row['count']."</td>\n";
  echo "<td><a href='#' onclick='javascript:jsRemoveProduct($PID)'>
        delete</a></td>\n";
  echo "</tr>\n";
  }

  $total_data = array('name' => 'total', 'id'=>'total', 'value' => $TOTALPRICE);
  echo "<tr valign='top'>\n";
  echo "<td colspan='3'> </td>\n";
  echo "<td colspan='2'>$TOTALPRICE ".form_hidden($total_data)."</td>\n";

  echo "</tr>\n";

  echo "<tr valign='top'>\n";
  echo "<td colspan='3'> </td>\n";
  echo "<td colspan='2'><input type='button' name='update' value='update'
        onClick='javascript:jsUpdateCart()'/></td>\n";
  echo "</tr>\n";

  echo "<tr valign='top'>\n";
  echo "<td colspan='3'> </td>\n";
  echo "<td colspan='2'>".form_submit('submit', 'checkout')."</td>\n";
  echo "</tr>\n";
}else{
  //just in case!
  echo "<tr><td>No items to show here!</td></tr>\n";
}//end outer if count
```

```
?>
</table>
</form>
<div id='ajax_msg'></div>
</div>
```

As a visual reminder, Figure 10-1 shows what the shoppingcart view might look like when loaded in a browser.

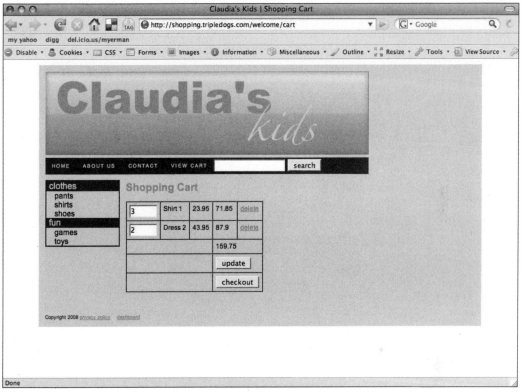

Figure 10-1

What you want is for the user to click the Checkout button and transfer all the information in the PHP session array called *cart* to a checkout process. For simplicity's sake, you're going to integrate the cart with Google Checkout, which is Claudia's preferred vendor.

There are many vendors out there that you can integrate a shopping cart with. The two best-known ones are PayPal and Google Checkout, but others, like PayPro Flow (from VeriSign) and Authorize.Net, also have significant followings. All of the systems work in fairly similar ways: You prepare the information to their specifications, and then you pass along that information in a way they can easily parse. Most of the lessons learned in this chapter will apply generally to most of these systems.

However, before you do all that, you need to make sure that all the data you're sending to the checkout process are good. For example, are all the products really in the database? Are the prices correct, as far as you can tell? If the prices have changed since the time the products were put in the Shopping Cart, is there a warning message? Also, are all prices properly formatted? (As you can see in Figure 10-1, *87.9* should really be *87.90*.)

The first order of business is to add a `checkout()` function to the Welcome controller. This function will be the place where you organize all of these features and to which your shoppingcart table will post. For right now, just create the function bare, as you'll be back to it in a minute:

```
function checkout(){
  //we'll be right back, folks!
}
```

Now open the shoppingcart view in an editor, and make sure that the Checkout button posts to welcome/checkout:

```
<h1>Shopping Cart</h1>
<div id='pleft'>

<?php echo form_open('welcome/checkout'); ?>
<table border='1' cellspacing='0' cellpadding='5'>
//snipped
```

Once you have that in place, it's time to build a verification function in the MOrders model. This verification function needs to make sure that everything in the model is a valid product and that each product has a valid price.

The easiest way to do that is to use whatever product IDs are stored in the session cart, extracting product IDs and prices only from the database, and doing a comparison. If the cart has a product ID that is not in the database, remove it from the cart. If the price is different in the database, update the Shopping Cart with the database price. If any changes take place, make a note for the user.

Notice that you'll be making use of the `id_clean()` *function here. It pays to be extra sure that you're not passing bogus IDs to the database.*

```
function verifyCart(){
  $cart = $_SESSION['cart'];
  $change = false;

  if (count($cart)){
    foreach ($cart as $id => $details){
      $idlist[] = id_clean($id);
    }
    $ids = implode(",",$idlist);
    $this->db->select('id,price');
    $this->db->where("id in ($ids)");
    $Q = $this->db->get('products');
    if ($Q->num_rows() > 0){
```

```
        foreach ($Q->result_array() as $row){
          $db[$row['id']] = $row['price'];
        }
      }
      foreach ($cart as $id => $details){
        if (isset($db[$id])){
          if ($details['price'] != $db[$id]){
            $details['price'] = $db[$id];
            $change = true;
          }
          $final[$id] = $details;
        }else{
          $change = true;
        }
      }

      $totalprice=0;
      foreach ($final as $id => $product){
        $totalprice += $product['price'] * $product['count'];
      }

      $_SESSION['totalprice'] = $totalprice;
      $_SESSION['cart'] = $final;
      $this->session->set_flashdata('change',$change);
    }else{
      //nothing in cart!
      $this->session->set_flashdata('error',"Nothing in cart! Please notify
          help@example.com to report this problem during checkout.");
    }
  }
}
```

In the above code, when you extract the products from the database and then loop through the cart, it's an opportunity to check to make sure that the product is valid and that the price is still good. If a price changes, then set the `$change` variable to TRUE. The same thing goes if you find that one or more products aren't in the database.

> Notice the `else` branch in the `verifyCart()` function? It serves a very important purpose, but the message it delivers to the end-user will hardly ever be seen because it only shows up if the Shopping Cart is empty. At the point at which the user checks out, he or she is doing so from a page that has already been loaded from the Shopping Cart, so it is highly unlikely that the Shopping Cart will disappear between then and the verification process.
>
> However, you might have a situation involving some kind of PHP session time-out or a malicious user trying to access the checkout page without first putting any items in the cart. If that's the case, you really want this little check in there. Feel free to customize the message any way you like.

At the end of the process, you are left with a brand-new array called `$final`, and that's what you write back to the PHP session.

Now that you have that in place, finish up the controller function:

```
function checkout(){
    $this->MOrders->verifyCart();
    $data['main'] = 'confirmorder';
    $data['title'] = "Claudia's Kids | Order Confirmation";
    $data['navlist'] = $this->MCats->getCategoriesNav();
    $this->load->vars($data);
    $this->load->view('template');
}
```

For right now, create a blank view called *confirmorder*, which you'll fill in below in the "Integrating Checkout" section. Right now, you need to do a bit more cleanup before moving on.

What kind of cleanup? Well, for starters, did you notice that dollar amounts aren't properly formatted if the pennies round to the nearest 10? For example, *19.90* is displayed as *19.9*, and that won't do. The easiest way to fix this is to go into the MOrders model and address it in every function where you do some math.

Because this would be a repetitive, error-prone process, the best thing to do is to create a function in your MOrders model that does the clean-up work and then use that function to implement the fix.

So here's a function that will convert any number into something that more closely approximates currency:

```
function format_currency($number){
    return number_format($number, ª2,ª'.',ª',');
}
```

The `number_format()` function is a handy PHP function that lets you format a number just about any way you want. You pass in the number as your first argument. The second argument is how many decimal places you want to display (it does all the work of rounding up or down). The third argument is the decimal point separator (and here you can make changes for your own locale — e.g., some European countries use a comma instead of a period). The fourth argument is the thousands separator (again, conveniently changeable to your locale).

Your new `format_currency()` function can now be used in your other functions. Just don't forget to invoke it as `$this->format_currency()`. Therefore, for example, in MOrders, you would do something like this throughout:

```
$_SESSION['totalprice'] = $this->format_currency($totalprice);
```

Don't forget to update your shoppingcart view. There's one place in there in which you are doing some math on the fly, and that still needs to be covered by this process. You won't be able to easily use the function you created in the MOrders model, but you can use the `number_format()` function:

```
echo "<td id='li_total_".$PID."'>".
    number_format($row['price'] * $row['count'], 2,'.',',')
    ."</td>\n";
```

Integrating Checkout

Because Claudia is using Google Checkout as her preferred eCommerce vendor, you're going to create a very simple integration with Google's HTML API. Essentially, the HTML API allows you to create a form with hidden fields that designate products and their prices.

The names of the fields are important. Google Checkout is expecting fields that are named like this:

```
item_name_1
item_description_1
item_quantity_1
item_price_1
```

Obviously, if you have more than one product, you would need item_name_2 and so on. You can also add some other fields for shipping:

```
ship_method_name_1
ship_method_price_1
```

For the purposes of this book (as opposed to working with a real, live customer), you're going to assume UPS Ground for shipping and a per-item cost of $5.00. You'll be able to adjust this easily for anything that you need to do.

Here's the confirmorder view. It's basically one big loop through the PHP session cart. Note that anywhere you see "change-this-now," you need to put in Claudia's actual Merchant ID from Google.

```
<h1>Please Confirm Your Order</h1>
<p>Please confirm your order before clicking the Buy Now button below. If you have
    changes, <?php echo anchor("welcome/cart", "go back to your shopping
    cart");?>.</p>


<form method="POST"
    action="https://checkout.google.com/api/checkout/v2/checkoutForm/Merchant/
        change-this-now"
    accept-charset="utf-8">

<p>
<?php
$TOTALPRICE = $_SESSION['totalprice'];

if (count($_SESSION['cart'])){
  $count = 1;
  foreach ($_SESSION['cart'] as $PID => $row){
    echo "<b>". $row['count'] . " "
      . $row['name'] . " @ " . $row['price']."<br/>";
    echo "<input type='hidden' name='item_name_".$count
      ."' value='".$row['name']."'/>\n";
    echo "<input type='hidden' name='item_quantity_".$count
      ."' value='".$row['count']."'/>\n";
    echo "<input type='hidden' name='item_price_".$count
      ."' value='".$row['price']."'/>\n";
    echo "<input type='hidden' name='item_currency_".$count
```

```
          ."' value='USD'/>\n";
      echo "<input type='hidden' name='ship_method_name_".$count
          ."' value='UPS Ground'/>\n";
      echo "<input type='hidden' name='ship_method_price_".$count
          ."' value='5.00'/>\n";
      $TOTALPRICE += 5;
      $count++;
   }
}

echo "<b>TOTAL (w/shipping): ". $TOTALPRICE;
?>
</p>
<input type="image" name="Google Checkout" alt="Fast checkout through Google"
src="http://checkout.google.com/buttons/checkout.gif?merchant_id=
      change-this-now&w=180&h=46&style=white&variant=text&loc=en_US"
height="46" width="180"/>
</form>
```

You end up with something similar to Figure 10-2.

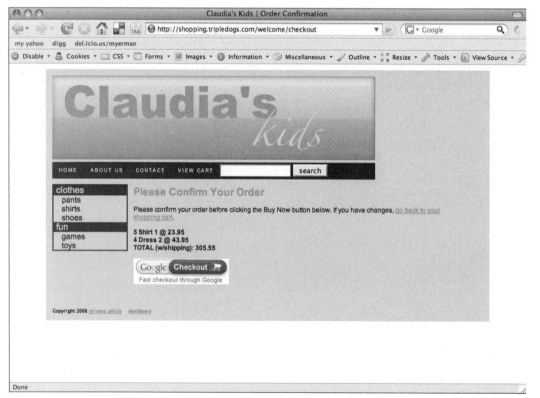

Figure 10-2

If you look behind the scenes at the HTML markup for this particular page, you'll see this:

```
<form method="POST"
action="https://checkout.google.com/api/checkout/v2/checkoutForm/Merchant/change-
this-now" accept-charset="utf-8">

<p>
<b>5 Shirt 1 @ 23.95<br/>
<input type='hidden' name='item_name_1' value='Shirt 1'/>
<input type='hidden' name='item_quantity_1' value='5'/>
<input type='hidden' name='item_price_1' value='23.95'/>
<input type='hidden' name='item_currency_1' value='USD'/>

<input type='hidden' name='ship_method_name_1' value='UPS Ground'/>
<input type='hidden' name='ship_method_price_1' value='5.00'/>

<b>4 Dress 2 @ 43.95<br/>
<input type='hidden' name='item_name_2' value='Dress 2'/>
<input type='hidden' name='item_quantity_2' value='4'/>
<input type='hidden' name='item_price_2' value='43.95'/>
<input type='hidden' name='item_currency_2' value='USD'/>
<input type='hidden' name='ship_method_name_2' value='UPS Ground'/>
<input type='hidden' name='ship_method_price_2' value='5.00'/>
<b>TOTAL (w/shipping): 305.55</p>

<input type="image" name="Google Checkout" alt="Fast checkout through Google"
src="http://checkout.google.com/buttons/checkout.gif?merchant_id=
        change-this-now&w=180&h=46&style=white&variant=text&loc=en_US"
height="46" width="180"/>

</form>
```

In other words, anyone in the world could take this HTML markup, create her own form, mess with the prices at will (making everything cost one penny and abolishing shipping), and then submit that form from anywhere, right?

That is 100 percent correct. At this point, this information is just in plain HTML for anyone to manipulate, and you need to do an extra bit of work to ensure that it doesn't happen. Google Checkout's XML API and digital signatures are good counters to this kind of tampering. Another safeguard is to monitor and review incoming orders before approving them (which is a good idea regardless of which vendor you use).

Google (and each of the other vendors, frankly) maintains an extensive knowledge base on how to secure shopping cart communications. You can explore the Google knowledge base to modify the code for various information and pointers that are specific to security when working with Google Checkout.

Last Remaining Issues

You get a call from Claudia. She's very excited because her team has successfully uploaded a great deal of information onto the site. "However, we have a little problem," she says.

It appears that whenever you create a new product in the system and don't upload a file, the system freezes. The same thing happens when you edit an existing product and don't upload a new image for it.

"One more thing," she says. "I know it's kind of a pain, but my mother got on the test site the other day, and nothing worked for her. I talked to her about it, and I think she's got a really old browser that doesn't support all the things we have on the site."

You assure Claudia that you will look into the file upload issue and that one of the last tasks you had before launch was the installation of a JavaScript and cookie sniffer to ensure that everyone had a browser that could handle the site's AJAX.

Debugging File Uploads

The file upload issue is a simple one to fix. You have two model functions that do the heavy lifting of adding/updating products in the database: addProduct() and updateProduct(). Both of these live in the MProducts model.

Each of these functions contains a section in which you set the config parameters for the incoming file. All you have to do is wrap those sections of the code that deal with file uploads with a simple test to see if $_FILES has something in it, and then, right before each specific upload, check to see if there is a name associated with each file. If there is, perform the upload. If not, move on. Here's the code:

```
function updateProduct(){
  $data = array(
    'name' => db_clean($_POST['name']),
    'shortdesc' => db_clean($_POST['shortdesc']),
    'longdesc' => db_clean($_POST['longdesc'],5000),
    'status' => db_clean($_POST['status'],8),
    'grouping' => db_clean($_POST['grouping'],16),
    'category_id' => id_clean($_POST['category_id']),
    'featured' => db_clean($_POST['featured'],3),
    'price' => db_clean($_POST['price'],16)
  );
  if ($_FILES){
    $config['upload_path'] = './images/';
    $config['allowed_types'] = 'gif|jpg|png';
    $config['max_size'] = '200';
    $config['remove_spaces'] = true;
    $config['overwrite'] = false;
    $config['max_width']  = '0';
    $config['max_height']  = '0';
    $this->load->library('upload', $config);

    if (strlen($_FILES['image']['image'])){
      if(!$this->upload->do_upload('image')){
```

```
        $this->upload->display_errors();
        exit();
    }
    $image = $this->upload->data();

    if ($image['file_name']){
        $data['image'] = "/images/".$image['file_name'];
    }
}

if (strlen($_FILES['thumbnail']['image'])){
    if(!$this->upload->do_upload('thumbnail')){
        $this->upload->display_errors();
        exit();
    }
    $thumb = $this->upload->data();

    if ($thumb['file_name']){
        $data['thumbnail'] = "/images/".$thumb['file_name'];
    }
}
}
//snipped for brevity

}//end of function
```

Detecting JavaScript and Cookie Compatibility

You may be expecting a huge dump of code to see if JavaScript and cookies are enabled. There's no way that you'd want to go through with something like that at this point in the project, so the following minimalist code is offered as a decent check for JavaScript compatibility:

```
<noscript>
    You will not be able to view this site if JavaScript is not enabled.
        Please turn on JavaScript to use this site.
</noscript>
```

That's it — that's all you need to put in your template view, and you're 100 percent covered. If they don't have JavaScript turned on, they get this message. There really is no way to test to see if JavaScript is turned on (after all, if it is off, you can't run a test to see if it is on). Even the following minimal test seems pretty bizarre:

```
if (true){
    //do something here, we must be on
}else{
    //well shucks, JavaScript turned off, there's no way to send an error message!
}
```

The <noscript> option is very straightforward and displays just the error message. You might want to add some branding to it, like the Claudia's Kids logo, maybe a phone number or other information, but that's about as good as it gets. (You could also contemplate removing the AJAX handlers from the shopping carts, but that seems a bit much.)

The same thing goes when checking for cookie support. You'll need just a small bit of code that will try to set a test cookie with a value (say, the integer 1). If the site can write the cookie and retrieve it OK, then cookies are supported. If not, display an error message.

```
<script>
    var tcookie = new Date();
    check_cookie = (tcookie.getTime() + '');
    document.cookie = "check_cookie=" + check_cookie + "; path=/";
     if (document.cookie.indexOf(check_cookie,0) < 0) {
        alert("You will not be able to view this site if cookies are not enabled.
                Please enable them now.");
        }
</script>
```

Conclusion

Congratulations! The project is now complete, and you know more than enough to continue working with CodeIgniter fruitfully for many years to come. You've also learned a great deal about working within an Agile context, coding iteratively without running yourself into the ground.

Some last parting thoughts on CodeIgniter:

❏   It's sometimes useful to leave third-party integrations (like the Google Checkout example) until the very end. At other times, you'll need to complete these kinds of integrations well before the final deadline, as they may need to be thoroughly tested.

❏   Because you're working in an iterative fashion, it also means you can fix things iteratively. Just apply the same common-sense rules for tackling fixes as you would for tackling any other sprint backlog item.

❏   It is always possible that your client might contact you in the months after you complete the project because they have thought of additional functionality that they would like to incorporate into their site. Working in an Agile way means being open to upgrades and updates after "going live" or "launching" a project. In the case of this project, Claudia may want to integrate with a different checkout process, or she might need more robust CSV import functions. Or she may come back to you for a look and feel upgrade. Or she may need extra databases. Whatever the changes might be, analyze what pieces are involved (models, views, controllers) and do the best work you can.

❏   A good rule to follow when working with CodeIgniter: Seek out a CodeIgniter library or helper to do what you need first. If you can't find that, seek out a PHP native function (like `number_format`). If you can't find anything there, seek out a third-party solution. Of course, you can always extend a native CodeIgniter library or helper too. Don't forget to tell the rest of the community about your extensions!

Index

categories.php

 powered by
books 24x7

Programmer to Programmer™

Take your library wherever you go.

Now you can access more than 200 complete Wrox books online, wherever you happen to be! Every diagram, description, screen capture, and code sample is available with your subscription to the **Wrox Reference Library**. For answers when and where you need them, go to wrox.books24x7.com and subscribe today!

Find books on

- ASP.NET
- C#/C++
- Database
- General
- Java
- Mac
- Microsoft Office
- .NET
- Open Source
- PHP/MySQL
- SQL Server
- Visual Basic
- Web
- XML

WROX™

www.wrox.com